RECEIVED

AUG 14 2003

ROLVAAG MEMORIAL
LIBRARY
ST. OLAF COLLEGE

"The Dreaming of the Bones" and "Calvary"

Manuscript Materials

THE CORNELL YEATS

Editorial Board

General Editors
Phillip L. Marcus
J. C. C. Mays
Stephen Parrish
Ann Saddlemyer
Jon Stallworthy

Advisory Editors
George Mills Harper
William M. Murphy
Series Editors
Plays: David R. Clark
Poems: Richard J. Finneran

Coordinating Editor Jared Curtis
Assistant Editor Declan Kiely

PLAYS

The Countess Cathleen, edited by Michael J. Sidnell and Wayne K. Chapman
The Land of Heart's Desire, edited by Jared Curtis
The Hour-Glass, edited by Catherine Phillips
Deirdre, edited by Virginia Bartholome Rohan
"The Dreaming of the Bones" and "Calvary," edited by Wayne K. Chapman
The Words Upon the Window Pane, edited by Mary FitzGerald
The Herne's Egg, edited by Alison Armstrong
Purgatory, edited by Sandra F. Siegel
The Death of Cuchulain, edited by Phillip L. Marcus

POEMS

The Early Poetry, Volume I: "Mosada" and "The Island of Statues," edited by George Bornstein
The Early Poetry, Volume II: "The Wanderings of Oisin" and Other Early Poems to 1895, edited by George Bornstein
The Wind Among the Reeds, edited by Carolyn Holdsworth
"In the Seven Woods" and "The Green Helmet and Other Poems," edited by David Holdeman
Responsibilities, edited by William H. O'Donnell
The Wild Swans at Coole, edited by Stephen Parrish
Michael Robartes and the Dancer, edited by Thomas Parkinson, with Anne Brannen
The Winding Stair (1929), edited by David R. Clark
Words for Music, Perhaps, edited by David R. Clark
"Parnell's Funeral and Other Poems" from "A Full Moon in March," edited by David R. Clark
New Poems, edited by J. C. C. Mays and Stephen Parrish
Last Poems, edited by James Pethica

"The Dreaming of the Bones"
and
"Calvary"
Manuscript Materials

BY W. B. YEATS

EDITED BY

WAYNE K. CHAPMAN

Cornell University Press

ITHACA AND LONDON

PR
5904
.D74
2003

The preparation of this volume was made possible in part by a grant from the Atlantic Philanthropies and the assistance in early stages by the Center for Electronic and Digital Publishing at Clemson University.

Copyright © 2003 by Cornell University
Previously unpublished material by W. B. Yeats © 2003 by Michael Yeats

All rights reserved. Except for brief quotations in a review, this book, or parts thereof, must not be reproduced in any form without permission in writing from the publisher. For information, address Cornell University Press, Sage House, 512 East State Street, Ithaca, New York 14850.

First published 2003 by Cornell University Press

Printed in the United States of America

Library of Congress Cataloging-in-Publication Data

Yeats, W. B. (William Butler), 1865-1939.
[Dreaming of the bones]
The dreaming of the bones ; and, Calvary : manuscript materials / by W. B. Yeats ; edited by Wayne K. Chapman
p. cm. -- (The Cornell Yeats)
Includes bibliographical references.
ISBN 0-8014-4173-0
1. Yeats, W. B. (William Butler), 1865-1939. Dreaming of the bones--Criticism, Textual. 2. Yeats, W. B. (William Butler), 1865-1939. Calvary--Criticism, Textual. 3. Yeats, W. B. (William Butler), 1865-1939--Manuscripts I. Yeats, W. B. (William Butler), 1865-1939. Calvary. II. Chapman, Wayne K. III. Title: Calvary. IV. Title.

PR5904.D74 2003
822'.8—dc21 2003048976

Cornell University strives to utilize environmentally responsible suppliers and materials to the fullest extent possible in the publishing of its books. Such materials include vegetable-based, low-VOC inks and acid-free papers that are recycled, totally chlorine-free, or partly composed of non-wood fibers. For further information, visit our website at www.cornellpress.cornell.edu.

52133021

THE CORNELL YEATS

The volumes in this series present all available manuscripts, revised typescripts, proof-sheets, and other materials that record the growth of Yeats's poems and plays from the earliest draftings through to the lifetime published texts. Most of the materials are from the archives of Senator Michael Yeats and the late Anne Yeats, now in the care of the National Library of Ireland; the remainder are preserved in public collections and private hands in Ireland and around the world. The volumes of poems, with a few exceptions, follow the titles of Yeats's own collections; several volumes of plays in the series contain more than one play.

In all of the volumes manuscripts are reproduced in photographs accompanied by transcriptions, in order to illuminate Yeats's creative process—to show the poet at work. The remaining materials—such as clean typescripts and printed versions—are generally recorded in collated form in an apparatus hung below a finished text. Each volume contains an Introduction describing the significance of the materials it includes, tracing the relation of the various texts to one another. There is also a census of manuscripts, with full descriptive detail, and appendixes are frequently used to present related materials, some of them unpublished.

As the editions seek to present, comprehensively and accurately, the various versions behind Yeats's published poems and plays, including versions he left unpublished, they will be of use to readers who seek to understand how great writing can be made, and to scholars and editors who seek to establish and verify authoritative final texts.

The Yeats Editorial Board

Contents

Acknowledgments

In 1985, I spent my first frenzied summer reading and transcribing poetry in Ireland for *Yeats and English Renaissance Literature* (Macmillan, 1991) and, in unforeseen ways, for the better part of my work since. I returned the next summer and often after that to pursue various lines of inquiry in the National Library of Ireland and in the poet's library, where Anne Yeats and the materials themselves helped me to understand the working relationship between her parents, an uncommon pair whose collaboration produced, arguably, the finest poetry and verse-drama written in English in the twentieth century. When Michael Sidnell and I began our collaboration, in 1990, as editors of *The Countess Cathleen: Manuscript Materials* (Cornell University Press, 1999), I was struck by how the nature of evidence in relation to principle encourages editorial invention. The magnitude of challenges posed by that project argued against the usual construction of a volume by facing individual folio reproductions and transcriptions. After six years constructing that book at Clemson University and with the work finished but for photographic scanning by David Garcia at New York University and another year to publication, I became interested in two other plays and simultaneously convinced that the production staff and facilities nearest to hand constituted an actual digital press. Hence, the present volume of two "plays for dancers," on the one hand, and the Center for Electronic and Digital Publishing, on the other, came into being.

In 1998, partnership with Warwick Gould to coedit a special issue of *Yeats Annual* (Palgrave, 2002) led to my first encounter with the manuscripts of *Calvary* except in fairly bad copies. However, as I explain in the introduction, original aims could not be sustained; the full story of which *Calvary* is a part depends on the textual genesis of *The Dreaming of the Bones*, in many ways a more interesting play and one of Yeats's best, as he said more than once. An edition of the manuscripts of both plays in one volume seemed appropriate when I proposed it to the Cornell Yeats editorial board. On principle, I owe much to the example of my friend Michael Sidnell.

I owe a great deal to the generosity, encouragement, and hospitality of the Yeats family over time. Besides Anne Yeats (now deceased), her brother Michael Yeats has been unfailingly helpful. I thank A. P. Watt Ltd. for permission to reproduce the unpublished materials included in this volume. Also, for permission to quote or reproduce materials in their possession, I thank the Council of Trustees of the National Library of Ireland; the Manuscript Collections of the British Library; the Henry W. and Albert A. Berg Collection of the New York Public Library (Astor, Lennox and Tilden Foundations); the Foster-Murphy Collection, Manuscripts and Archives Division, New York Public Library; the Harry Ransom Humanities Research Center, University of Texas, Austin; the Houghton Library, Harvard University; Special Collections, the Robert W. Woodruff Library, Emory University; and Special Collections and Archives, the Frank Melville Jr. Library, State University of New York at Stony Brook.

I am especially grateful to Stephen Parrish, first of all, for the wisdom of his editorial guidance and many kindnesses. For prompting my initial work on the *Calvary* side of this project, I owe thanks to Janis Tedesco Haswell, and to James Pethica and Declan Kiely for great favors in collections at the Melville Library in Stony Brook and in the New York Public Library, respectively. For various types of information, I am grateful to James Doan, Carmel Jordan, Ann Saddlemyer, Roy Foster, Phillip Marcus, and Warwick Gould. I also thank the staff of the Office of Resource Sharing, R. M. Cooper Library, Clemson University, as well as the librarians and curators of the repositories listed above.

Over three years, the project enlisted Clemson graduate assistants David Ritter, Heather Hicks, Ladson Stringfellow, Nicole Kirkham, and Nicole Hall to do much of the initial keyboarding before my daughter, Charis Chapman, undertook in the Center for Electronic and Digital Publishing nearly all of the computer typesetting prior to submission to the series' coordinating editor, Jared Curtis, whose technical wizardry and amazing speed I value greatly.

Finally, I thank the Department of English, Clemson University; the Department of English, Cornell University; the College of Architecture, Arts and Humanities, Clemson University; the Harry Ransom Humanities Research Center, University of Texas; and Atlantic Philanthropies for providing generous financial support.

WAYNE K. CHAPMAN

Clemson, South Carolina

Abbreviations

BL	British Library archives
Chapman 1	Wayne K. Chapman, "W. B. and George Yeats: The Writing, Editing, and Dating of Yeats's Poems of the Mid-1920s and 1930s, with a Chronology of the Composition of the Poems," in *Yeats's Collaborations: Yeats Annual* 15 (2002): 120–158 (ed. Warwick Gould and Wayne K. Chapman; London: Palgrave, 2002).
Chapman 2	Wayne K. Chapman, "Authors in Eternity: Some Sources for Yeats's Creative Mysticism," *Yeats's Collaborations: Yeats Annual* 15 (2002): 288–312 (ed. Warwick Gould and Wayne K. Chapman; London: Palgrave, 2002).
E&I	W. B. Yeats, *Essays and Introductions* (London: Macmillan, 1961).
FPD	W. B. Yeats, *Four Plays for Dancers* (London: Macmillan, 1921).
Letters	*The Letters of W. B. Yeats*, ed. Allan Wade (London: Rupert Hart-Davis, 1954; New York: Macmillan, 1955).
NLI	National Library of Ireland archives
P&C	W. B. Yeats, *Plays and Controversies* (London: Macmillan, 1923).
VP	*The Variorum Edition of the Poems of W. B. Yeats*, ed. Peter Allt and Russell K. Alspach (New York: Macmillan, 1957; 3d printing, 1966).
VPl	*The Variorum Edition of the Plays of W. B. Yeats*, ed. Russell K. Alspach, assisted by Catharine C. Alspach (London: Macmillan, 1966).
VSR	*The Secret Rose, Stories by W. B. Yeats: A Variorum Edition*, ed. Phillip L. Marcus, Warwick Gould, and Michael J. Sidnell (Ithaca: Cornell University Press, 1981).
Wade	Allan Wade, *A Bibliography of the Writings of W. B. Yeats*, ed. Russell K. Alspach, 3d ed. rev. (London: Rupert Hart-Davis, 1968).
YL	Edward O'Shea, *A Descriptive Catalog of W. B. Yeats's Library* (New York: Garland, 1985). Followed by a number assigned by O'Shea to the titles listed in his catalog; transcriptions of Yeats's annotations in these volumes are my own.

Census of Manuscripts

Paper Types for Loose Folios Used in Both Plays

Type 1: 20.4 cm by 12.8 cm, with three holes punched in one margin for a three-ring notebook, unlined and watermarked WALKER'S / LOOSE / LEAF.

Type 2: 22.8 cm by 17.8 cm, torn from an exercise booklet, twenty-three blue-gray horizontal lines on each side, 0.85 cm apart, and no watermark.

Type 3: 26.0 cm by 20.5 cm, unlined typing paper, watermarked COWAN.

Type 4: around 26 cm by 20.2 cm; somewhat irregular in shape from being torn from a tablet at the top; unlined, plain white paper; without watermark.

Type 5: 27.0 cm by 20.5 cm, lightweight writing paper, with twenty-six ruled lines on the recto side only, without watermark.

Type 6: 26.0 cm by 20.4 cm, unlined typing paper, watermarked COWAN / MERCANTILE BOND.

Type 7: 25.7 cm by 20 cm; unlined, lightweight, plain white typing paper; without watermark. Unlike type 4 in that it was not issued in tablet form.

Type 8: 19.7 cm by 15.9 cm, torn from an exercise booklet, twenty dark blue horizontal lines on each side, without watermark.

Type 9: 22.2 cm by 15 cm, torn from an exercise booklet, twenty-two light blue horizontal lines on each side, without watermark.

Type 10: 24 cm by 18.5 cm; removed from a bound notebook; with twenty-four light blue, horizontal, ruled lines on each side; watermarked BALLYCLARE / CO ANTRIM.

Type 11: 27.3 cm by 21.6 cm, with twenty-eight light blue horizontal lines, spaced 0.9 cm apart, and with a vertical black rule to establish a left margin at 3.4 cm from left edge of the paper. No discernible watermark. Used as backing sheets for the Harvard(A) pasteup copy.

Type 12: 27.3 cm by 21.3 cm, with thirty-one gray horizontal lines spaced 0.8 cm apart. No discernible watermark.

Type 13: 26.2 cm by 20.3 cm, lightweight, semitranslucent typing paper, bearing watermark UNWIN / EXTRA STRONG / LONDON.

Type 14: 26.8 cm by 20.2 cm, with twenty-six ruled gray lines to the side, spaced 0.8 cm apart; removed from an exercise notebook; no watermark.

Type 15: 26.7 cm by 21.2 cm, plain white typing paper, watermarked, by the American manufacturer, MAZE / LINEN BOND.

Type 16: 26 cm by 22.2 cm, plain white typing paper with no discernible watermark.

Part I. *The Dreaming of the Bones*

BL Add. MS 55879 An unbound set of the marked page proofs of *The Collected Plays of W. B. Yeats* for the first edition of 1934 (Wade 177), part of the Macmillan Archive (vol. 1,094) in the British Library. All gatherings are stamped "FIRST PROOF," and the upper right corner of each folded gathering bears the notation "marked proof" (or simply "marked") in black ink. The first folded gathering is also marked, in George Yeats's hand, "Revise to / T. Mark / c/o M & Co." All corrections are in black ink. In *The Dreaming of the Bones* (pp. [431]–445), there are several corrections in punctuation, capitalization, and spelling. The correction "Dervorgilla" to "Dervagilla" is everywhere made but not subsequently printed in *Collected Plays*. On page 437, the typeset word "jail" is circled in black ink (at *VPl* 87), and "They" is circled, beside which "That?" is inscribed (at l. 89) but not substituted in *Collected Plays*. On page 439, "Connaught" is circled in black ink, agreeing with the spelling of "Connacht" in *Collected Plays*. Numerous printer's notations—including the renumbering of odd pages by leaf, [431] to 221, 433 to 222, 435 to 223, and so on—and spacings are indicated in pencil. In *Calvary* (pp. [447]–457), several corrections in punctuation, capitalization, and versification are made (the latter negotiated between a querying party in one hand and Yeats in another, both in black ink). In the opening stage direction, the words "the preceding plays" are circled in blue ink, noted by a black check mark, but not followed in *Collected Plays*.

BL Add. MS 55884 Page proofs for volumes 3 and 4 (marked principally by Thomas Mark?): *Plays* for the unpublished Coole edition, part of the Macmillan Archive (vol. 1,099) in the British Library. *The Dreaming of the Bones* portion consists of pages [83]–99. The entire *Four Plays for Dancers* segment of this proof set ([37]–112) has been renumbered twice: once in blue crayon (153–228, crossed out, in lower right-hand corners) and once in pencil (30–68 in upper right-hand corners) but only on rectos, as if to account solely for leaves. In the preface (p. 39), a pencil inscription is made in response to the printed spelling "Dervagilla": "as other Gaelic names, Lady Gregory's spelling, also others." To this is attached a slip noting, in black ink and another hand: "Dervagilla is impossible!! No / one has ever spelt it like that — / Dervorgilla is universal. / Also Dermot should / <u>really</u> be DIARMUID / though Dermot is <u>just</u> possible. Lady G. always used / DIARMUID." Beside this in pencil: "(Dreaming of the Bones / p. 201 H —,"

201 being the blue crayon number inscribed on page 85 of the proofs, the first page of the play. Besides corrections of these two names to "Dervorgilla" and "Diarmuid," "Donogh" was emended to "Donough" and "jail" to "gaol." The typeset state of the text suggests that *Plays and Controversies* (1923), and neither BL Add. MS 55879 nor *Collected Plays*, was the copy text. The *Calvary* portion consists of pages [101]–112, where a few slight corrections and printed anomalies point to *Four Plays for Dancers* (1921) as well as *Plays and Controversies* (1923) for authority, not BL Add. MS 55879.

BL Add. MS 55891 Another set of page proofs for the unpublished Coole edition, part of the Macmillan Archive (vol. 1106) in the British Library. Marked on a blue slip: "Vol II [of Plays] / Latest / Corrected / Proof. // Marked by / Mrs. Yeats." On the first gathering (vol. 4, "B"), the half title page of "*The Hour-Glass / (in verse) / 1914*," the notation "~~IV~~ / ~~Plays II~~ / *1939 sit*" appears in blue ink above the words "Marked / [?July] / ~~1939~~ Vol. IV correct / 1945 // 1939" in pencil. In *The Dreaming of the Bones* (pp. [83]–99 for text, 93–202 for music); corrections by Mrs. Yeats are few and generally compare with BL Add. MS 55884. Likewise, the preface to *Four Plays for Dancers* compares with that in BL Add. MS 55884, save that Mrs. Yeats has not changed the spelling of "Dervagilla" to "Dervorgilla," even when misprinted "Dergavilla" at line 274. A note on page 202 of the music speaks to the issue of authority in spelling: "cf pp. 85 and 87 where this is corrected by the author to Dervagilla." Printing is the same as in BL Add. MS 55884. The *Calvary* segment consists of pages [101]–112 and agrees with BL Add. MS 55884, bearing only one correction by Mrs. Yeats.

Emory A corrected copy of *Two Plays for Dancers* (Dundrum: Cuala Press, 1919) prepared as copy text for *Four Plays for Dancers* (London: Macmillan, 1921). Pages [1]–[16] constitute *The Dreaming of the Bones* segment, with the title page and preface marked for omission. In the Robert W. Woodruff Library, Emory University. Follows Texas(C).

Harvard(A) A file containing a complete holograph version of the play in verse derived from different draft states and pasted together and augmented with matter on interposed leaves. Twenty-five folios (the same number of pages) quarto, signed and dated at the end "August 1917"; some leaves carry both typed and handwritten versions of the same interpolated lines (often not agreeing with one another); unbound and boxed in half red morocco. In the Houghton Library, Harvard University. Purchased from Mrs. Yeats and received at Harvard on March 1, 1950. The contiguous sequence of folios 1–24 is followed by a duplicative folio 1a, a somewhat revised fair-hand version made from Yeats's copying out again folio 1. The earliest states preserved in this mixed version are removed from notebooks and sometimes bear indecipherable writings on the sides that have been pasted down. Types 2, 8, and 12 paper, in various combinations, have been attached to type 11 paper. The reconstruction of the four layers of manuscript stratum is given in the transcription notes below.

Harvard(B) A file containing an unsigned carbon copy of a typescript of the play on twenty-one sheets (twenty-one pages) of type 13 paper, prepared by Misses Jacobs and Oldroyd, Literary and Typewriting Office (47 Great Russell Street, London) and carrying the bookplate of John Quinn. The typescript compares with the others typed for Yeats by that office—NLI 8775(3), NLI 8775(4) and Texas(B)—but is an entirely different typed state, prepared for printing (not acting) and bearing some nonauthorial corrections in pencil to make uniform such things as character headings. Other corrections, such as the movement of half lines and changes in punctuation, are made in pencil and black ink, the latter almost certainly by the poet. Once received by John Quinn in New York, Harvard(B) became the copy text for yet another typescript of the play (hereafter called "Quinn") used in the *Little Review* printing. Sewn in a brown paper cover with ribbon of same color, the typescript has been in the Houghton Library, Harvard, since October 1935.

NLI 8775(1) A folder containing part of a large brown envelope, inscribed on one side: "Cover of packet which contained items now Ms. 8775"; inscribed on the other: "Dreaming of the Bones — / W. B. Yeats // 2 corrected typescripts / both corrected by WBY // Some corrections dictated to G.Y. / & in her writing // a few stage directions by Lennox / Robinson / in his writing / MSS. Note on play — // MSS Fragments — listed by Trinity College / (No. 84)." Includes fourteen sheets of type 1 paper, numbered 1 to 14 in pencil, bearing in holograph and in black ink a two-part prose Subject (or theme) of the play and a complete prose draft of speeches by the chorus (notably without the songs), a stranger called "Mac Dermit," the Young Man, and the Young Girl. The contiguous order of the manuscript is 1^{r}, 1^{v}, 2^{r}–9^{r}, 9^{v}, 10^{r}–14^{r}. Leaf 14^{v} consists of a canceled paragraph, evidently prepared for a letter on the subject of Hugh Lane. Also contains a note on a slip of paper: "I have placed / 'p. 15' in folder / 8775(2), where it / apparently belongs. / David R. Jones / 12/5/67" (see NLI 8775[2], leaf 5^{r}); as well as a notation on each side of a envelope flap, as follows: "Dreaming of the Bones — / Stray pages only" and "Watt / June 20 — Nov 2 / 1923" (entirely canceled). "Stray pages" might refer to the vagrant lyrics and set pieces composed for them in NLI 8775(2).

NLI 8775(2) A folder containing five leaves of various holographic drafts, including four units of work on songs and associated speeches as defined below. These units anticipate the earliest of the multiple draft states compounded in Harvard(A), the only complete version of the play extant in holograph. If, as seems probable, a verse draft of the play had been undertaken before the fragments of NLI 8775(2) were written, that draft is lost. The four units are as follows:

> Unit 1: on type 1 paper, two drafts (in black ink) of the passage beginning "Why should the heart take fright . . . " (leaves 1^{r}–2^{r}/2^{v}; cf. *VPl* 90–129).
>
> Unit 2: on type 5 paper (leaf 3^{r}), the following drafts in pencil of the songs and integrating speeches correspondent with *VPl* 90, 92–95*sd*, and 96–99 (with first song from 2^{r}, "Why should the heart take fright," copied over with slight correction), concluding with a version of lines 108–111.
>
> Unit 3: on a half sheet of type 5 paper (leaf 4^{r}) in pencil, a transitional speech for the third song, with revision of the song itself as it was copied out (cf. *VPl* 119–129; only "Calamity," in line 126, remains to be developed).
>
> Unit 4: on type 5 paper (leaf 5^{r}) in pencil, reworked passages that were heavily revised on 3^{r} and correspondent with *VPl* 96–100 and 108–111.

NLI 8775(3) A folder containing a corrected typescript of the play (bound with red ribbon), endorsed in black ink on a brown paper cover measuring 26.7 cm by 21.5 cm: "Corrected copy

/ 1931"; inscribed again (in red ink): "Some corrections WBY / (dictated to) G.Y.— / Stage directions Lennox Robinson." Besides the cover, this typed ribbon copy of the play consists of twenty sheets of type 3 paper, text with typed numbers [1]–18, with title page and a blank sheet forming endpapers. This corrected version, in its first typing, anticipates the 1919 printings in *The Little Review* and *Two Plays for Dancers*, although some revisions, as in the Stranger's last line (282) and in a half-page paste-over at lines 246–256, generally bring the text into conformity with *Collected Plays* (1934). The scenes and stage directions are in red, and none of the pencil substitutions of "Stranger" for "THE GIRL" were made near the end in any printing, including the unpublished Coole edition. The text as originally typed compares with Texas(B), which lacks later revisions, and with NLI 8775(4), another carbon copy bearing the corrections made in 1931.

NLI 8775(4) A folder containing another typescript of the play, a carbon copy of NLI 8775(3) on type 3 paper (though with brown ribbon), assembled identically and bearing a similar inscription, in red ink: "Corrected by WBY / Some corrections dictated to GY / & in her writing." The twenty sheets are numbered [1]–18 (the title page and endpaper go without numbering). The scenes, directions, and character names in headings are, of course, not in red in this carbon copy, although they are underscored in red on the ribbon copy. Both the paste-over passage at lines 246–256 and the underlying original may be discerned, because the carbon undertext is darker than the characters on the overlying slip, confirming use at two different times. Like NLI 8775(3), this typescript predates Harvard(B) and Quinn in its first use but was recycled for later production and editions of the play.

NLI 8775(5) A folder containing a holograph draft of Yeats's note on the play, in four numbered pages in black ink and on type 4 paper, possibly anticipating a typescript now lost. However, the note might easily have been set up directly into galley proof from this more than usually legible manuscript. At two points are printer's notations on fonts to be used in 1921 for *Four Plays for Dancers* (Wade 129).

NLI 13,583 A file containing various fragments and drafts of unpublished poems, with some fragments of published material, including a holograph fragment, on a single leaf of type 2 paper, of an early version of the First Musician's song at the opening of *The Dreaming of the Bones*, in black ink with corrections in pencil, and the second verse of his second song, at (roughly) *VPl* 112–118, in pencil.

NLI 30,007 A folder containing corrected page proofs of *Plays* from the Coole edition. The relevant portions in volume 4 are date stamped November 27 to December 7, 1931, and July 20 to October 7, 1932. Marked by Yeats, with his autograph note: "I think I had better see a / 'revise' of ~~the~~ this volume. / WBY." On the half title page, at the top: "Marked by author." There are various superimposed notations, including the correct (i.e., roughly chronological) sequence of the plays for the volume, beginning with *The Hour-Glass* and concluding with *The King of the Great Clock Tower*; the order of plays in *Four Plays for Dancers* is retained. *The Dreaming of the Bones*, stamped "FIRST PROOF," is missing much of the lower corners of all pages ([133]–145, including some printed and handwritten matter). Occasional marginal queries, in another hand, presumably those of Mrs. Yeats; these are usually crossed out when responded to by Yeats. All corrections are introduced in black ink. The play is given the date 1919. The *Calvary* segment (pp. [147]–158) is damaged but without the lacunae in *The Dreaming of the Bones*, the most damaged play in this set of proofs. Queries by Mrs. Yeats are canceled when responded to. All corrections are in black ink. The play is assigned the date 1920.

NLI 30,051 An envelope containing two typescript fragments of the play. The first, on type 2 paper, consists of a ribbon-copy transcript of the opening scene and the First Musician's song (*VPl* 1–16); the second, on type 8 paper, consists of a ribbon-copy transcript of early dialogue between the Stranger and the Young Man (ll. 46–59a) agreeing with all printings save for one word: "Finvara" appears as "Kinvara" at line 51. Neither fragment is corrected.

NLI 30,071 An envelope containing a torn sheet of paper bearing two autograph fragments of dialogue from the play, in black ink, corresponding to *VPl* 152–154 and 173–175. An ellipsis before the first part and ellipses before and after the second suggest that this sheet was prepared to introduce revisions into an otherwise complete version, perhaps the mixed, multistate version of Harvard(A) or one of several typescripts. The fourteen gray ruled lines on both sides of this slip (spaced 0.8 cm apart), plus the torn edge at right, confirm the slip's origin to be a bound notebook. No watermark, 12.5 cm by 20.5 cm (at maximum width). A pin hole in the upper left corner shows that it was once attached to other papers.

NLI 30,079 An envelope containing manuscript notes and fragments on type 9 paper, mostly for *The Only Jealousy of Emer* but also a handwritten "Order of Contents" for *Four Plays for Dancers* (1921; Wade 129), a typed "Contents" for same (bearing autograph corrections in black ink) and a note on a sheet of type 10 paper: "Four/~~Three~~ designs for masks or costumes will be sent for this book by Edmond Dulac, & two photographs of players wearing the masks." The directions on the typed contents also concern Dulac's designs and, like the handwritten list, depart from chronology and the final order by leading with *The Dreaming of the Bones*.

NLI 30,545 A white vellum manuscript notebook begun on November 23, 1930, and containing working drafts of poems and prose, including a one-page holograph draft entitled "Note for Abbey Programe (Dreaming of Bones)." The program note, written for a revival of the play in the 1930s, was copied out of the notebook and revised as NLI 30,820. The 387-page notebook, now privately owned, is on the NLI accession list but was sold by Michael Yeats. It is described in Sotheby's sale catalog on *English Literature and History* (London), Thursday, July 19, 1990, lot 210, pages 134–139. The program note is listed as item 24 (for p. 132) in an index to contents made by Curtis Bradford.

NLI 30,820 An envelope containing a holograph draft of a program note for the play. The note refers to text as reprinted in *Plays and Controversies* (1923). The one-page draft is a revision of the note in NLI 30,545. The sheet measures 20.2 cm by 16.4 cm and bears round corners and double red lines printed 2.2 cm from the top, followed by thirty-one light blue horizontal lines; made for a three-ring notebook, with three holes on the left and watermarked WALKER / LOOSE / LEAF.

Quinn A folder containing a twenty-one-page typescript (on type 15 paper) made for the poet by John Quinn at Z. & L. Rosenfeld (New York), for the first American printing of the play in *The Little Review* (January 1919), part of the Foster-Murphy Collection (box 14; Yeats, William Butler, TS. 913) at the New York Public Library. On a gray cover, folded over at 27.9 cm by 21.5 cm to a side and attached to the play by two brass pins, as were other typescripts commissioned by Quinn near his law office in Manhattan. The inscription, "Yeats, W. B." (in pencil), is not in Yeats's hand. This version of the play was derived from retyping Harvard(B) with unusual exactness, making corrections marked in the former by Yeats, but repeats overlooked typographical errors such as "zitha" for "zither," a fault also found in Texas(B), NLI 8775(3), and NLI 8775(4), though caught by Yeats in the last instance.

Texas(A) A folder containing a holograph draft of the lyric "At the grey round of the hill" (the song of the First Musician at the end of the play) with emendations in black ink (one page, torn in two and then mended with a strip of the same type 16 paper). Inscribed in another hand in the lower left margin of the manuscript: "Composed Ely Place / ~~10~~ 9.vii.'17." Part of the Yeats collection at the Harry Ransom Humanities Research Center, University of Texas at Austin.

Texas(B) A folder containing a typed carbon copy of the play, with autograph emendations, signed and dated August 1917, on type 3 paper and identical with NLI 8775(3) and (4) save for the later amendments made on those two typescripts and for differences in the correction of punctuation. A brown paper cover (26.5 cm by 21 cm) is sewn to the typescript at five points and bears the typed title, centered and underscored twice in red ink. All textual changes in speeches and directions are in pencil; scorings in red ink are ruled beneath headings and directions; some scorings beneath amendments are in blue crayon, as are vertical scorings and bracketings in the margins. Above the title are the following notes in Yeats's hand: "Flute = The Life [?as] Elemental in Principle / Plucked Instr. = The Soul Element / Bow Instr. (nasal) = The Spirit Element / Drum (Cymbal) = The Body Element."

Texas(C) A folder containing page proofs with autograph emendations, sixteen pages printed, and a typed title page bearing (at lower left) the credit: "From / The Paget Literary Agency / 25 West 45th Street / New York City"; as well as the note (in ink and not in Yeats's hand): "Proof sheets corrected by the author of the / First Edition as it appeared in 'Two Plays / for Dancers' " (Cuala Press, 1919).

Texas(D) A folder containing the preface and preliminary pages of *Four Plays for Dancers*, "First Proof" copy in ten pages; printer's stamp: "1920 October 14" (by R. & R. Clark, Edinburgh).

Texas(E) Scribner box 2, folder 2, containing a clean printed copy of the play as part of a unit removed from *Collected Plays* (1934), reorganized and numbered according to the sequence in *Four Plays for Dancers*—that is, 4–7, in the order of plays for volume 4 of Scribner's never-realized "Dublin Edition," rather than 8, 11, 15, 16, in *Collected Plays*. Also includes notes on the plays and music to *The Dreaming of the Bones*, apparently removed from *Plays and Controversies* (1923).

Part II. *Calvary*

BL Add. MS 55879 See the general description in part I, above.

BL Add. MS 55884 See the general description in part I, above.

BL Add. MS 55891 See the general description in part I, above.

Harvard(C) An autograph manuscript (unsigned), consisting of thirteen folios (or sixteen pages) of type 14 paper and constituting one complete draft of the play, postdating the two drafts of NLI 30,361 and anticipating the typescripts NLI 8776(3) and (4). The folios are remounted in half red morocco from an exercise notebook. Titled "On the Road to Calvary," the manuscript has been in the Houghton Library since March 1, 1950, after being purchased from Mrs. Yeats.

NLI 8776(1) A folder containing (in five folios of type 4 paper) a holograph draft of Yeats's note on the play, in black ink, anticipating typescripts NLI 30,789 and NLI 8776(2). These pages of lightweight typing paper are numbered 2 to 5, starting with the second page, and were fastened together by a rusting paper clip at one time. For *Four Plays for Dancers* (1921; Wade 129).

NLI 8776(2) A folder containing (in five sheets of type 4 paper) a corrected ribbon copy of the note on the play typed from NLI 8776(1). These pages are numbered 2 to 5, starting with the second page, and were fastened by a pin that has left a hole in the upper left-hand corner of all the sheets. All corrections are in black ink and correspond with the ones made on the last page of NLI 30,789. A printer's notation on sheet 1^r—"Pica Cas" (in pencil)—suggests that this copy was used in typesetting *Four Plays for Dancers* (1921; Wade 129).

NLI 8776(3) A folder containing (in six sheets of type 6 paper) a mixed set of two typescripts to produce one complete version of the play (1^r–2^r and 4^r are ribbon copies; 3^r and 5^r–6^r are carbon copies), with substantial autograph corrections in black ink throughout. Unnumbered and with a pin hole in the upper right corner of each sheet. This carries on from Harvard(C) and leads to NLI 8776(4).

NLI 8776(4) A folder containing (in eight sheets of type 6 paper) another typed version of the play (carbon copy), incorporating the amendments and corrections of NLI 8776(3), with three autograph revisions (in black ink) and a few further corrections and notations for printing (in pencil and in another hand). Typed page numbers [1]–8 are canceled and superseded by autograph numbers in upper right-hand corners (in black ink), 2–9. The missing page 1 might have carried the opening scene and dramatis personae. These eight sheets were attached by means of a pin in the upper left-hand corner, as a small hole attests.

NLI 30,007 See the general description in part I, above.

NLI 30,079 See the general description in part I, above.

NLI 30,125 An envelope containing a large folded sheet of galley proof (51 cm by 76 cm) for

Yeats's note on *Calvary*, with autograph corrections in black ink, for *Four Plays for Dancers* (1921; Wade 129), stamped "FIRST PROOF" and "7 OCT 1920" by the printer, R. & R. Clark, Edinburgh.

NLI 30,361 A quarto-size manuscript notebook of sixty leaves, without watermark, measuring 20 cm by 16.5 cm and bearing twenty light blue, horizontal, ruled lines on both sides of each page. The first page of this exercise book presents an astrological chart inscribed: "Horary 8.50. August 30. 1919. / Ballylee." But, having made this entry, Yeats turned the notebook over and worked from back to front. The assigned folio numbers, therefore, proceed from the earliest extant holograph version of *Calvary* (in two drafts), called "The Road to ~~Al~~ Calvary" (on leaves 1–26, and, intermittently, leaves 28, 29, and 30), and including a sketch of a door opened to a dark interior (27^{v}; see frontispiece on p. 117, below), the first draft of "Solomon and the Witch" (sideways and partly upside down on 30^{v} and 31^{v}), much material related to *The Player Queen* (31^{r} and 32–41), and a draft of the essay "A People's Theatre: Letter to lady Gregory" (42–60). The horary appears on 60^{v}, entered with the notebook reversed.

NLI 30,789 A folder containing (in five sheets of type 7 paper) Yeats's "Note on the Symbolism of 'Calvary,'" a carbon copy of the typescript NLI 8776(2), with autograph revisions (in black ink) on page 5 only, roughly comparable to those made in his hand on the ribbon copy, although the unique amendments made on the carbon were not printed in *Four Plays for Dancers* (1921) or in later printings.

Texas(D) A folder containing the preface and preliminary pages of *Four Plays for Dancers*, "First Proof" copy (10 pp.); printer's stamp: "1920 October 14" (by R. & R. Clark, Edinburgh).

Texas(E) Scribner box 2, folder 2, containing a clean copy of the play as part of a unit removed from *Collected Plays* (1934), reorganized and numbered according to the sequence in *Four Plays for Dancers* (that is, 4–7, in the order of plays for volume 4 of Scribner's never-realized "Dublin Edition," rather than 8, 11, 15, 16, in *Collected Plays*). The folder also includes notes on each of the plays, apparently removed from *Plays and Controversies* (1923).

Introduction

I. General Conception of the Plays

It is commonplace, especially for last Romantics as beholden to Shelley and Keats as was Yeats, that strong poets should declare themselves wedded to the muse. It is also characteristic of Yeats's Irishness as a poet that he should equate the spousal muse with Ireland. Enduring the young Joyce's parody of him, in the "The Holy Office" (1904), as one who indeed would "accounted be . . . of that mumming company . . . to appease / His giddy dames' frivolities" and be consoled "when he whinges / With gold-embroidered Celtic fringes" (ll. 23–28),[1] Yeats similarly derided his imitators by 1914. So there was "more enterprise / In walking naked" (*VP* 320, ll. 9–10). "[C]lose on forty-nine" and childless (*VP* 270, ll. 20–21), he reckoned that his muse of yore, "that reed-throated whisperer / Who comes at need, although not now as once" (*VP* 320, ll. 1–2), might still inspire in defense of Lady Gregory a lacerating invective against the enemies of Romantic Ireland. Consequently, Yeats became a modern poet according to his protégé and companion at the time, Ezra Pound—"making it new" but rededicating the work of his life to ancient principles in the conception of a national tradition. The same can be said of Yeats the playwright because of the novel direction he took after 1914 in composing several highly experimental, one-act, lyric plays.

Right from the beginning, Yeats makes clear his dedication to country in the introduction to *Certain Noble Plays of Japan*, "translated by Ernest Fenollosa and finished by Ezra Pound" for initial publication by the Cuala Press "in the year of the Sinn Fein rising" (1916):

> In the series of books I edit for my sister I confine myself to those that have I believe some special value to Ireland, now or in the future. I have asked Mr. Pound for these beautiful plays because I think they will help me to explain a certain possibility of the Irish dramatic movement. . . . In fact with the help of these plays . . . I have invented a form of drama, distinguished, indirect and symbolic, and having no need of mob or press to pay its way. . . . When this play and its performance run as smoothly as my skill can make them, I shall hope to write another of the same sort and so complete a dramatic celebration of the life of Cuchulain planned long ago. . . . It is an advantage of this noble

[1]James Joyce, *Poems and Shorter Writings*, ed. Richard Ellmann, A. Walton Litz, and John Whittier-Ferguson (London: Faber and Faber, 1991), p. 97.

form that it need absorb no one's life, that its few properties can be packed up in a box, or hung upon the walls where they will be fine ornaments.[2]

Moreover, the incidence of war in 1916—the one in France and the Sinn Fein uprising in Dublin—made Yeats's adaptation of the Noh in *At the Hawk's Well* only the beginning of invention.[3] For the Japanese paradigm at hand "arose in an age of continual war and became a part of the education of soldiers" (*E&I* 235). Perhaps he had no inkling that he had a play within him on the passion of Christ; nevertheless, Yeats recognized working in such dramatic forms "the most vivid and subtle discrimination of sense and the invention of images more powerful than sense"; "the Deity gives us, according to His promise, not His thoughts or His convictions but His flesh and blood" (235). Although intertwined with *The Dreaming of the Bones*, the making of *Calvary* was still years off. On the other hand, the former, the second of Yeats's "plays for dancers," is anticipated by his observations on one Noh play in particular:

> The adventure . . . is often the meeting with ghost, god, or goddess at some holy place or much-legended tomb; and god, goddess, or ghost reminds me at times of our own Irish legends and beliefs . . . . [A]nd the ghost-lovers in *Nishikigi* remind me of the Aran boy and girl who in Lady Gregory's story[4] come to the priest after death to be married. These Japanese poets, too, feel for tomb and wood the emotion, the sense of awe that our Gaelic-speaking countrypeople will sometimes show when you speak to them of Castle Hackett or of some holy well; and that is why perhaps it pleases them to begin so many plays by a traveller asking his way with many questions, a convention agreeable to me, for when I first began to write poetical plays for an Irish theatre I had to put away an ambition of helping to bring again to certain places their old sanctity or their romance. . . . But in the *Nishikigi* the tale of the lovers would lose its pathos if we did not see that forgotten tomb where "the hiding fox" lives among "the orchids and the chrysanthemum flowers." The men who created this convention . . . measured all that time had taken or would take away and found their delight in remembering celebrated lovers in the scenery pale passion loves. . . . When a traveller asks his way of girls upon the roadside he is directed to find it by certain pine-trees, which he will recognise because many people have drawn them. . . . In

[2]The American edition of Ernest Fenollosa and Ezra Pound, *"Noh" or Accomplishment: A Study of the Classical Stage of Japan* (New York: Alfred A. Knopf, 1917), was reissued as *The Classic Noh Theatre of Japan* (New York: New Directions, 1959), from which the passage is quoted, pp. 151–152; see *E&I* 221–222, where the initial two sentences are missing and, as elsewhere, numerous other variants occur.

[3]Although his preface to the play is dated October 24, 1916, the play itself was first performed in April, the endpapers of a copy of *Responsibilities: Poems and a Play* (Dublin: Cuala, 1914; Emory, copy 2) being used to choreograph the Japanese dancer, Mr. Ito, in relation to the musicians, just as revisions elsewhere constituted partial copy text for the so-called standard edition of *Responsibilities* (1916). Contracts for the last and for a projected complete works were issued by Macmillan virtually on the eve of the Easter Rising. Publication of *At the Hawk's Well* in March and June 1917, when Yeats's first Rebellion poems began circulating privately, coincides with the writing of *The Dreaming of the Bones*, which deviated from his plan to complete "the life of Cuchulain" in such plays.

[4]The story is told by Old Deruane in Lady Gregory's *Visions and Beliefs in the West of Ireland Collected and Arranged by Lady Gregory: With Two Essays and Notes by W. B. Yeats* (1920; 2d ed., Gerrards Cross, U.K.: Colin Smythe, 1970), p. 79. Yeats contributes the following note there (p. 359, n. 36): "The same story as that in one of the most beautiful of the 'Noh' plays of Japan. I tell the Japanese story in my long terminal essay." Indeed, the whole plot of *Nishikigi* is summarized at length by Yeats on pp. 334–335 of Lady Gregory's book (with another allusion to the Aran story) in "Swedenborg, Mediums, and the Desolate Places."

> the *Nishikigi* the ghost of the girl-lover carries the cloth she went on weaving out of grass when she should have opened the chamber door to her lover, and woven grass returns again and again in metaphor and incident. The lovers, now that in an aëry body they must sorrow for unconsummated love, are "tangled up as the grass patterns are tangled." Again they are like an unfinished cloth: "these bodies, having no weft, even now are not come together; truly a shameful story, a tale to bring shame on the gods." (232–234)

In *The Dreaming of the Bones*, the Three Musicians begin their first "Song for the folding and unfolding of the cloth" by asking "Who can have trod in the grass? / What rogue is night-wandering?" (*VPl* 763, ll. 4–5), questions connected with both the grass motif of *Nishikigi*'s "girl-lover" (Tsure) and the "traveller" (the Waki) who "seems an Aran fisher" (l. 28) in Yeats's play. The tangling of bodies that have no "weft" signifies the closing dance of forlorn lovers and the concluding "Songs for the unfolding and folding of the cloth." The dream-cloth grass weaving of the Japanese heroine resembles the rope making of Yeats's early story "The Twisting of the Rope" to such an extent that we might suppose that he thought of that, too, delighted that his invention had such a precedent.

So let us consider briefly Red Hanrahan's relation to mythic Echtge and his devotion to the Ireland of fairy lore in stories of *The Secret Rose* (1897) as preliminary to Yeats's revisiting in 1917—when inspired by the *Nishikigi* translation—the legend of notorious Diarmuid and Dervorgilla as told by Yeats in the story "Hanrahan's Vision." From 1917 to 1921, the later Yeats found himself absorbed personally and politically in the subject of betrayal, having recently taken an English wife, a young muse who inspired "metaphors for poetry" but who was not Maud Gonne nor any personification of Ireland. Siring children during the Anglo-Irish war and expecting his nation to call him to duty as a statesman, he worked on his credentials (in England, for the most part) as both a father of his country and a citizen of the world, styling himself as an ironic patriot in several Rebellion poems and a spokesman for such citizenship in the philosophical "plays for dancers," *The Dreaming of the Bones* and *Calvary*. These plays about betrayal really have their origin in Yeats's return, in *The Dreaming of the Bones*, to the place of Hanrahan's meeting with the lovers whose "sin brought the Norman into Ireland" (*VSR* 116, 220). Though Yeats's sympathy is palpable, it is equivocally hedged in the closing speech of this play about modern Ireland: "I had almost yielded and forgiven it all— / This is indeed a place of terrible temptation" (*VPl* 775, ll. 281–282 in *apparatus criticus*).

Owen Hanrahan, whom "men call . . . the Red," or, in time, simply Red Hanrahan after Lady Gregory helped revise the stories of *The Secret Rose* (1897) into the more idiomatic *Stories of Red Hanrahan* (1907), was largely based on the eighteenth-century bard Owen Roe of Munster, also known as Eoghan Ruadh ó Súilleabháin. Hanrahan's Sidhe mistress was called "Cleena of the Wave" in the 1897 printing (*VSR* 190) and thereafter "Echtge, daughter of the Silver Hand" (92); like Fand to Yeats's Cuchulain, she is in both versions a sort of Irish Venus to counterpoint Hanrahan's worldly desire for a flesh-and-blood woman, Oona or his lost sweetheart, Mary Lavelle. His heart's desire being thus conflicted, he is tempted by the blandishments of the fairy queen of Slieve Echtge but does not wholly give himself to such favoritism, to his misfortune: "It is a pity for him that refuses the call of the daughters of the Sidhe," the voices foretell, "for he will find no comfort in the love of the women of the earth to the end of life and time" (102). Still, his songs are a curse to the inhospitable and praise to Ireland and her "ancient defeated gods" (114). He is dangerous and a power among the folk, "for he is a poet of the Gael" (100). His songs are about "Ireland and her griefs, under one name or another" (103), love songs of

"Hanrahan's Rosary," "poems disguising a passionate patriotism under the form of a love-song addressed to the Little Black Rose or Kathleen the Daughter of Hoolihan or some other personification of Ireland" (207).

The Steep Place of the Strangers, a covert, fabled vantage spot on Lugnagall from which to view "the white door that is in the side" of Ben Bulben headland, Sligo (115), recurs as an important site in the Hanrahan stories, like the forgotten tomb among "the orchids and the chrysanthemum flowers" in *Nishikigi*. In "Hanrahan's Vision," with a flutter of wild rose petals in the air, "the gateway of Eternity" opens and closes "in one beat of the heart" (117), a Blakean "pulsation of the heart" (220). Instructive for Hanrahan because of his conflicted feelings for Mary Lavelle and for his Dé Danann muse, a procession of lovers makes whirling flight toward this gateway, including "tall beautiful young men, and . . . queen-women" (114) whose aspect appears all the more strange for the glinting in starlight of "heart-shaped mirrors" they have "instead of hearts" (115). These couples, Hanrahan learns from one of two standing "dark and half-hidden forms" (115), "are not put in songs by the poets, because they sought only to triumph one over the other, and so to prove their strength and beauty, and out of this they made a kind of love" (116). The confession she makes is moving, but it also invokes cathartic terror in the poet she addresses:

> All these are unhappy, but I am the unhappiest of all, for I am Dervagilla, and this is Dermot, and it was our sin brought the Norman into Ireland. And the curses of all the generations are upon us. . . . It was but the blossom of the man and of the woman we loved in one another, and so when we died there was no lasting unbreakable quiet about us, and the bitterness of the battles we brought into Ireland turned to our own punishment. We go wandering together for ever, but Dermot that was my lover sees me always as a body that has been a long time in the ground, and I know that is the way he sees me. Ask me more, ask me more, for all the years have left their wisdom in my heart, and no one has listened to me for seven hundred years. (116–117)

Red Hanrahan screams three times into the night in "great terror" to avaunt the shades of Ireland's damned (117). The story ends, but in the sequence of tales Yeats remains ambiguously attentive to the problem of divided loyalties. To which object of devotion—that is, to muse or to beloved—should one be true?

Hanrahan eventually dies, as the fairies have foretold: "the cold of the grave is in his heart for ever. It is death he has chosen; let him die, let him die, let him die" (102). Discovered by turf cutters, this bard of the Gael is given "a burying worthy of so great a poet" of Mother Ireland, though he had lived miserably in poverty and was father to no one (123).

Middle-aged and determined to change the circumstances of his own life, Yeats made perhaps the first unmistakable reference from which to date the writing of *The Dreaming of the Bones* in a letter to Lady Gregory, dated June 11 [1917], wherein he says:

> I have almost finished my Dervogilla play[,] I think the best play I have written for years. It has grown greatly since you ~~say~~ saw it & is I am afraid only too powerful politically. I have nothing more to write but the lyrics & must leave London for that. (Berg Collection, box 13, folder 900973; cf. *Letters* 626)

It follows that this might be the play he had written about the month before, on May 15, to Olivia Shakespear, his former lover and the step-aunt of his eventual bride: "I have . . . started another play in the manner of *The Hawk's Well*" (*Letters* 626).[5] On July 6, 1917, he stayed in Dublin with his physician and close friend Oliver St. John Gogarty, in whose house Yeats is supposed to have read the play in an unfinished but very advanced state to the mostly appreciative James Stephens.[6] Possibly *At the Hawk's Well* was read instead, accompanied by musicians, since the manuscripts date the last song in *The Dreaming of the Bones* as "Composed Ely Place / ~~10~~ 9: VII: '17"—i.e., written at George Russell's Dublin residence on 9 July 1917, three days later—and date completion of the play as a whole as occurring in "August 1917" (Texas [A] and Harvard [A], 24^{r}), more than a month *after* Yeats's reading at Gogarty's. Moreover, in a letter to Lady Gregory of August 12, 1917, Yeats announced: "I have finished my play. I think of calling it 'The dreaming of the bones.' I have greatly improved it since you saw it—improving & adding to the lyrics & strengthening the atmosphere" (Berg Collection, box 13, folder 900935). The letter was sent from Maud Gonne's home in Calvados, France, and reports the play's reception there as his "best" because of "some popular quality." He was pleased that the music was to be written by Walter Morse Rummel on Edmund Dulac's recommendation and that Maud and Iseult Gonne, two of the objects of his matrimonial pursuit in that year, were once again on "good terms." By September 8, from the Hôtel Gavarni, Paris, he wrote again to say that he expected to bring back at least part of the music Rummel was still writing for the "Noh play," *The Dreaming of the Bones*, and that "Sooner or later I shall want to get it up in Dublin but not yet" (Berg Collection, box 13, folder 900988).

Yeats continued to revise text and work on notes to the play for another year or more, in preparation for publication, as Mrs. Yeats (starting in October) recorded on the composition of the work in his library: "August 1917 / re-written 1918 summer" (*YL* 2350). With this activity extended and publication stalled in *The Little Review* and *Two Plays for Dancers* until January 1919, its overall writing collided with and elided into other projects, including *The Only Jealousy of Emer*. The writing of *The Only Jealousy of Emer* had given place to *The Dreaming of the Bones* until shortly after Yeats's marriage to Georgie Hyde-Lees, through whom the spirit guides instructed him in the completion of work and counseled him out of depression weeks after he had abandoned pursuit of Maud and Iseult Gonne. Indeed, new work on a "philosophical dialogue" from which *A Vision* (1925) originated had to be stopped temporarily to relieve insomnia and to write verse once more, including "another rebellion poem," as he reported to Lady Gregory, from London, on December 16, 1917, noting that the way had cleared to "finish my play & then return to the dialogue" (Berg Collection, box 13, folder 900995).[7] Also relevant to the textual-genetic climate are philosophical poems such as "The Phases of the Moon," which emerged in dialogic form with the mystical papers that fictitiously stood at the center of *A Vision*. As Yeats said when reprinting the play in *Four Plays for Dancers* (1921),

---

[5]On June 7, [1917], Yeats wrote to Lady Gregory from the Savile Club, London, and reports working "every morning" on it (New York Public Library, Berg Collection, box 13, folder 900972). By June 30, he was still in London but anticipating his departure for Ireland (folder 900981), and, just prior to July 10, 1917, from George Russell's address at 15 Ely Place, Dublin, he wrote to her of his plans to take the train to visit her at Coole Park after seeing people in Dublin on business and to collect information for a lecture on Padraic Pearse.

[6]See James Stephens, *Letters of James Stephens*, ed. Richard J. Finneran (London: Macmillan, 1974), p. 219. Stephens's letter of the next day, as a cover to verses promised Gogarty at the reading, found Yeats's as yet untitled play "marvellous" and "beautiful" but defective for its excessive "artifice"—the drum, the unwinding of the cloth, and "little journeys round the stage"—that got between the play and the audience.

[7]Possibly the play Yeats alluded to was *The Only Jealousy of Emer*, which had been interrupted by the writing of *The Dreaming of the Bones* and which, like *Calvary*, required the collaborative genius of the automatic script to get Yeats's writing into verse.

> I wrote my play before the Robartes papers came into my hands, and in making the penance of Dermot and Dervorgilla last so many centuries I have done something for which I had no warrant in these papers, but warrant there certainly is in the folk-lore of all countries. (*VPl* 778)[8]

When Yeats said in June 1917 that he was "afraid" that *The Dreaming of the Bones* was "only too powerful politically," he was acknowledging that the play was another instance, like the incendiary group elegy "Easter, 1916" and several poems on the subject of the insurrection, in which he had been careful not to compromise negotiations with the British Government over the contested Hugh Lane paintings. Lady Gregory had asked him to be discreet—hence he deferred publishing the Rebellion poems in standard editions and in the press for four years[9]—and it is clear that his decision to delay publication of "the best play I have written for years" was similarly motivated. His limited edition of 1919 at the Cuala Press and Macmillan's *Four Plays for Dancers* of 1921 are exactly coincident with *The Wild Swans at Coole*, from which his Rebellion poems were withheld although part of the original plan, and *Michael Robartes and the Dancer*, in which those lyrics appeared together for the first time.[10]

On February 9 [1918], Yeats wrote to Iseult Gonne, noting the death of Robert Gregory, an expected trip to London over the Lane pictures, progress on the spiritual exercises with Mrs. Yeats, and completion of "a Cuchulain poem full of this new philosophy. I wish I could tell you of what has come but it is all so vast and one part depends upon another" (Stony Brook, box 56, folio 107). The "Cuchulain poem" to which the letter refers is probably not a Noh play but "The Phases of the Moon," which in early fragments took the form of a dialogue in which Cuchulain listens to the recitation of a master much as Aherne listens to that of Robartes in the poem's familiar state. Seemingly lifted from draft materials of *The Only Jealousy of Emer*,[11] the early "Phases of the Moon" manuscript was certainly part of a network of projects on which *The Dreaming of the Bones* depended. After writing *At the Hawk's Well*, in 1916, on the model of the Japanese theater of the Noh, Yeats might refer to any of his "plays for dancers" as a "Cuchulain play" yet perhaps less probably a "Cuchulain poem." Mrs. Yeats's dating of "Phases of the Moon"

---

[8]See Liam Miller, *The Noble Drama of W. B. Yeats* (Dublin: Dolmen, 1977), p. 240, where it is argued that divergence from the more realistic and historically accurate play *Dervorgilla*, by Lady Gregory, accounts for Yeats's failing to cite his friend as a source, although crediting the Abbey secretary W. A. Henderson "with great kindness" for providing "all historical [a]llusions to 'Dervorgilla'" (see appendix E). Probably, Henderson included excerpts from the histories of Edmund Campion (1571) and Meredith Hanmer (1571); see *Ancient Irish Histories, The Works of Spencer, Campion, Hanmer, and Marleburrough* (Dublin: Hibernia, 1809; rpt., Port Washington, N.Y.: Kennikat, 1970), vol. 1: [Campion] bk. 2, chap. 1, pp. 79–84; and vol. 2: [Hanmer] part 2, pp. 218–240. Counterintuitively, perhaps, all but Yeats's final touches to *The Dreaming of the Bones* seem to have been made before he became acquainted with one of the main sources of his doctrine of "the dreaming back"; the Yeatses' reading of Theodor Fechner's *On Life after Death* (1914; *YL* 665) will be discussed accordingly, in part III (below), in relation to Yeats's *Calvary*.

[9]See Wayne K. Chapman, "The Annotated *Responsibilities* . . . ," *Yeats Annual* no. 6, ed. Warwick Gould (London: Macmillan, 1988), 108–133.

[10]See the detailed account in the introduction to W. B. Yeats, *The Wild Swans at Coole: Manuscript Materials*, ed. Stephen Parrish (Ithaca: Cornell University Press, 1994); see also Chapman 1:151, for dates of composition for the other deferred Rebellion poems.

[11]The textual affinities are reported in "The Miltonic Crux of 'The Phases of the Moon,'" *Yeats Annual* no. 8, ed. Warwick Gould (London: Macmillan, 1991), 59–77. The unusual paper type used in the early fragment of the poem (in NLI 13,587[21]) finds its complement in only three disjunctive fragments of the play: NLI 8774 folders 8, 14, and 16 (of 23). Folder 14, bearing a dialogue between Cuchulain and a Woman of the Sidhe, proceeds from a gap of ten pages, as the surviving numbered pages of the scene suggest. Folders 8 and 16, respectively, relate to the choral unfolding and folding of the cloth and to a scene between the Woman of the Sidhe and the Evil Genius.

and the second, third, and fourth dance plays (see Chapman 1:124 and 150) also allows that Yeats might have been referring to an early stage of *Calvary* as an outgrowth or extension of his Dervorgilla play, then almost entirely finished but undergoing revisions. On January 14, 1918, when his latest Noh adaptation was *The Only Jealousy*, he was "full of plans" and projected a collection of "my four or five Noh plays" (*Letters* 644). Writing again to Lady Gregory, on the next day, he reported enthusiastically:

> To-day I finished my new Cuchulain play and am hesitating on a new one, where a Sinn Feiner will have a conversation with Judas in the streets of Dublin. Judas is looking for somebody to whom he may betray Christ in order that Christ may proclaim himself King of the Jews. The Sinn Feiner has just been persuading a young sculptor to leave his studio and shoulder a rifle.
>
> Judas is a ghost, perhaps he is mistaken for the ghost of an old rag-picker by the neighbourhood. I will not know whether the idea is too theoretical and opinionated (?) till I have made prose draft. Before that I shall write a couple of lyrics. . . . (*Letters* 645)

It is not clear what the fifth Noh play was, because the "Judas play," as Yeats called it in the notes to his wife's automatic script, certainly became in two drafts "The Road to Calvary," or simply *Calvary*, finished with fanfare in July 1918 (see *Letters* 651).[12] The Easter conjunction of Jerusalem and Dublin in time of rebellion might not have differed technically from the meeting of a Sinn Feiner (as Waki) with the disgraced Irish ghosts of *The Dreaming of the Bones* or, twenty years later, from the transformation of the Morrigu to the Dublin Street-Singer at the end of *The Death of Cuchulain*. Perhaps it looked in February 1918 as if the Dublin scenario with a Sinn Feiner confronting the specter of betrayal personified should bifurcate into two plays, the choral speeches of the first draft and those of the First Musician in the second being all that remains of conversation "in the streets of Dublin." Possibly Yeats realized how derivative the situation might seem in a play published beside *The Dreaming of the Bones*, and *Calvary* never appeared otherwise in Yeats's lifetime. Walter Rummel had "written very fine music for . . . [the] play about a Sinn Feiner and a ghost" by February 8, 1918 (*Letters* 645), so we see how Yeats's schemes conflated. For Rummel's music, of course, was set to the songs of *The Dreaming of the Bones* and published as such in 1921. As Yeats appears to have regarded them, the two plays were part of a single construct.

Moreover, an eastern setting near Dublin more than a century before the Easter Rising of 1916 is evident in the first prose draft of the play. To emphasize his nationalist sympathy with a contemporary audience familiar with recent events at home, Yeats reverted to the struggle of Romantic Ireland that he had treated symbolically, in 1902, in *Cathleen Ni Houlihan*. A stranger who has "fought at Vinegar Hill" (NLI 8775[1], 6^r), a battle fought in Wicklow "marked by horrific and unforgotten atrocities" in the popular rebellion of 1798,[13] sleeps by day and roams the hills by night. On a lonely stretch of road in the hour before dawn, he encounters a man and

[12]Paraphrasing Mrs. Yeats, Birgit Bjersby provides a thumbnail sketch that suggests that the fifth Noh play was entirely different and "might be called a summary of 1918" in two dialogues, one between an old man and a young girl who lives in a tower on a hill, and the other between a mother and her son (*The Interpretation of the Cuchulain Legend in the Works of W. B. Yeats* [Upsala, 1950; rpt., Darby, Pa.: Folcroft Library Editions, 1970], p. 35, n. 3.

a woman who bring him to a "hollow between two little hills" and tell him that these are "the two houses of [?Slieve] & since this last trouble began in the country its said that there are devils here" (9^{r}). The stranger's name is Mac Dermit and the couple gradually reveal themselves to him as "Darmuid & . . . Dervagilla" (11^{r}) just as "the horizon behind Howth [?~~whitens~~] becomes bright" (12^{r}). When the ghost of the young man first speaks to Mac Dermit, who has come from fighting in the south, the locale is explicitly given: "The lesser sugar lo[a]f is over your head. If it were day light you would see Yonder the sea, & Dublin lies over there. . . . Delgar is there, and the village by the downs is yonder" (5^{r}). They meet in the shadow of the western slope; the couple are haunted by "terrible temptations / That beset [them] there," Mac Dermit being a hunted man with "the gallows before [him]" (7^{r}).

Yeats's return to the situation but not quite the location of Hanrahan's vision lends to the patriotic impression of the play more of Yeats as a man and poet than can be discerned in the first draft. The play's twilight setting shifts from the east to the west of Ireland, to contemporary time, and to environs closer to Coole demesne and "the stranger's room" (*Letters* 686) in Thoor Ballylee castle than to "the Steep Place of the Strangers" (*VSR* 113) looking on Ben Bulben headland. Adapting elements of the Noh play *Nishikigi* does not obscure the impression of the man nor interrupt the thought train Yeats invokes to connect the local legend of the itinerant poet Raftery and the beautiful Mary Hynes with kindred pairings. Only a short distance away, the fifteenth-century Cearbhall O'Dalaigh and his beloved Eibhlin Kavanagh haunt the spot of their secret wedding and murder at Corcomroe Abbey, County Clare.[14] Incongruously, the twelfth-century Dermot Mac Murrough, king of Leinster, and his mistress, the queen of Meath, encounter on "the white road" or "pathway . . . to the ruined Abbey of Corcomroe" (*VPl* 763, l. 20; 766, ll. 90–92) the 1916 rebel who finally recognizes them and is almost moved to forgiveness. But Yeats had suggested, on July 10, 1917, that Thoor Ballylee's restoration, the play's transposed setting, and the anticipated completion of his play were related: "While here I shall start the builders at the castle and walk over a mountain side where I have laid the scene of a new play" (*Letters* 627). "The conception of the play," he said, evoking a sense of the national in the context of the universal (and making use of an idea he and his wife had worked out after he had finished the play), "is derived from the world-wide belief that the dead dream back . . . through the more personal thoughts and deeds of life. . . . The lovers in my play have lost themselves in a . . . self-created winding of the labyrinth of conscience" (*VPl* 777). It is not primarily their abnormally strong sexual appetite for one another that they must concede here, as Dervorgilla had confessed to Hanrahan; rather, their guilty consciences engender a spiritual desolation that is proportionate to their desire for physical reenactment. Their disgrace is not merely personal but national, tribal. "If some one of their race forgave at last / Lip would be pressed on lip" and "They were not wholly miserable and accursed / If somebody of their race at last would say, / 'I have forgiven them'" (773). Mac Dermit (meaning "son of Dermot," presumably, in the first draft) is *chosen* to hear the testimony of his kinsman and the abducted queen. The Young Man's judgment is momentous because it concerns Ireland herself.

---

[13]R. F. Foster, *Modern Ireland, 1600–1972* (London: Penguin Group, 1988), p. 279.

[14]For a geneological account of the O'Dalaighs and the local bardic tradition, see James E. Doan, *Cearbhall ó Dálaigh: An Irish Poet in Romance and Oral Tradition* (New York: Garland, 1990); on how some of those traditions still live in the vicinity of Corcomroe Abbey, see Carmel Jordan, "Monastery of the Moon: Corcomroe Abbey and *The Dreaming of the Bones*," *Yeats: An Annual of Critical and Textual Studies* 16 (1998), ed. Richard J. Finneran (Ann Arbor: University of Michigan Press, 2001), pp. 17–32, as well as Natalie Crohn Schmitt, "'Haunted by Places': Landscape in Three Plays by W. B. Yeats," *Comparative Drama* 31.3 (1997): 337–366 (illustrated).

Thus, our discussion ends where it began, stressing Yeats's tendency to father songs about Ireland from analogues in national folk culture. One's beloved and country are not the same but they might coexist in the order of progression from the humane to the possessed, politics falling somewhere between. Without citing Dervorgilla beside analogous women, Yeats's unpublished prose Subject gives the issue of the play to be "The evil of love — Dierdre & Grania & all the ruin they brought — Helen[.] Why should love that so uplifts the heart bring so great evil[?] Is it of God or is it of the evil one[?]" (NLI 8775[1], 1[r]). In the second draft, the fugitive Mac Dermit confers to Dermot the appellation "Stranger," with characteristics of Judas or Satan. Shown the grave of Donough O'Brien, who "knew the secrets of women" and rebelled against his Irish master (*VPl* 769), the Young Man curses "all that troop" of men who made Mother Ireland "weak" (769). Only when the Young Girl, Dervorgilla, pleads the abject loneliness of seven hundred years is he tempted to make pardon, like a priest (The Waki in *Nishikigi*) absolving sin that had led to the English invasion of Ireland. Yeats marvels us by having the young patriot come to his senses just as we realize the irony of his refusal to acknowledge likeness and culpability in his participation in violent political insurrection in the 1916 Easter Rising, as one scholar notes.[15] "O, never, never / Shall Diarmuid and Dervorgilla be forgiven" (773), the Young Man swears, repeating it like an oath to make himself believe it as doctrine. Had God engendered such evil in His love for Ireland, Yeats added in the scratch notes of his prose Subject, "it may be little for the . . . happiness of the world or for anything but for a heart exalted, & moved." The Sinn Feiner has not such a heart, being human. He cannot forgive the sin and stop the violence, for God "alone" can love the joy that "coe[xists] with sorrow" (NLI 8775[1], 1[r]).

Given the inscrutable nature of such love and the enormity of evil, the dead ask too much of the living, who renounce the question and the particular holy, or merely haunted, place that summons it. The curtain line of *Nishikigi*—"A wild place, unlit, and unfilled"—is emulated in all versions of the Young Man's closing speech: "This is indeed a place of terrible temptation" (*VPl* 775, l. 282 in *apparatus criticus*). Like "terrible beauty," the epithet in the declaration gesturės two ways at once. Intact from the first draft to late revisions for a performance in 1931, the line retained its resemblance to the precursor: (1) "I leave this place of terrible temptation" (NLI 8775[3]); (2) "A place of terrible temptation, a dreadful place" (NLI 8775[4]); and, most emphatically and idiomatically Irish, (3) "Terrible the temptation and the place!" (BL Add. MS 55879). The renunciation resembles the protests of Lazarus and Judas in *Calvary*, although these protests are fraught with the philosophical questions that Yeats and his young wife raised with the spirit guides between late 1917 and July 1920, when the preface and notes to *Four Plays for Dancers* were finished (see part III, below).

II. *The Dreaming of the Bones*: Manuscripts and Revisions

Having written to Olivia Shakespear, on May 15, 1917, about beginning "another play in the manner of *The Hawk's Well,*" and to Lady Gregory, on June 11, 1917, about having "almost finished my Dervorgilla play" (*Letters* 626), Yeats appears to have completed within that time the prose Subject and draft of NLI 8775(1) and probably much more. The earliest drafts of songs and choral settings to survive—in NLI 13,583, NLI 8775(2), and Texas(A)—were composed

[15]See Joseph Chadwick, "Family Romance as National Allegory in Yeats's *Cathleen ni Houlihan* and *The Dreaming of the Bones*," in *Twentieth Century Literature* 32, no. 2 (summer 1986): 163.

between June 11, essentially apart from the body of speeches (since he had "nothing now to write but the lyrics and must leave London for that" [626]), and July 9, 1917, when "At the grey round of the hill" was written at George Russell's home in Dublin. Though Yeats dated completion of the play as occurring in France in August 1917, it is impossible to say exactly how much of the mixed holographs of Harvard(A) existed at that time. Part of that version is lost, and other parts are irrecoverable short of undoing Yeats's pastings from summer 1918, when George Yeats, who might have had a hand in the matter, says that he rewrote the play. The procedure, in any case, was systematic, distinguishing recent fair copies (in B, D, and inserted C* and D* states) from the earlier state (C) in the mechanics of construction. Three types of paper used for writing were usually affixed to a fourth type (A) to render an almost complete text suitable for publication, after typing, in *Two Plays for Dancers* (January 1919; Wade 123) and in *The Little Review* (January 1919). The following table indicates that almost all lines and stage directions (sd) are accounted for in Harvard(A) in the aggregate of numbered, interposed, and partly typed folios taken as a whole (see the description of Harvard[A] on p. xv, and the transcription on pp. 47–85).

folio	state	*VPl* lines		page number
1a	D	sd–ll. 16	song	none
1	B	sd–ll. 16	song	(1)
2	B/A	ll. 17–25	song	(2)
3	C/A	ll. 26–33sd		(3)
4	C/A	ll. 35b–43		(4)
5	C*	ll. 34–35/44–45		none
6	C	ll. 47b–59a		none
7	C/A	ll. 59b–67		(5)
8	D*	ll. 67b–69a		none
9	C/A	ll. 69b–76b		(6)
10	C/A	ll. 78b–90		(7)
11	C*	ll. 90b–95sd		none
12	B/A	ll. 94–107sd	song	(8)
13	B/A	ll. 108–118	song	(9)
14	B/A	ll. 118sd–140	song	(10)
15	C/A	ll. 141–161		(11)
16	C/A	ll. 162–173b		(12)
17	C/A	ll. 174–189/del 184–189		(13)
18	C/A	ll. 184–199		(14)
19	B+C/A	ll. 200–208a/208b–211b		(15)
20	C+B/A	ll. 212–223a/223b–229a		(16)
21	C/A	ll. 229b–243		(17)
22	C+B/A	ll. 244–246/247–262		(18)
23	B/A	ll. 263–287	song	(19)
24	B	ll. 288–310	song	(20)

The uniqueness of some significant variants in the B state of this mixed version in *The Little Review* printing suggests that the Cuala Press version of *Two Plays for Dancers* permitted Yeats the opportunity to make revisions that, after 1919, were transmitted to *Four Plays for Dancers*, *Plays and Controversies*, *Collected Plays*, *Variorum Edition of the Plays*, and most galleys of the unpublished Coole (Macmillan) and Dublin (Scribner) deluxe editions.

Yeats's publication of the play in *The Little Review*, a dead end only in the sense that the text falls outside the stream of transmission, served the purpose of securing American copyright when *Calvary* was brought out in Ireland. The strategy had as its precedent the United States publication of *At the Hawk's Well* in *Harper's Bazaar* (March 1917), followed soon after by printings in *To-Day* (London) and in the limited edition of *The Wild Swans at Coole* published at the Cuala Press. Coordination of these several printings was a feat because Yeats also needed to place *The Only Jealousy of Emer* in an American magazine as he brought it out, together with *The Dreaming of the Bones*, in *Two Plays for Dancers*. Revisions for the latter publication have not survived, and only one marked copy (at Emory) represents a state between it and *Four Plays for Dancers*. On the other hand, the extant typescripts are an extraordinarily rich source of information about the evolution of *Calvary*.

From the complete verse version in mixed states to the first printings of 1919, Yeats engaged his London typists[16] to make a ribbon copy (NLI 8775[3]) and at least two carbon copies (NLI 8775[4] and Texas[B]), which were retained for immediate use in London and Dublin. He had another typed version (Harvard[B]) made to send to New York, where his friend John Quinn served him as liaison if not agent. Generally speaking, Pound had served Yeats in placing work with American journals. Not surprisingly, in the January issue of *The Little Review*, these clever men were able to lay in related contributions of their own: Pound on the subject of "Tariff and Copyright" and Quinn ("J. Q.") as publicist for Yeats, Pound, Fenollosa, and the whole translation/adaptation enterprise. On October 17, 1918, Quinn received the play, marked in pencil for printing, from Pound with instructions to send it to *The North American Review*, which he promptly did and confirmed in a letter to Yeats.[17] When the editor rejected it, "filled up for months ahead," or perhaps after Quinn was obligated to withdraw the manuscript from *The Dial,* because he was made to feel how keenly Pound wanted the play in *The Little Review*, with Yeats's consent, the play was retyped at Quinn's direction by a stenographer near his New York law offices; by then *The Bookman* had also considered the play and had rejected it "because of politics."[18] The typing of the Quinn manuscript from Harvard(B) is slavish to a degree seldom seen, reproducing minute aspects of formatting, including some obvious typographical faults, in the new transmission copy.

Typographically, the printing in *The Little Review* seems to be more dutifully observant of the typescripts than are texts set at the Cuala Press and for Macmillan by R. and R. Clark, Limited, Edinburgh, between 1919 and 1934, including the de luxe editions. The *Variorum Edition of the Plays* shows that the number of variants declines substantially with publication of *Four Plays for Dancers* and *Plays and Controversies*. Moreover, the corrected proof copies of *Collected Plays* (BL Add. MS 55879) and the unfinished de luxe editions (BL Add. MSS 55884 and 55891, NLI 30,007, and Texas[E]) confirm that significant shifts toward the final state given as the base text of *Variorum Edition of the Plays* had been effected and substantially completed by 1921 and 1923. After that, the editing Yeats supervised was very largely delegated and in the hands of Macmillan editor Thomas Mark and of George Yeats. By 1931, the prevailing issues for the

---

[16]Misses Jacobs and Oldroyd, 47 Great Russell Street, London.

[17]John Quinn, *The Letters of John Quinn to William Butler Yeats*, ed. Alan Himber, with assistance by George Mills Harper (Ann Arbor: UMI Research Press, 1983), p. 192. Receipt confirmed on October 22, 1918.

[18]Quinn, *Letters*, p. 195 (November 14, 1918); and Richard J. Finneran, George Mills Harper, and William Murphy, eds., *Letters to W. B. Yeats* (New York: Columbia University Press, 1977), 2:353–354. See the context of the episode as given in B. L. Reid, *John Quinn and His Friends* (New York: Oxford University Press, 1968), p. 348. Quinn employed Z. and L. Rosenfeld, Stenography and Typewriting, at the Times Building, 42d Street and Broadway, New York, to retype the play for him. They were nearby his law offices on Broadway and on Nassau Street and specialized in court proceedings, legal and technical translation, and customized work for the theater.

three of them were standardizing punctuation and making uniform the spellings of Irish names in the play and in the canon as a whole. The problematic spelling of Dermot and Dervorgilla, where precedent in Lady Gregory's writings is cited as an authority and used as a bludgeon to force a reversion to corrections that had been implemented in one set of page proofs (in BL Add. MS 55891, after having been marked in NLI 30,007), is recorded in the notes and collation of variants given in appendix E, below (especially p. 268).

Appendix B gives two versions of a program note written for the Abbey Theatre production of *The Dreaming of the Bones* that played on December 6, 1931. Yeats refers the audience to the words and music "in my book 'Plays & Controversies' " (*P&C*), for those who were interested, rather than distracting them from the play by putting too much in the program. Indeed, while he was pleased with Rummel's settings and made much ado about gathering them for publication since their commissioning in 1917 (*Letters* 629, 645), they were not essential to the play, which was published without them until 1921, and then only in *Four Plays for Dancers* and *Plays and Controversies*. Moreover, they were "too difficult" in rehearsals and so abandoned during the Abbey's only production of the play in Yeats's lifetime.[19] In September 1921, Yeats sent to Nugent Monck at the Norwich Theatre a bound copy of "some proofs of my new plays" (*FPD*), recommending *The Dreaming of the Bones* as "the simplest [of the four] but . . . most damnably Irish" and *The Only Jealousy of Emer* as "the most interesting technically"; he did not recommend *Calvary* because he doubted that Monck would understand it without its note (appendix C).[20] He said that he did not suppose he would ever get a studio or drawing room of his own in which to present such experiments to the "non-existent audience who know my symbols." By 1931, without saying so in the program, he had withheld his note (appendix A) as well as music, acknowledging a limited audience for, but not recondite matter in, *The Dreaming of the Bones*. Perhaps reflecting his recent impatience with the problem of accommodating words and music to one another and knowledge that Rummel's music had been dropped, Yeats commented: "There was a time when I wanted every word sung to be as audible & intelligible as the spoken dialogue; but now I let the musician write as the theme moves him; [?and] I think of my words as a half secret between myself and the singer" (NLI 30,820). Understandably, the playwright's and director's prompt copies for this production, including instructions for musicians, were materials consulted in the revision of the play for the Macmillan and Scribner deluxe editions and *Collected Plays*.

It seems extraordinary that the ribbon copy and one of the carbon copies of the first typescript made in 1918 were recycled into use for these late projects when they had been superseded by *Four Plays for Dancers* and *Plays and Controversies* in the complicated textual schema of significant projects undertaken by Macmillan in 1930 (see Chapman 1:128–131). Bearing pasted-over revisions at lines 249–259, NLI 8775(3) and (4) had been amended, probably in 1921, but still bore evidence of numerous jottings, at various times, in the hands of Yeats, his wife, and Abbey director Lennox Robinson. Consequently, typescript NLI 8775(3) is an ideal base text for the complete version (1918–1935) in this volume. The frequent stage directions are easily reconciled

[19]*Letters* 785. See appendix D, p. 263, on Dulac's masks, which Yeats wanted to use in *FPD*, as he wanted to use the music Dulac recommended to him. Lennox Robinson, in *Ireland's Abbey Theatre: A History 1899–1951* (1951; Port Washington, N.Y.: Kennikat, 1968), p. 146, lists the music for the performance as by J. F. Larchet, who handled music for the September 21, 1931, production of *The Cat and the Moon*.

[20]Letters from W. B. Yeats to Nugent Monck, September 1, [1921], and September 6, [1921], discovered by Michael Sidnell while conducting research on our Cornell volume *The Countess Cathleen: Manuscript Materials* (1999); now in the Berg Collection, New York Public Library.

in the two typescripts, and they are interesting vestiges of a performance that bestowed credit, in *The Irish Independent* and *The Irish Times* (both on December 7, 1931), to Yeats and to program opener Ninette de Valois, head of the Abbey School of Ballet. The Sunday dance programs that Yeats announced at closing curtain were not the envisioned platform for his plays for dancers.[21] There is, however, a contemporary note in the Coole edition proofs that sanctions a procedure that Yeats and Robinson implemented in the production to allow Dervorgilla's part, played by Nesta Brooking, to be committed more to dancing: "Dervorgilla's few lines can be given . . . to Dermot [that is, the Stranger], and Dervorgilla's part taken by a dancer who has the training of a dancer alone, nor need that dancer, if masked, be a woman [after Michio Ito in *At the Hawk's Well*]" (appendix E, p. 268; cf. appendix A, p. 236). A 1950 revival of *The Dreaming of the Bones* was cast in this way by Ria Mooney at the Abbey, using new automated technology to generate scripts.[22] Perhaps the wonder of the 1931 production, in light of the play's pairing with *Calvary* from 1921 onward (see appendix D), is that the audience found it beautiful and *un-Christian*, and did not seem to worry about the latter.

III. *Calvary*: Manuscripts, Notes, and Revisions

Not to forgive those who may engender evil with their love is un-Christian, and the connection with Easter week violence to liberate Ireland makes it no less so. If not "of the evil one," such love is God's, coexists in joy and sorrow, and offers little happiness for the world save to "a heart exalted, & moved" (NLI 8775[1], 1^r). The thesis would serve two plays, and surely, as a passion play to challenge the liberator of souls and epitome of love, *Calvary* might have seemed to its maker beyond the tolerance of the orthodox. The arguments Lazarus and Judas make to Christ *are* unorthodox, to acknowledge the obvious. Not one to be shy about controversy, Yeats had endured offended sensibilities and charges of heresy, for example, at the inaugural performance of *The Countess Cathleen*, some twenty years before, when more point could be made in defending blasphemous characters and forgiving the sale of a virtuous soul to alleviate the suffering of the Irish folk. Dealing with the agents of the devil in famine times was like dealing with the agents of British rule during the Great Hunger. The precedents were there, too, in Marlowe, Goethe, and Byron. But nothing so theologically original or provocative as *Calvary* had stirred opponents to rowdiness and petition signing in 1899, when the national theater was at stake. Because *Calvary* was never brought to the stage in Dublin in Yeats's lifetime and was published nowhere before *Four Plays for Dancers*, the play is here a relatively straightforward piece of work to describe. Its origin, however, no longer a mystery in itself, was largely an intensely private matter for the poet, his wife, and the initially "non-existent audience who [knew Yeats's] symbols." In point of fact, from 1917 to 1919, he was only just beginning to formulate those symbols for himself.

Like the tone formulas specified in Rummel's music for *The Dreaming of the Bones* (see *FPD* 108, *P&C* 435–436) and like Yeats's equations inscribed above the title in Texas(B)—

---

[21]See Kathrine Sorley Walker, *Ninette de Valois* (London: Hamish Hamilton, 1987), pp. 117–119, on the 1931 production; and Sylvia C. Ellis, *The Plays of W. B. Yeats: Yeats and the Dancer* (London: Macmillan, 1995), for occasional references to de Valois's work at the Abbey, including a performance of Yeats's *Fighting the Waves*, also in December 1931.

[22]Abbey Theatre file, NLI 29,547.

Flute = The Life [?as] Elemental Principle
Plucked Inst. = The Soul Element
Bow Inst. (nasal) = The Spirit Element
Drum (Cymbal) = The Body Element

—symbols proliferated with his occult studies, which were informed by the spirit guides and particular books in his private library. Forms and essences from Jacob Boehme's *The Forty Questions of the Soul and the Clavis* (*YL* 236) and spectral configurations from Swedenborg's *Arcana Coelestia* (*YL* 2037), for instance, proved to him that the sources communicating through the medium of Mrs. Yeats could be confirmed by authority. As Yeats undertook to write his Judas play, derived from the Dervorgilla one on the theme of betrayal, he became, by self-acclamation, a "creative mystic" in the tradition of William Blake (Chapman 2:288–289). By February 1918, his encounter with Theodor Fechner's *On Life after Death* (*YL* 665) provided him with the doctrine of "dreaming back" that he applied first in the poem "Shepherd and Goatherd," next in the new play, and eventually in the revision of *The Dreaming of the Bones* in summer 1918 and its note of around July 1920. In chapter 2 of Fechner, Yeats was drawn to the following passage, marking it as indicated:

> In the moment of death . . . when man has to part with <u>those organs in which his powers of acting lay</u>, he will, all at once, become conscious of all the ideas and effects which, produced by his manifold actions in life, will continue living and working in this world, and <u>will form</u> . . . <u>an organic individuality</u> which only then becomes alive, self-conscious, self-active, ready to act through the human and natural world, of its own will and power.[23]

Three pages later, Fechner drew Yeats's attention to Christ as a "great spirit," as distinct from the actual, or "historical," man who died:

> The most striking instance of a great spirit living and working on through the ages we see in Christ. You must not think it an empty saying, that He liveth in those who believe in Him. Every true Christian carries Him within him, not in a symbolical meaning, not in life and reality; every one that thinks and acts according to His mind is a partaker in Him; for it is the spirit of Christ that causes in him such thinking and acting.[24]

In another four pages, the following passage (also annotated by Yeats) brought to the Christian notion of divinity the contentiousness of antic vices, or "the wicked":

> <u>When other spirits rest in peace with God</u>, partaking of His thoughts, <u>the wicked</u> ones <u>will go about restless, through the sorrows and changes of earthly life</u>, and their spiritual disorder will infect other men with error and superstition, with folly and vice.[25]

---

[23]P. 36; Yeats's underscorings, with the marginal note, "Dreaming Back / and / Return."

[24]Pp. 39–40; accompanied by a short marginal stroke and Yeats's thought, "One has to consider the individuality created in transmission. Only Christ is more than the historical Christ. Yet the dead do not create (it seems)."

[25]P. 43; marginal stroking and underscoring by Yeats, besides his contextual observation, "Dreaming / Back."

These three passages relate to Yeats's extensive interrogation of the spirits, in the automatic script, on the subject of Christ as "CG" (Creative Genius) and the antithetical Judas as His "evil mask" or the "EG" (Evil Genius). Generally speaking, research on the subject went well enough. But when Yeats wanted to know the meaning of the money Judas had taken to betray Christ, a muddle occurred. The spirit, "Thomas," or Mrs. Yeats (as many prefer), became evasive; hence, George Mills Harper sees a pivotal moment in Yeats's thinking about *Calvary* in the sitting of October 26, 1918:

> the theme was subtly but drastically altered: a seemingly simple contrast of Antithetical and Primary to the question of free will versus determinism. A play planned as a "Judas play" became a Christ play. Peter, who would have destroyed the symmetry of the first plan (his Evil Genius and Judas's Good Genius in opposition to Christ's Ego), was replaced by Lazarus and the Roman Soldiers, dramatic parallels of Judas. The logic is improved, but the intensity lowered. Although Judas may still be conceived as "the personified origin of action—the one who causes pity to act," he cannot . . . be cast as the agent who "pities jewish race & so would have christ become their king."[26]

Harper's observations about *Calvary* as a "Christ play" are less speculative, of course, than are his assumptions about an abandoned "Judas play," because no actual "plan," scenario, or draft of one has survived to attest to St. Peter's being part of it. Still, traces of the conception of such a play, irrespective of its link to *The Dreaming of the Bones* in an Irish setting of Easter week 1916, exist in the automatic script, as Janis Haswell has persuasively argued recently, using both versions of *A Vision* as a gloss for "reconstructive interpretation" and drawing on a good many transcriptions found in the present Cornell volume.[27]

For symbolism, there was Fechner's color wheel, or "many-coloured star," and, no less systematic, there were the birds of Swedenborg's *Arcana Coelestia* (*loc. cit.*, p. 19): "*Birds* signify things rational and intellectual," paralleling Yeats's note (on p. 55): "spiritual = [air symbol] hence birds." On the flyleaf of *The Principia* (*YL* 2039A) Yeats was moved to draft "A Needle's Eye" (titled "A Crowded Cross"); and a reference to Fechner by Yeats in Swedenborg's *The Spiritual Diary* (*YL* 2040, p. 431) goes with the veritable bestiary, or aviary, that the Yeatses recorded in the automatic script and its attendant card file (see Chapman 2:291). The spiritual world, as Yeats noted in his copy of *On Life after Death*, resembled the "Cabalistic / Edane's / Tree—birds / in branches / Etc." (69). "God has not appeared to the birds," the Second Musician sings as a refrain (*VPl* 787–788, ll. 174, 179, 184) to bring down the curtain. And birds of sea and air were symbols of "intellectual intellect" and "intellectual love," according to the spirit Thomas on January 14, 1918. So when Thomas told Yeats to "read Fechner" on June 16, 1918, Yeats probably had already started writing "The Road to Calvary" and might have finished the first two drafts

---

[26]George Mills Harper, *The Making of Yeats's* A Vision: *A Study of the Automatic Script* (Carbondale: Southern Illinois University Press, 1987) 2:153; see also p. 177.

[27]Janis Haswell, "Resurrecting *Calvary*: A Reconstructive Interpretation of W. B. Yeats's Play and Its Making," *Yeats's Collaborations: Yeats Annual* no. 15, ed. Wayne K. Chapman and Warwick Gould (London: Palgrave, 2002), 159–189. Although our collaboration gave impetus to more metaphysics than either one of us originally imagined, my work is limited here to the resources of Yeats's library and to manuscripts as physical evidence. The evidence makes clear that Yeats obtained "metaphors for poetry" by deliberate study, for a profusion of details were arrayed in a number of sources.

of NLI 30,361,[28] rewriting and polishing *The Dreaming of the Bones* as he did so.

The earliest manuscripts of *Calvary* exist in two principal locations today: in the National Library of Ireland, as part of the folder designated NLI 30,361; and in the Houghton Library at Harvard University, as MS Eng 338.8 (or Harvard[C] here) due to a direct purchase from Mrs. Yeats in 1950. Since the writing of the play relates to the couple's psychic inquiries on the subject of the avatar, or "Second Master" (Christ being the first), which Yeats and his wife thought they were to conceive in a child, one appreciates their maintaining the prepublication states of the play with circumspection. As a matter of priority, NLI 30,361 came first, followed by Harvard(C). A complete accounting would therefore proceed from the two holograph versions of the former (consisting of twenty-nine folios, or thirty-nine pages) to the full-length draft of Harvard(C) (in thirteen folios, or sixteen pages) and, thereafter, the typescripts from which copy was derived for the first printing in *Four Plays for Dancers* (1921; Wade 129). The other materials include an autograph note and a preface for *Collected Plays* in maroon notebook NLI 30,336; a five-page, five-folio, handwritten note on the play titled "The Road to Calvary," NLI 8776(1); a five-page typescript, NLI 8776(2), or corrected ribbon copy of NLI 8776(1), anticipating NLI 30,789 ("Note on the Symbolism of 'Calvary' "), a carbon copy that bears Yeats's corrections only on the last page; a six-page typescript, NLI 8776(3), following Harvard(C) but introducing substantial revisons of the play in holograph; an eight-page typescript, NLI 8776(4), incorporating the corrections and revisions of NLI 8776(3) but, with the exception of a comma deletion and page numbering by Yeats, carrying minor corrections (in pencil) by the copy editor at Macmillan in preparation for typesetting the first published version. A galley proof of the note for *Four Plays for Dancers*, date stamped October 7, 1920, survives in NLI 30,125.

Only at the advanced stage of revision in NLI 8776(3) did the early, longer title become the contracted, final one: "~~ON THE ROAD TO~~ CALVARY." Perhaps the choral speeches in NLI 30,361, and those of the First Musician in the second draft, are all that remains of a Sinn Feiner conversing "in the streets of Dublin" (*Letters* 645) from the play's origin. However, the first of two complete drafts in that manuscript develops a scene involving Christ (not Judas) and the chorus of bystanders and then Christ and Lazarus by the roadside, with Lazarus standing with the chorus. Because of the substantial discrepancies between Yeats's account to Lady Gregory on January 14, 1918, and the earliest version of *Calvary*, it seems probable that his "hesitating" to write a new play for dancers eventually led him to discard altogether any writing he might have done on a fifth Noh play. Apart from that loss, the manuscript record for *Calvary* seems to be intact.

The earliest drafts are in fact secured in a bound notebook with an horary at one end of it dated "August 30. 1919. / Ballylee." Other materials include a short passage of dialogue for *The Player Queen*, two oddly positioned pages from the 1918 first draft of "Solomon and the Witch" (see Chapman 1:151), and, abutting the horary, an early draft of the essay "A People's Theatre: Letter to Lady Gregory" (published for the first time in *The Irish Statesman*, November 29 and December 6, 1919). Amid the final run of *Calvary* folios is a drawing of a door ajar and dark interior, reproduced below as a frontispiece to part II (p. 117) and associated by Yeats (*Letters*

[28]Steve L. Adams, Barbara J. Frieling, and Sandra Sprayberry, eds., *Yeats's 'Vision' Papers*, vol. 1: *The Automatic Script: 5 November 1917–18 June 1918* (London: Macmillan, 1992), transcribe Thomas's symbols and directive on Fechner from Mrs. Yeats's hand (on pp. 251 and 508); and Robert A. Martinich and Margaret Mills Harper, eds., *Yeats's 'Vision' Papers*, vol. 3: *Sleep and Dream Notebooks, 'Vision' Notebooks 1 and 2, Card File* (London: Macmillan, 1992), give a composite of symbols from those and other sittings on p. 405 and passim.

729–730) with a reading of the play at Gogarty's (like Yeats's recitation of *The Dreaming of the Bones* in 1917), when the house ghost suddenly threw open the door of the room, as if prompted to do so by the following lines:

> Who is this from whom the crowd has shrunk,
> As though he had some look that terrified?
> He has a deathly face, and yet he moves
> Like a young foal that sees the hunt go by
> And races in the field.
> [*A player with the mask of Lazarus has entered.*
> *Lazarus.* He raised me up.
> I am the man that died and was raised up;
> I am called Lazarus. (*VPl* 782, ll. 38–44)

Nearby in manuscript notebook NLI 30,361, and possibly related to the performance, are sketches that offer two views of a mask.

In the first draft of this passage, the chorus asks no such questions, offers no incantatory rhetoric or opportunities for dramatic entrances for the masked Christ and Lazarus. Generally speaking, the whole first draft ranges from free verse to blank verse and prose. But that it is a "Christ play" is beyond doubt from the beginning:

> Every year at Easter
> With the coming again of the year
> With the sprouting of grain & the blossoming of the
> fruit trees
> The savior of men dreams his bitter dream
> Sees those that mocked him, those chosen he saved
> Even at coming of the year
> Even at sprouting of the grain. (NLI 30,361, 1^{r})

This "Song of folding & unfolding [of the cloth]" emulates the dream-cloth grass weaving of the heroine of *Nishikigi*, but transgendered and transferred to a ghostly Christ who, dreaming back through the psychic trauma of the last moments of his life, must repeatedly endure the mockery of those whom he has saved. Thus he carries an invisible cross in an "Asiatic street," not a Dublin roadway. The gist of the plot is borne by the arguments of the ungrateful Lazarus and the arch betrayer, Judas. In nine folios, the Roman Soldiers conclude the mockery with a rhetorical query: "are we not your best / worshippers[,] god, who ask nothing of ~~your will~~ / your power or your love[?]" (9^{r}).

Then, like nature after the sacrifice of the god of generation, the manuscript starts all over again in verse (on 11^{r}), following the chorus's closure of draft one by asking that Christ call on our Father in Heaven to "tumble all the mockers / And all mocking now into the pit" (10^{v}). This pronouncement on mockery anticipates Yeats's vituperative treatment of the subject in the poem "Nineteen Hundred and Nineteen": "Mock mockers after that / That would not lift a hand maybe / To help good, wise or great / To bar that foul storm out, for we / Traffic in mockery" (*VP* 432, ll. 108–112). The "dreamer" climbs the "road to Calvary" on Good Friday, a "yelling crowd upon a narrow road" egging him on as he pantomimes the stations with a "cross that does not exist" (11^{v}), the chorus singing as if one with the mockers:

> We are the mockers & the tale
> Is but the tale we choose to tell
> ~~What raging~~ where is there raging miracle
> or burdened breast that can . . . prevail
> In ballance with our enmity
> That bids man take his natures rest
> And loose the burden from his heart
> Because we are heavens enemy. (11^{v})

Thus the irony of Christ's sacrifice is increased in the revision.

By the third draft, Harvard(C), this song is redeployed but cut in preference to a solo by the First Musician:

> O but the mockers cry
> Makes my heart afraid
> As though a flute of bone
> Taken from a herons thigh
> A heron crazed by the moon
> Were cleverly softly played. (Harvard[C], 2^{r})

Only recently, the chorus had been divided into the contrapuntal trio of musicians at the end of the second draft, remaining divided ever after. The shift away from an engaged, conventionally righteous chorus to a detached one holds with Yeats's conception of water birds as symbols of "intellectual intellect." A mystery might be maintained as a biblical apocryphus, but the shift made artistic sense because it traded a heavy frame for a lighter one and avoided mimicking recent successes. One such success was "The Wild Swans at Coole," evoked to a fault in the play in draft two: "Where have last year[']s cygnets gone? / . . . Now the lakes / ~~Coole lakes~~ empty" (NLI 30,361, 25^{v}), which at least is an improvement over "Father swan & swan the mother / Mount above Coole lake" (26^{r}), perhaps an emblem of the Yeatses' role in the gospel of the avatar, as they interpreted that story from various spirit guides.

By revision, Yeats strove for effects he admired in the Noh plays of Fenollosa's and Pound's translation; the invention was to be "distinguished, indirect, and symbolic" (*E&I* 221). The logic of Lazarus, Judas, and the Roman Soldiers had been worked out in the first draft, a logic that exactly served the purpose of prose composition. The chorus's mediation of this logic with songs such as the one above was a comparatively difficult business. The chorus and, later, the First Musician had to narrate the pivotal dumb show of Martha and the three Marys between Lazarus's exit and Judas's entrance. Naturally, this scene takes place as a simple juxtaposition in draft one (NLI 30,361, 5^{r}). In draft two, the choral movement at this point gets mired for nearly three pages (15^{v}–17^{r}) in the women's "half ecstasy," as the metaphysical conceit of "Solomon and the Witch" (at 30^{v} and 31^{v}) works feebly to convey the passion Christ had "lit" in them: "~~Even as your own flame~~ / . . . Our passion & our will / But coal always [?lit]" (15^{v}). The metaphor was not working, and the device of the chorus seems to break down in mimicry of the several women. Hence, the pivotal sequence was simplified by draft three (Harvard [C]), where the bird symbol and talismanic feather were substituted for the incandescent lamp in the

First Musician's second song (at 6^{r}). After typing, where significant revisions were made in the lyric setting (in NLI 8776[3], 3^{r}; see pp. 223–224), the song itself had achieved its final form, save for issues of punctuation:

> "Take but his love away
> Their love becomes a feather
> Of eagle, swan or gull
> Or a drowned heron's feather
> Tossed hither and thither
> Upon the bitter spray
> And the moon at the full[."] (cf. *VPl* 784, ll. 90–96)

With this solution also came, in draft three, a new "Song for the folding and unfolding of the cloth," transplanting the free-verse one in the first draft. Like the song the First Musician sings in sympathy for the women, the new opening song of the musicians was initially written near the end (28^{r}–30^{r}) but outside the compass of the second draft (NLI 30,361). Once Yeats copied the opening lyrics into Harvard(C) and positioned the other songs according to his three-point progression, the play became an articulated body of parts integrated by the bird motif. Anticipating Christ, "the white heron / Shivers in a dumbfounded dream" (*VPl* 780, ll. 3–4). In the first important revision in typescript, four lines on the efficacy of the Father to exact retribution were replaced by two lines mocking the Son: "Call on your father now before your bones / Have been plucked ~~clean~~ <bare> ~~by~~ the great desert birds" (NLI 8776[3], 1^{r}). At both ends of the work, with the ritual folding of the cloth, the Second Musician sings refrains that are equally uncompromising in their detachment: first, "God has not died for the white heron" (*VPl* 780–781, ll. 5, 10, 15); finally, "God has not appeared to the birds" (787–788, ll. 174, 179, 184). Enigmatic and chilling, the last line could not be the last word. Consequently, in 1927, Yeats published a long sequel titled *The Resurrection* (*VPl* 900–936).

As a postscript, the note that Yeats prepared for the first printing of *Calvary* speaks of the symbolism of the birds and how that symbolism relates to the dramatic action of the characters. Aside from general inventions based on supposed letters from the deserts of Arabia, by which he meant the automatic script, Yeats reported that

> Certain birds, . . . such lonely birds as the heron, hawk, eagle, and swan, are the natural symbols of subjectivity, especially when floating upon the wind alone or alighting upon some pool or river. . . .
>
> I have used my bird-symbolism in these songs to increase the objective loneliness of Christ by contrasting it with a loneliness, opposite in kind, that unlike His can be . . . sufficient to itself. I have surrounded Him with the images of those He cannot save, not only with the birds, who have served neither God nor Caesar, and await for none or for a different saviour, but with Lazarus and Judas and the Roman soldiers for whom He has died in vain.[29]

The rest of the note is a kind of phantasmagoria of the type we associate with the 1925 edition of *A Vision*. One might read the notes of *Four Plays for Dancers* straight through as if they were

---

[29] *VPl* 789–790; cf. appendix C, pp. 254–255, below.

chapters of a thesis, because three of the notes were written for the occasion, around the summer of 1920. Only the one for *At the Hawk's Well* amounted to a reprinting, having been published with the play in 1917. The preface is included (in appendix E) to facilitate such a reading. The assembly of four plays and their notes was not inevitably the one elected for *Four Plays for Dancers*, as appendix D suggests, because two drafts of the contents list differed from the order that Yeats eventually chose. When he finally yoked the Cuchulain plays and made another pair of *The Dreaming of the Bones* and *Calvary*, he reached a sensible arrangement, right for the collected work but, in one sense, unsatisfying in its first application in *Four Plays for Dancers* in 1921. One imagines how much more politically assertive and contentious a book he might have made had he stuck with his original plan to begin and end with an Easter play.

Transcription Principles and Procedures

Over an eighteen-year period, Yeats's writing, revising, and editing of *The Dreaming of the Bones* and *Calvary*, including their respective commentaries for *Four Plays for Dancers* and the unpublished deluxe edition, were a complex business in which personal and adaptive theatrical aims were reconciled with thematic concerns. *The Dreaming of the Bones*, in particular, poses an interesting complication in the way that materials for an early production were revised for a later one and figured at two points, after a considerable interval, in the development of the text. The published states of the two plays are preceded by many manuscripts of different types, depending on the circumstances or even the practical objective of the playwright at various times.

In the case of *The Dreaming of the Bones*, there was Yeats's need to work out the whole action in prose from a thematic Subject (or prose draft), as was his custom to do when writing poetry. Then followed the songs, written separately; then a complete verse version in holograph made of two or more mixed states of the play, with typed slips added to bridge passages; then typescripts, some made under Yeats's supervision and others not; then stage prompt copies made from two of these scripts for productions at the Abbey Theatre; then, finally, a series of corrected proofs, mainly in his handwriting, intended for printing in his lifetime.

In the case of *Calvary*, we have Yeats's effort to complete a fourth "play for dancers" for publication rather more than for production; so his original choral device quickly gave way to an invention developed in the others. In turn, three complete drafts (more or less in verse) ensued, in holograph and in bound as well as loose-leaf notebooks, before the play emerged in two typed states: the first, in part, significantly rewritten in the margins by Yeats; the second, derived from the first, bearing notation by the printer in 1921. The rest of the story is about W. B. and Mrs. Yeats marking proofs for the English edition of *The Collected Plays* (1934) and, from 1931 to 1935, for the closely affiliated Coole (Macmillan) and Dublin (Scribner) editions.

Because the works are one-act plays and short, the editor has been able to match photographs of the holograph materials and facing transcriptions throughout, as is usual in the Cornell Yeats series. The only exceptions are in the appendices, where Yeats's notes, when extant in holograph, are given only in transcription. Otherwise, certain patterns by M. J. Sidnell and W. K. Chapman in *The Countess Cathleen: Manuscript Materials* (1999) have been adapted to save space (for instance, the use of partially streamed photography and transcriptions to present short passages written on versos and on manuscript insert slips). Idiosyncrasies of Yeats's spelling, punctuation, and manner of revising are retained as much as possible, and his drawn lines and arrows are depicted graphically to help the reader relate the transcriptions to their originals. Blots, bleeds, and physical damage are noted only when text is affected.

In sum, the principles and conventions employed are several:

1. The following conventions represent the physical features of Yeats's texts in transcription:

roman type	black ink
italic type	pencil
boldface type	typescript or print
background shading	for one of two draft states mixed by pasting
[. . .]	vertical space omitted in streamed transcriptions

2. The whole word is given when that seems intended, even though letters are missing or elided with a stroke, as often with the "-ing" ending. When a precise spelling is unclear, standard spelling is used, but when Yeats's misspellings are clear, these are preserved—such as "stary" for "starry," "stepp" for "steps," "boyed" for "buoyed," etc. The spelling of names may represent his pronunciation (as with "Dierdre" and "Lazerus"), his uncertainty (as with "Dermid"/"Darmuid" and later forms "Dermot"/"Diarmuid"), or his attempt to show derivation (as in variants "Mac Dermit"/"Mc Dermot," with or without space). A word is left incomplete if Yeats seems to have abandoned it after writing only a part of it, as frequently occurs in his speech headings, which are often variously abbreviated.

3. Overwritings are formalized thus: Thomond$\left\{\begin{matrix}.\ \mathrm{B}\\ ,\ \mathrm{b}\end{matrix}\right\}$eing, where Yeats has decided to end a sentence and begin anew by superimposing a period and capital letter.

4. Yeats's cancellations of letters, words, parts of words, parts of lines and whole lines are represented by straight horizontal lines through the deleted matter, in accordance with the principle of reading discussed above. Cancellation of part of a line followed by cancellation of more of the line, or the whole of it, is represented by a vertical bracket in the left margin. Frequently there are earlier cancellations within such canceled blocks, and these are represented with horizontal lines.

5. Yeats's underlinings and "stet" notations are retained, and his caret symbols are raised to the line level when (as usual) they are placed below the line. The line spacing in the transcriptions is always sufficient to accommodate one extra line or part of a line inserted by Yeats. Where he has inserted extra lines, or parts of lines, the line spacing is expanded to accommodate his interlineations.

6. Illegible words are represented as follows:

[?]	an illegible word
every[?thing]	a partly illegible word
[~~?~~]	an illegible canceled word
[?Martha]	a conjectural reading

7. In transcribing typescripts, errors and corrections such as strikeovers are only recorded when significant, but all holograph corrections are indicated.

8. In collations and notes, "*sd*" is an abbreviation for "stage direction," "*dp*" for "*dramatis personae*," "*del*" for "deleted," "*rev from*" for "revised from," and "*rev to*" for "revised to." Editorial queries and glosses related to the revision of textual matter are noted parenthetically.

I. *The Dreaming of the Bones*

Photographs and Transcriptions of the Early Manuscripts (1917–1918)

A. Complete Prose Version, NLI 8775(1) (1917)

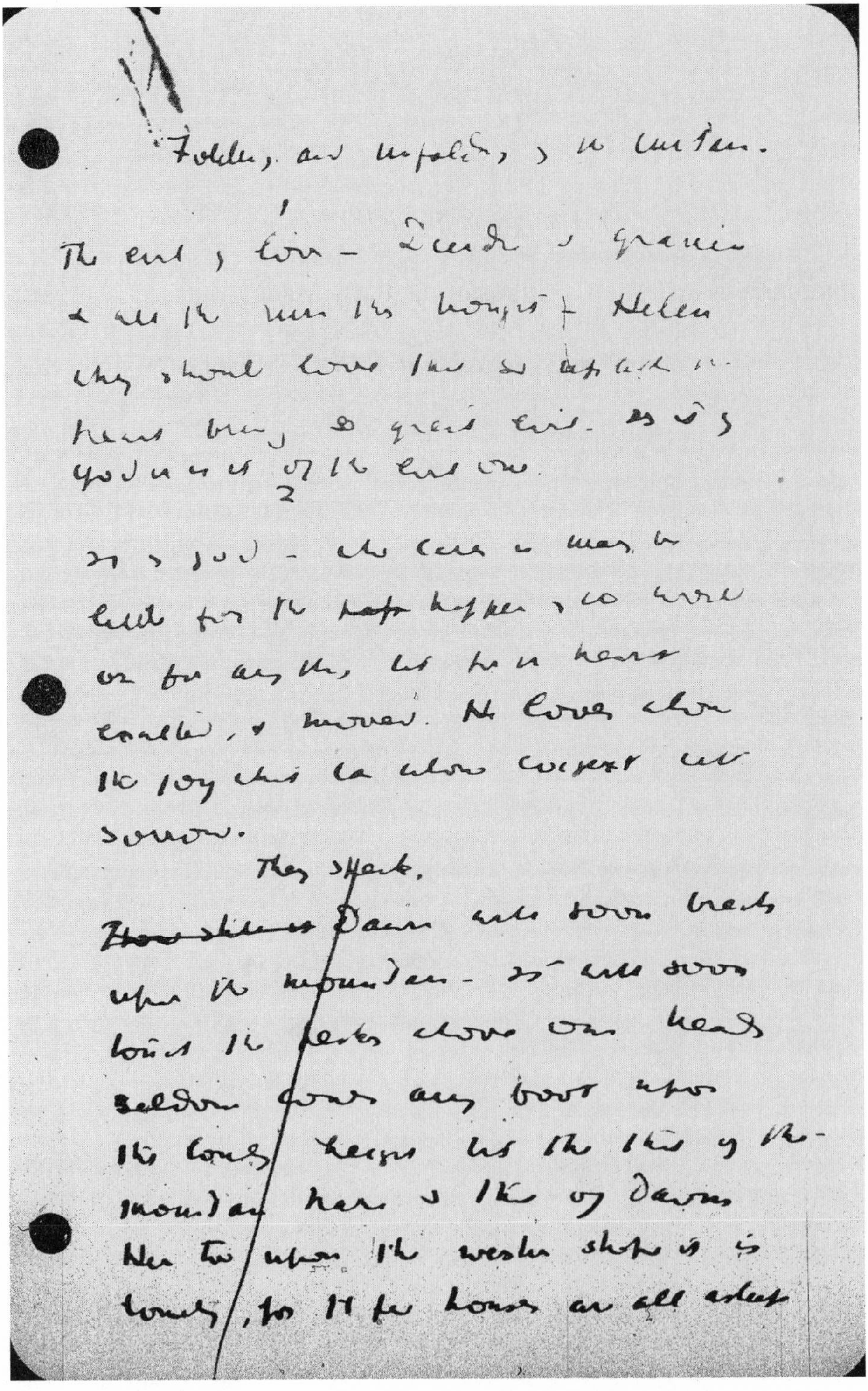

[NLI 8775(1), 1^{r}]

1

Folding and unfolding of the curtain

1

The evil of love – Dierdre & Grania
& all the ruin they brought – Helen
Why should love that so uplifts the
heart bring so great evil. Is it of
God or is it of the evil one.

2

If of god – who cares it may be
little for the ~~hap~~ happiness of the world
or for anything but for a heart
exalted, & moved. He loves alone
The joy which can alone coegexst with
sorrow.

They speak

~~How still is~~ Dawn will soon break
upon the mountains – It will soon
touch the peaks above our heads
seldom comes any foot upon
The lonely height but the that of the
mountain hare & that of dawn.
Here too upon the western slope it is
lonely, for the few houses are all asleep

---

10 "coexist" intended in "coegext"?

11*sd* "They" (as in 2^{r}) refers to persons of the chorus. See 3^{r} and elsewhere.

11*sd*–19 Superseded by 2^{r}, ll. 1–15, followed by dialogue on 1^{v}, 3^{r}, 4^{r} . . . et seq.

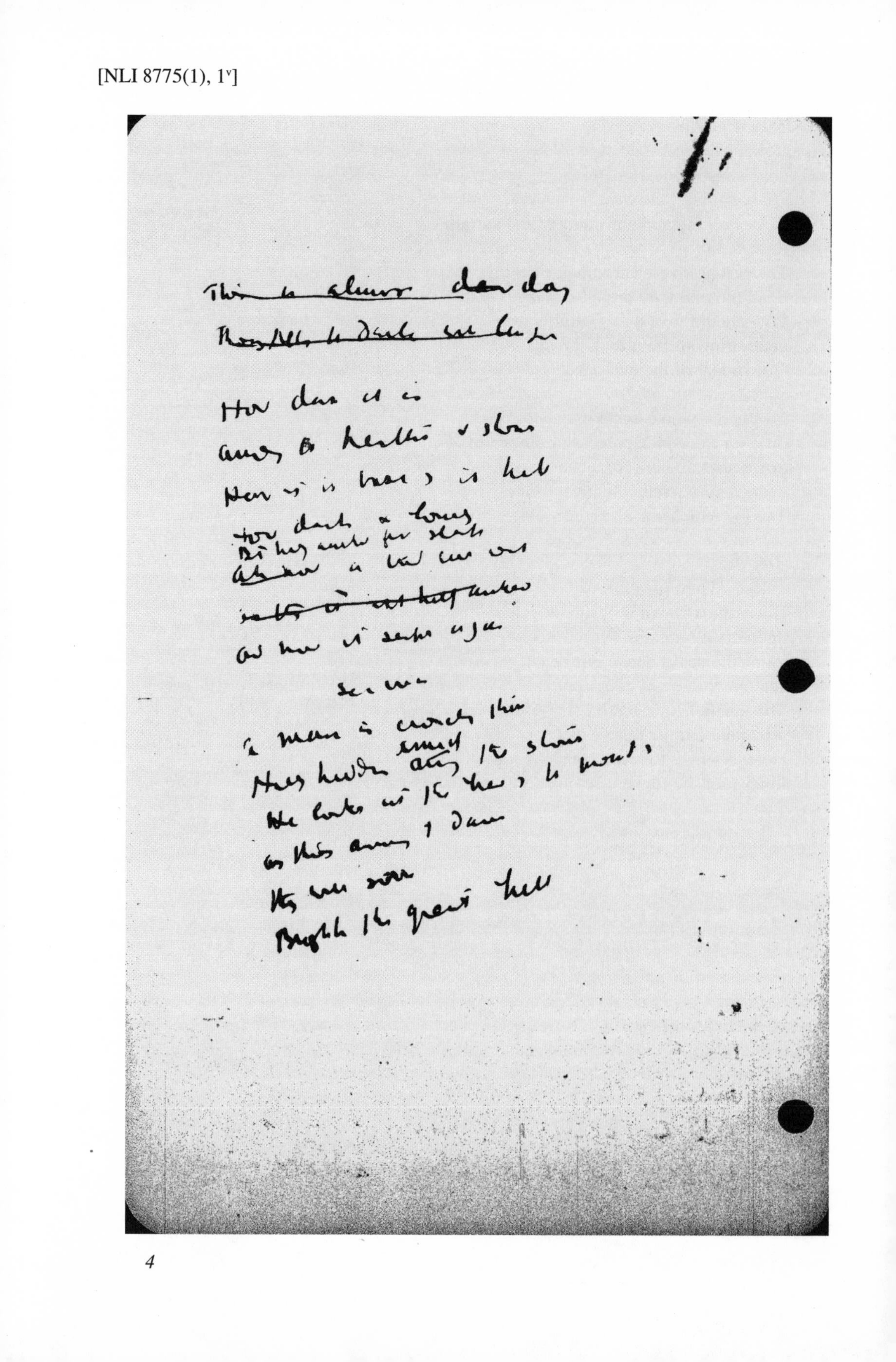

[NLI 8775(1), 1v]

[NLI 8775(1), 1^{v}]

~~This is almost dawn~~ day
~~Though [?late] the dark will linger~~

How dark it is
Among the heather & stones
Here at the base of the hill
How dark & lonely
But half awakened from sleep
~~And now~~ a bird cries out
~~As though but half~~ awakened
And now it sleeps again

Second Man

A man is crouching there
amid
Half hidden ~~among~~ the stones
He looks at the head of the [?mountains]
as though [?awaiting] the dawn
That will soon
Brighten the great hill

1–10 Continues from 2^{r}, ll. 18–19, evidently in same voice though possibly that of chorus.

11–16 The Second Man (or a member of the chorus speaking individually) is anticipated by 2^{r}, ll. 18–19, and perhaps 1^{v}, ll. 1–10, where the [First] Man, a member of the chorus, speaks singly.

[NLI 8775(1), 2r]

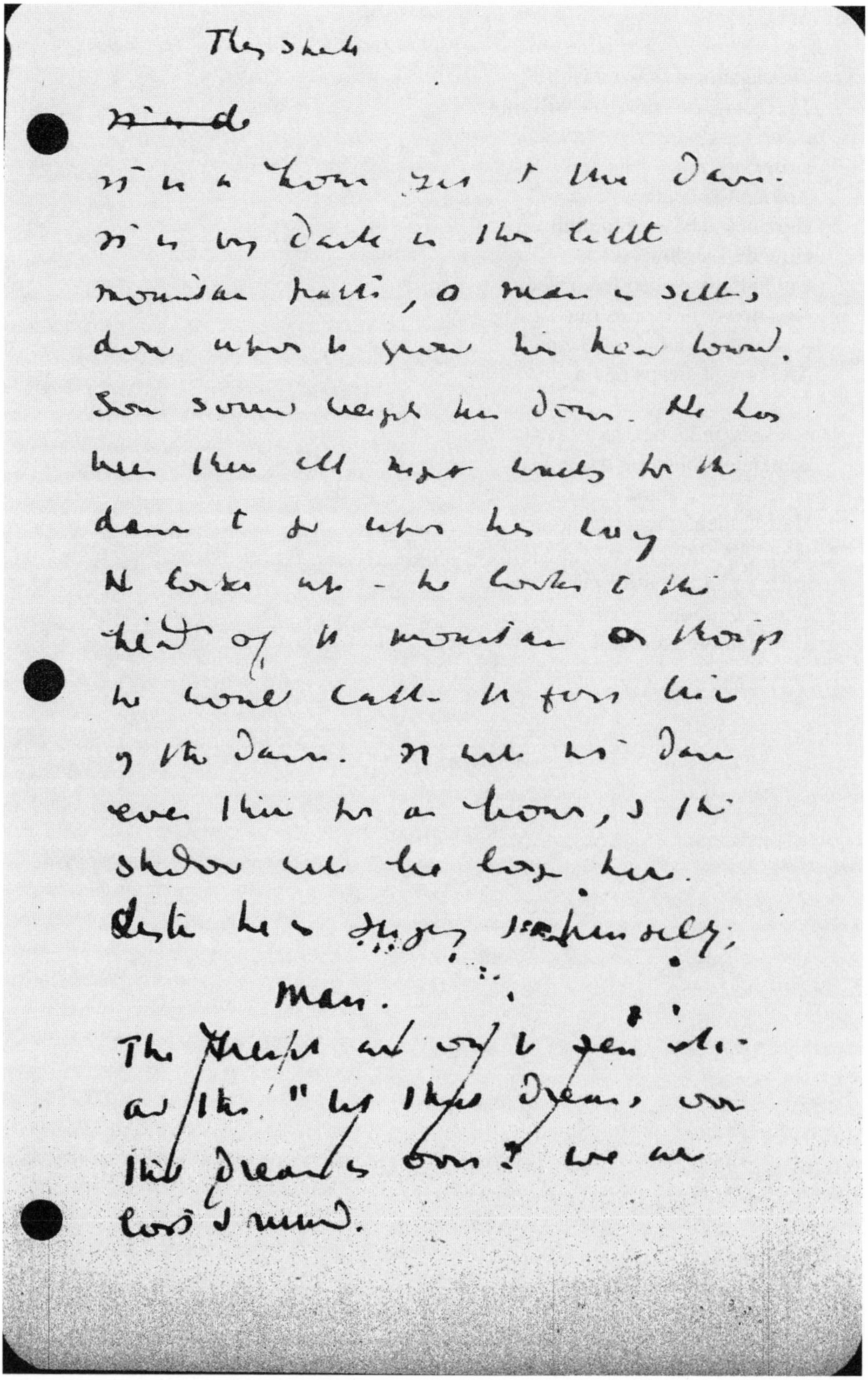

[NLI 8775(1), 2[r]]

2

They speak

~~It is d~~
It is an hour yet to the dawn.
It is very dark on this little
mountain path, a man is sitting
down upon the ground his head bowed.
Some sorrow weighs him down. He has
been there all night waiting for the
dawn to go upon his way
He looks up – he looks to the
head of the mountain as though
he would call the first trace
of the dawn. It will not dawn
even there for an hour, & the
shadow will be longer here.
Listen he is singing to himself.

Man.

The French are on the sea etc
And then "but that dreams over
That dream is over." We are
lost & ruined.

---

sd "They" (as in 1[r]) refers to persons of the chorus. See 3[r] and elsewhere.

16–18 References to external lyric pieces are evidently intended.

18–19 The words "We are lost & ruined" are not canceled but substituted for Yeats's direction on two external lyrics sung by the seated figure (Mac Dermit), whom the chorus has just described. The first of the two individuals from the chorus to speak, possibly the Man, continues on 1[v], ll. 1–10, before the Second Man succeeds him.

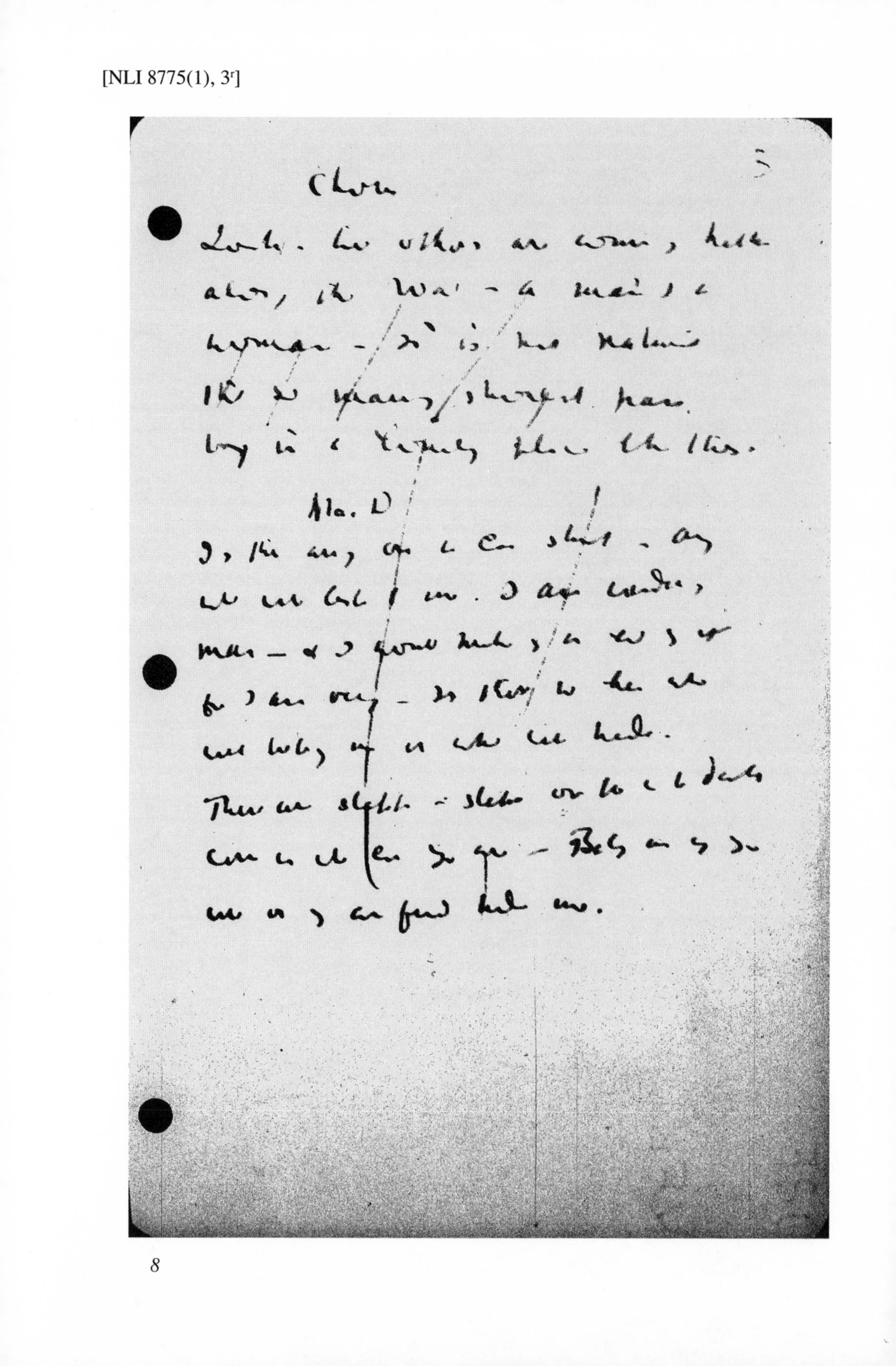

[NLI 8775(1), 3[r]]

[NLI 8775(1), 3[r]]

Chorus *3*

Look – two others are coming hither
along the road – a man & a
woman – Is it not natural
that so many should pass
by in a lonely place like this.

Mac D

Is there any one in ear shot – Any
who will listen to me. I am wandering
man – & I would make [?up] an end of it
for I am [?weary] – Is there [?none] here who
will betray me or who will hide.
There are stepp – steps over there in the dark
Come in who ever you are – Betray me if you
will of if are friend hide me.

1–5 Follows from 1[r], ll. 12–19 and 2[r], ll. 1–15 as the second collective speech of the chorus.

6–13 "Mac D," later "Mac Dermit" (also "Mc Dermit"), has just been spied crouching (by the Second Man) and heard singing songs of the 1798 Rebellion.

11 "stepp" for "steps"?

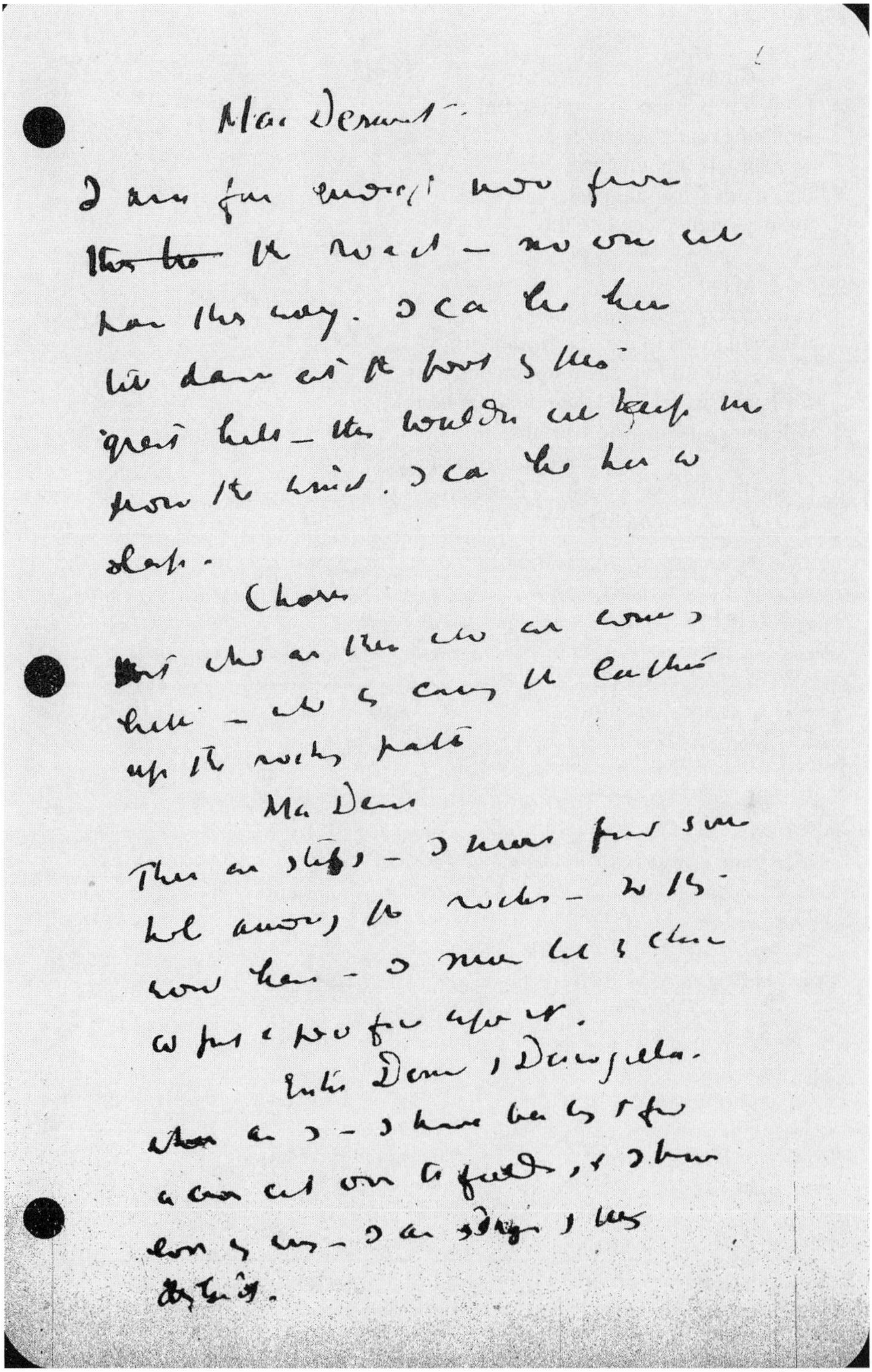

[NLI 8775(1), 4[r]]

4

Mac Dermit

I am far enough now from
~~This tra~~ the road – no one will
pass this way. I can lie here
till dawn at the foot of this
great hill – this boulder will keep me
from the wind. I can lie here to
sleep.

Chorus

But who are these who are coming
hither – who is carrying the lanthern
up the rocky path.

Mac Dermit

There are steps – I must find some
hole among the rocks – [?for] they
would hear – I must take a chance
And put a good face upon it.
Enter Dermid & Dervogilla.
Where am I – I have been trying to find
a cross cut over the fields, & I have
lost my way – I am stranger to this
district.

4[r] Supersedes the dialogue initiated on 3[r], in effect proceeding from revisions on 1[v].

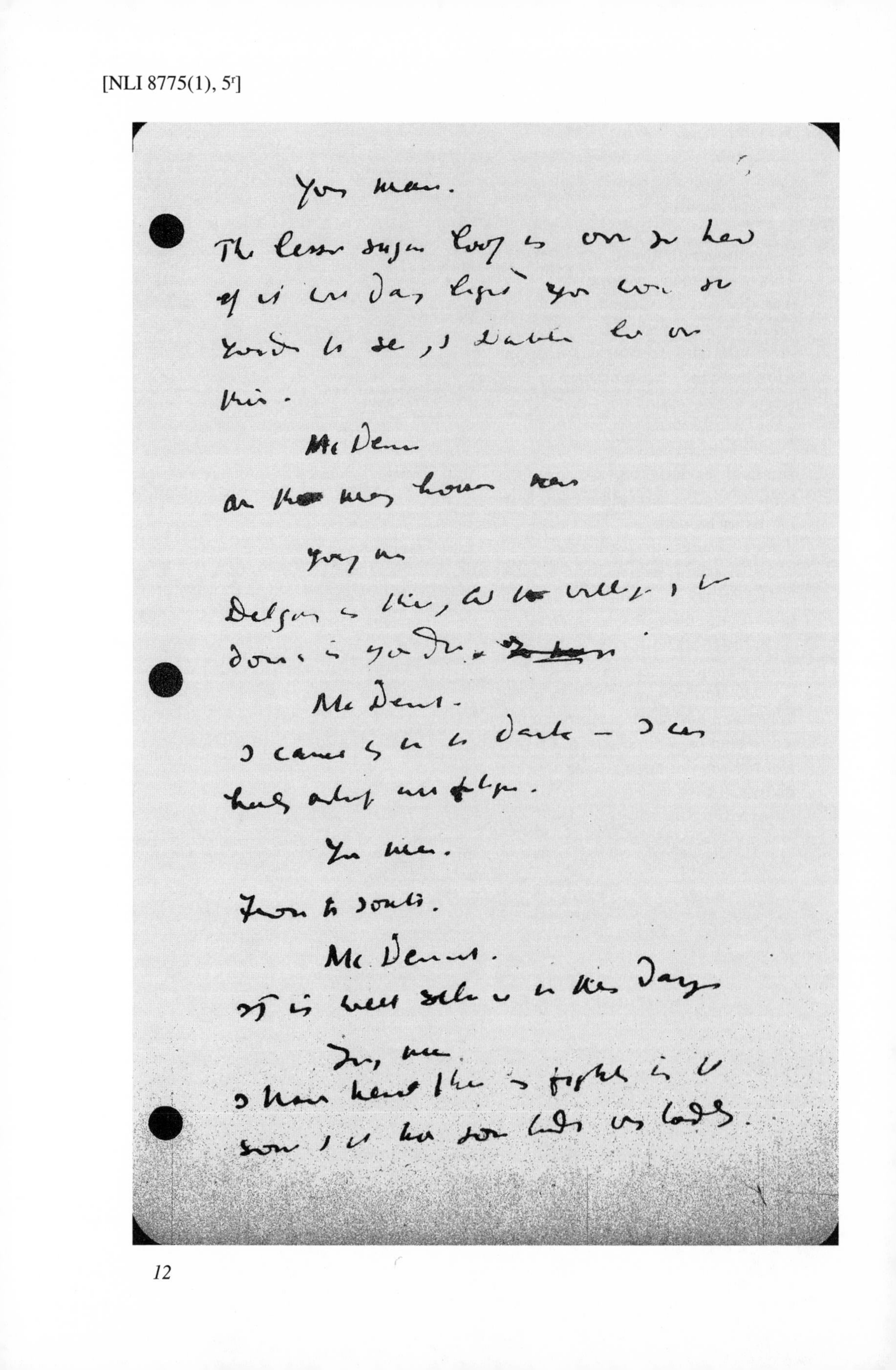

[NLI 8775(1), 5[r]]

5

Young Man.
The lesser sugar loof is over your head.
If it were day light you would see
Yonder the sea, & Dublin lies over
there.

Mc Dermit
Are there many houses near

Young Man
Delgar is there, and the village by the
downs is yonder. ~~To pass~~

Mc Dermit
I came by in the dark – I was
half asleep with fatigue.

Young Man.
From the south.

Mc Dermit
It is with silence in these days

Young Man
I have heard there is fighting in the
south & have heard some birds cry loudly.

---

1 "loof" for "loaf"?

[NLI 8775(1), 6r]

[NLI 8775(1), 6^{r}]

6

[?Yonder] – son husband, father or
brother – you meet here among these
rocks and at night, ~~before~~ because
the road & the daylight are
forbidden to you. We will not
judge one another, we both have
the same enemies, the dawn
~~& the sound of whistles, or of the~~
~~and~~ and human voices. I do not
see you well by this lanthern
but you are not dressed like
the people of my village.

Young Man

Where we live – there is no dress
but this.

Mac Dermit

Why should I fancy a strange dress
– when I must put my trust in the
~~strangers~~ faces I have never seen before
I am called Mac Dermit I
have fought at Vinegar Hill. I have
hill on my feet. I have slept in

1–12 Speaker is Mac Dermit?

1 "son husband," for "son, husband," or "some husband"? See 9^{r}, ll. 12–14.

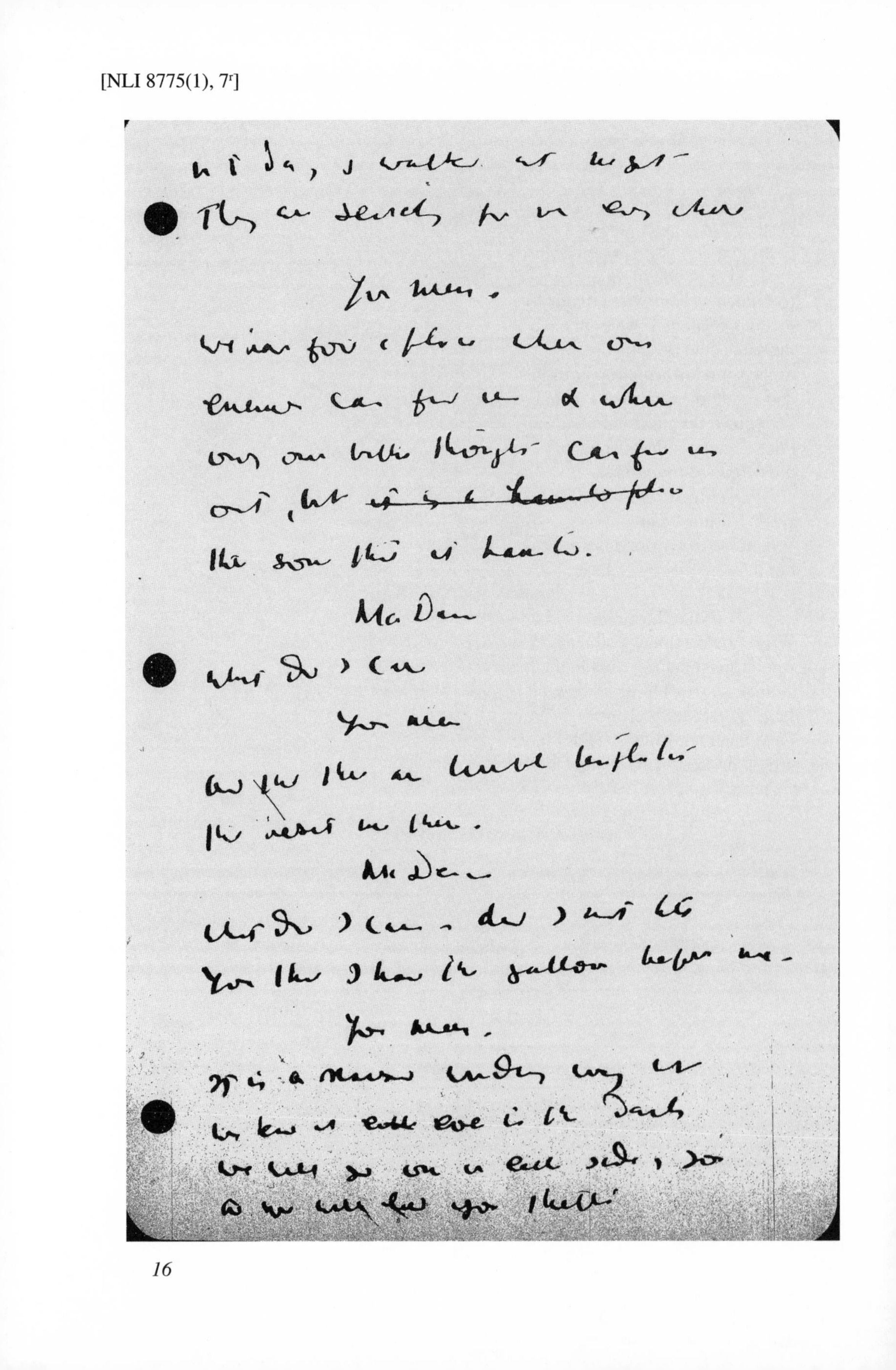

[NLI 8775(1), 7r]

[NLI 8775(1), 7^{r}]

7

in the day & walked at night
They are searching for me every where

Young Man.

We have found a place where our
enemies can find us & where
only our bitter thoughts can find us
out, but ~~it is a haunted place~~
[?There's] some think it haunted.

Mac Dermit

What do I care

Young Man

And that there are terrible temptations
That beset [?me/?us] there.

Mc Dermit

What do I care – did I not tell
You that I have the gallows before me.

Young Man.

It is a narrow winding way up
We know at ~~early~~ eve in the dark
we will go on on either side of you
And we will lend you shelter

---

4 "can" for "cannot"?

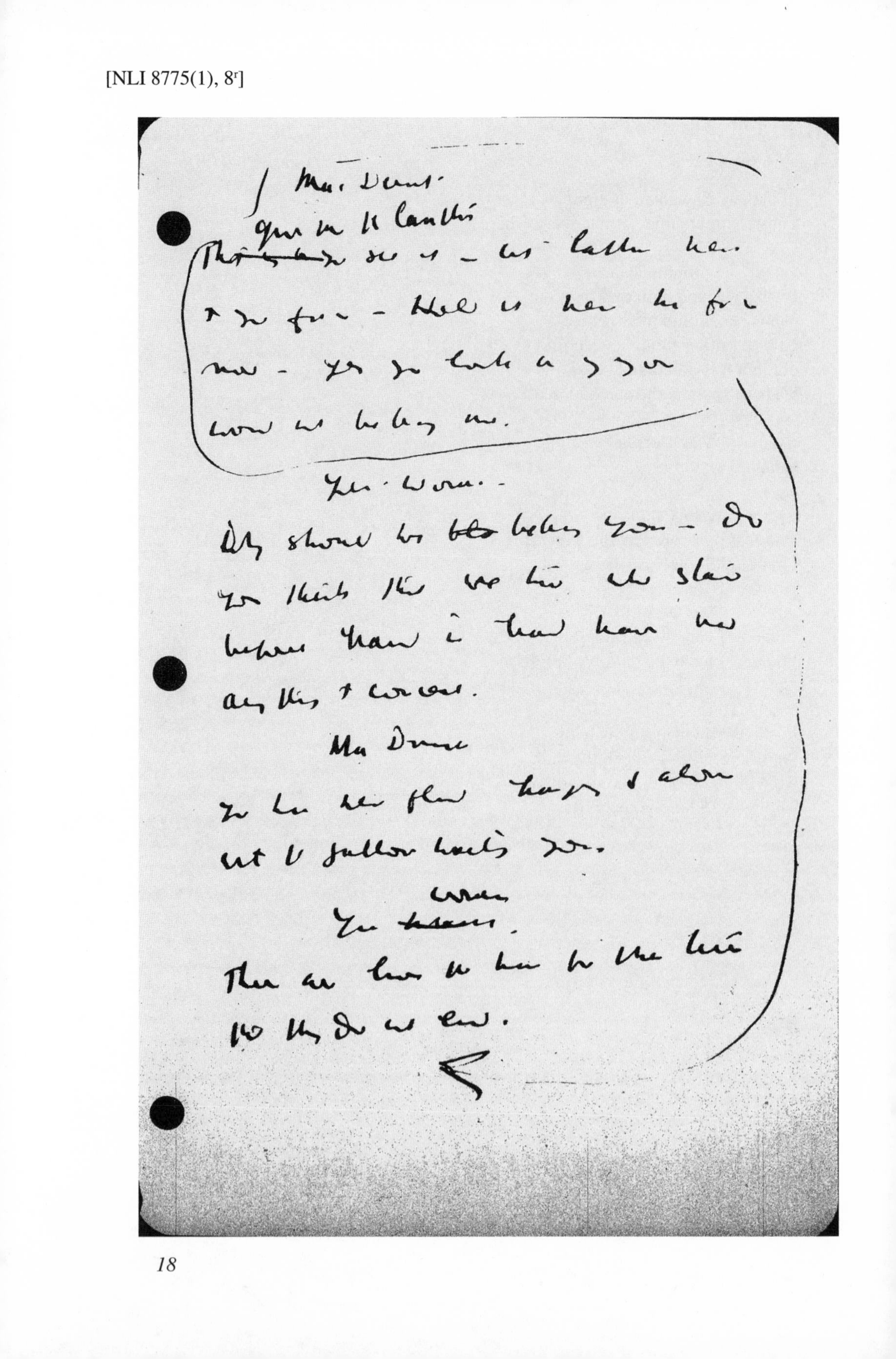

[NLI 8775(1), 8r]

[NLI 8775(1), 8r]

8

Mac Dermit
Give me the lanthern
~~That is on~~ You see it – that lanthern near
to your face – Hold it near her face
now – yes you look as if you
would not betray me

Young Woman.
Why should we ~~ble~~ betray you – do
You think that we two who stand
before hand in hand have had
any thing to conceal.

Mac Dermit
You have never fled hungry & alone
with the gallows waiting you.

Woman
Young ~~Man~~.
There we live that [?hunger] for the [?times]
that they do [?but] end.

1–5 Fully circumscribed in ink and marked with an arrow to indicate that the speech is to succeed l. 13.
12 "we live" or "are lives"?

[NLI 8775(1), 9r and 9v]

[NLI 8775(1), 9^{r} and 9^{v}]

[9^{r}]

9

~~Chorus~~

Chorus.

Mac Dermit

1 You have brought me to a hollow
2 between two little hills.

Young Man.

3 You are between the two houses of [?Slieve]
4 & since this last trouble began in
5 the country its said that there are
6 devils here – most evil devils
7 & that is why you will be safe.

Mc Dermit

8 ~~Do you live here always – is~~
9 ~~There some hole in the mountain where~~
10 ~~You hide – where you have found~~
11 ~~a bed – or do you creep out or~~ Does
12 ~~do~~ she creep out of her fathers or
13 her husbands house in the morning
14 hour to meet you here.

[9^{v}]

Mac Dermit

1 & when you meet here you think
2 of those old lovers, & [?later]
3 you like each other the better for
4 the thought – I too have been young &
5 remember – strange that old
6 passions intoxicate us when
7 we are young like old wine

9^{v}, 1–7 Partially inscribed on the right with a line leading off to indicate an insertion, as shown, into the Young Man's speech at 10^{r}, l. 12.

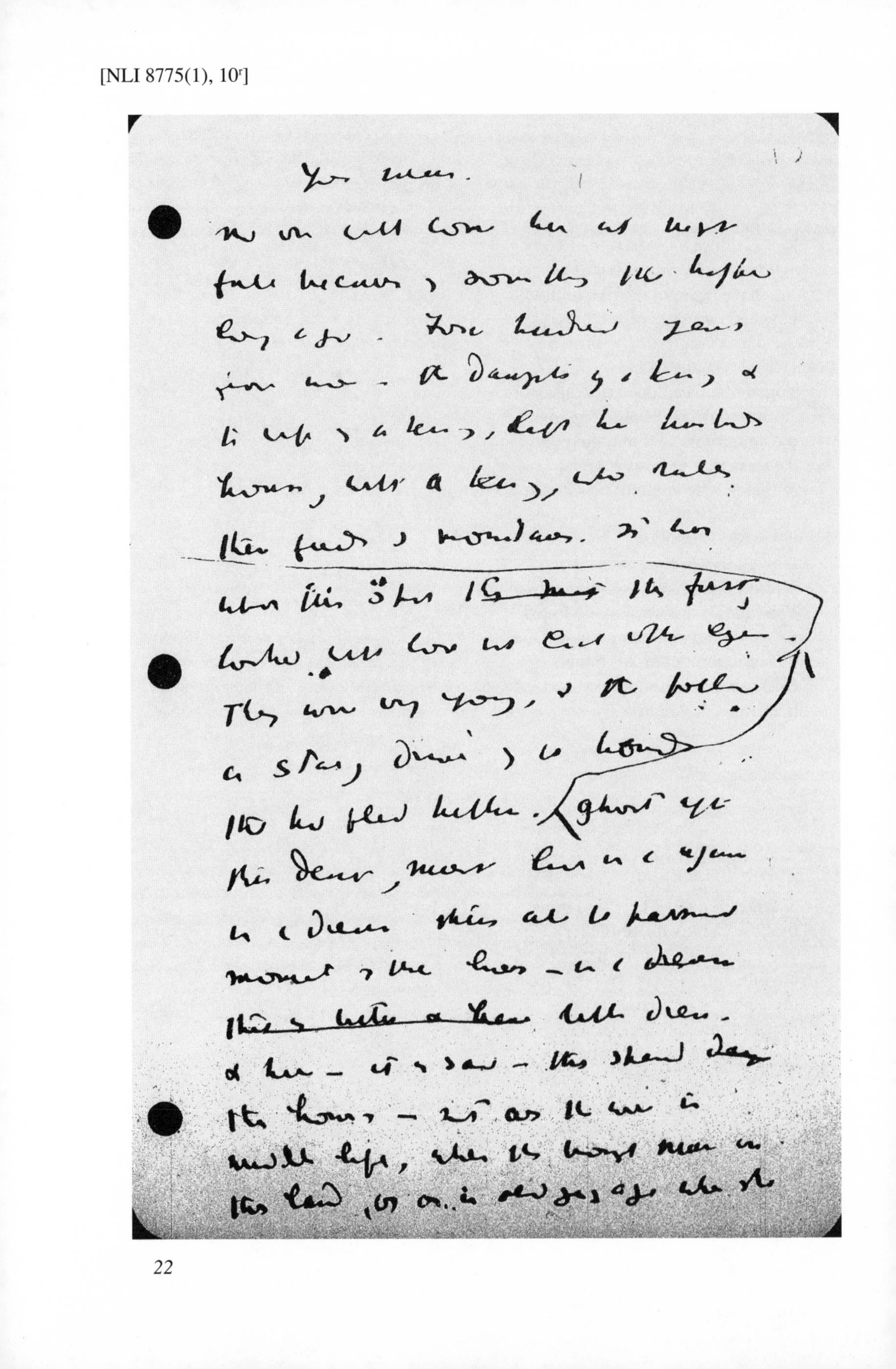

[NLI 8775(1), 10r]

[NLI 8775(1), 10r]

10

Young Man.

No one will come here at night
fall because of something that happened
long ago. Four hundred years
from now – the daughter of a king &
the wife of a king, left her husbands
house, with a king, who rules
these fields & mountains. It was
upon this spot ~~they met~~ they first,
looked with love in each others eyes –
They were very young, & they followed
a stary dream of the hounds
that had fled hither. ^ Ghosts after
their death, must live once again
in a dream stirring all the passionate
moments of their lives – in ~~a dream~~
~~that is bitter & have~~ bitter dream.
& here – it is said – they spend ~~days~~
their hours – not as they were in
middle life, when they brought man on
this land, or as in old gay age when she

4 "from" bears the sense of "before"?

11 "stary" for "starry"?

12 Caret and curving arrow indicates insertion of Mac Dermit speech worked out on 9v. After the interpolation, the speech here continues as the Young Man.

20 "gay" for "grey"?

[NLI 8775(1), 11r]

[NLI 8775(1), 11r]

11

in sack cloth, but as at their first
glance.

Mac Dermit

You speak of Darmuid & of Dervagilla
who brought in the English my curse
upon them.

Young Man.

But for one day in every year – they
dance a mournful dance, dancing
in a dream – a perpetual recognition
a perpetual ~~come~~ covering of the
face – love & the knowledge of
sorrow. They dreamed & they are
punished by a dream.

Mac Dermit

May their punishment never end
You have chosen your meeting place
badly.

[NLI 8775(1), 12r]

[NLI 8775(1), 12^{r}]

12

Young Girl.
It is said – there in the valley – and
if any of the race of Darmuid would
forgive them – they would ~~for believe~~
forgive themselves, & then death could
end in change.

Mac Dermit
None of the race of Darmuid
will ever forgive them – look the
dawn there is beggining to brighten.
The sun is still below the sea, but
the horizon behind Howth [?~~whitens~~]
becomes bright. Before long the dawn
will be upon us – But why do you
gaze at one another – Why ~~let~~
those dream like shapes – Why do
you cover your faces.

Young Girl.

[NLI 8775(1), 13r and 14r]

[NLI 8775(1), 13r and 14r]

[13r]

13

O you are not living man & woman

~~Mc Dermit~~
{G/Y}irl

We are those old lovers – In but a
Moment we must begin our dance –
Forgive us & we will find peace.
It is terrible in the one glance
to know all love & all miseries
to rejoice, & to be full [?remorse]
to be alone & see but one another
& then to stay remembering all the
misery that we brought upon the land

Mc Dermit.

~~You~~ Hundreds of years – that is a
long repentance – to [?~~spe~~] have nothing
left but a dream – no no – no no
~~[?Should] any~~ one Darmuid s race will
Ever forgive us. They begin to dance
They move slowly covering their eyes ~~They~~
[?~~dancing~~].

[14r]

14

Chorus describes the dance

Perhaps there is uttermost joy
in that sorrow – [?ecstasy] in the
thought of all that misery – here upon
this [?barren] [?hill]. (They go)

T Mc Dermot

They are gone – This is indeed
a place of terrible temptation.

13r, 11 See 10r, l. 3, above.

14–15 "one" for "one of"? The lines might be spoken by the Young Girl, rather than by the speaker indicated.

15–17 The words "They begin to dance" etc. introduce a further undifferentiated element of amalgamation into the designated speech of Mac Dermit, that of stage directions.

14r, 2 "ecstasy" derived from "ecsatsy"?

I. *The Dreaming of the Bones*

Photographs and Transcriptions of the Early Manuscripts (1917–1918)

B. Songs and Choral Settings, NLI 13,583, 38^{r}; NLI 8775(2); Texas(A) (1917)

[NLI 13,583, 38r]

Ms 13,583

There is no man but may
meet sudden face to face
In any out of the way
Woods and desolate places
Of those night wanderings
Old learned books have said
The dizzy dreams that spring,
From the dry bones of the dead
And many a night it seems,
That all the valley fills
~~With~~ That those phantastic dreams,
Can overflow the hills
So passionate is a shade
Like wine that fills to the top
A grey green cup of jade
Or maybe an agate cup.

[NLI 13,583, 38r]

There is no man but may
Meet suddenly face to face
In an out of the way
Windy and desolate place *mad*
If these night wandering
Old learned books have said
The dizzy dreams that spring
From the dry bones of the dead
And many a night it seems
That all the valley fills
That
~~With~~ those phantastic dreams
Can over flow the hills *Have over flowed*
So passionate is a shade
Like wine that fills to the top
A grey green cup of jade
Or maybe an agate cup.

~~*O lonely clouds of the night*~~
~~*Why has my heart run wild*~~
~~*When star*~~

There is no sound or sign
And yet hearts run wild
O lonely clouds of the night
My rascal hearts run wild
Remembering remembering
Old learned books have said
These

1–16 With revisions in pencil; these lines anticipate the First Musician's second song, installed in the text at *VPl* 1–16; especially correspondent are ll. 8–16.

17–19 In pencil; anticipate lines worked out in the First Musician's second song, *VPl* 101–107.

20–26 In pencil; anticipate verses of the First Musician's second song, *VPl* 101–107 and 114–115.

[NLI 8775(2), 1r]

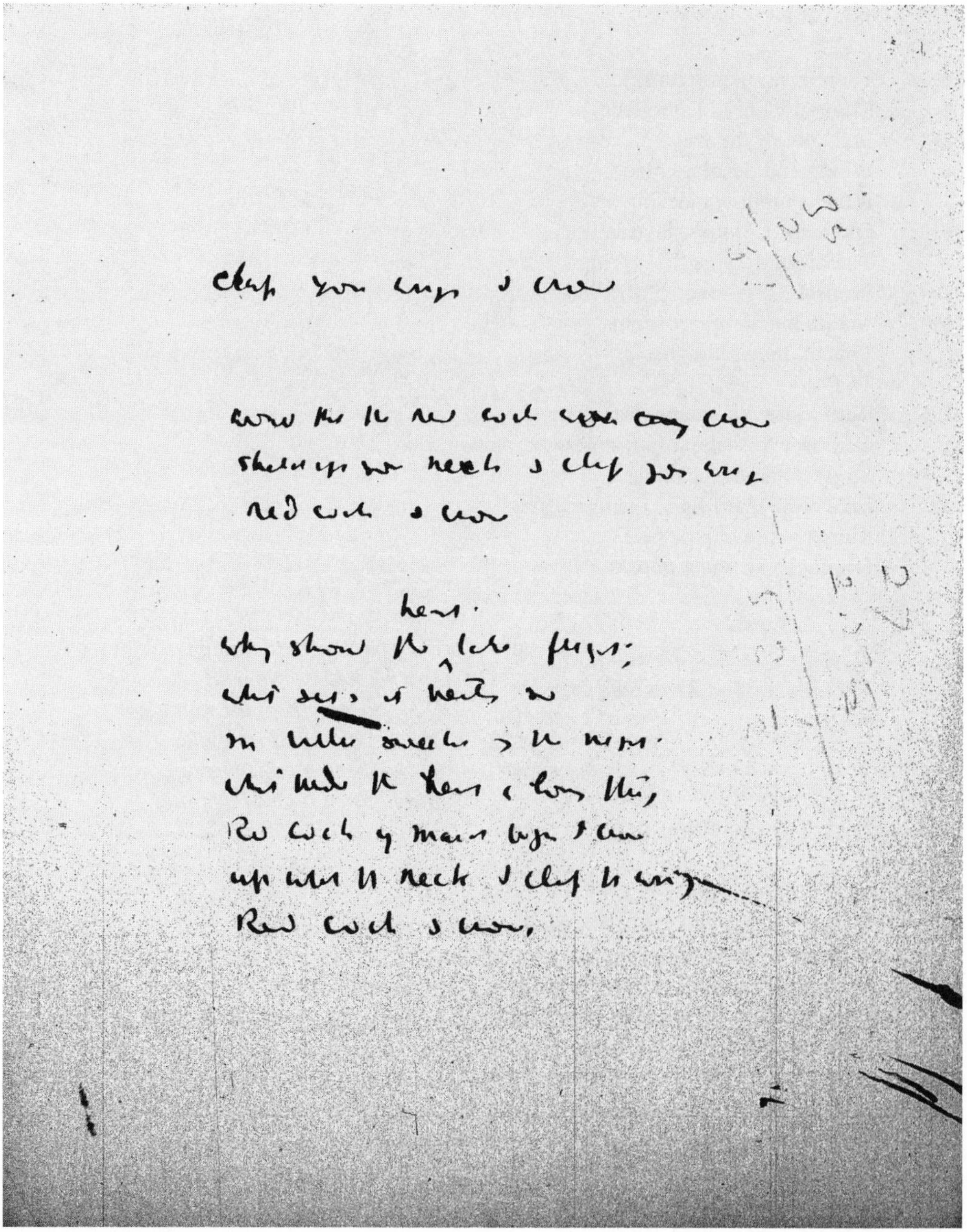

[NLI 8775(2), 1^{r}]

Clap your wings & crow

Would that the red cock ~~with every~~ crow
Stretch up your neck & clap your wings
red cock & crow

heart
Why should the ^ take fright,
What sets it beating so
In bitter sweetness of the night
What made the heart a lonely thing
Red cock of March begin to crow
Up with the neck & clap the wing
Red cock & crow.

1–4 Rehearse the refrain lines of the three verses of the First Musician's second song, *VPl* 101–107, 112–118, and 123–129.

5–11 Draft of the entire first verse of the First Musician's second song, *VPl* 101–107.

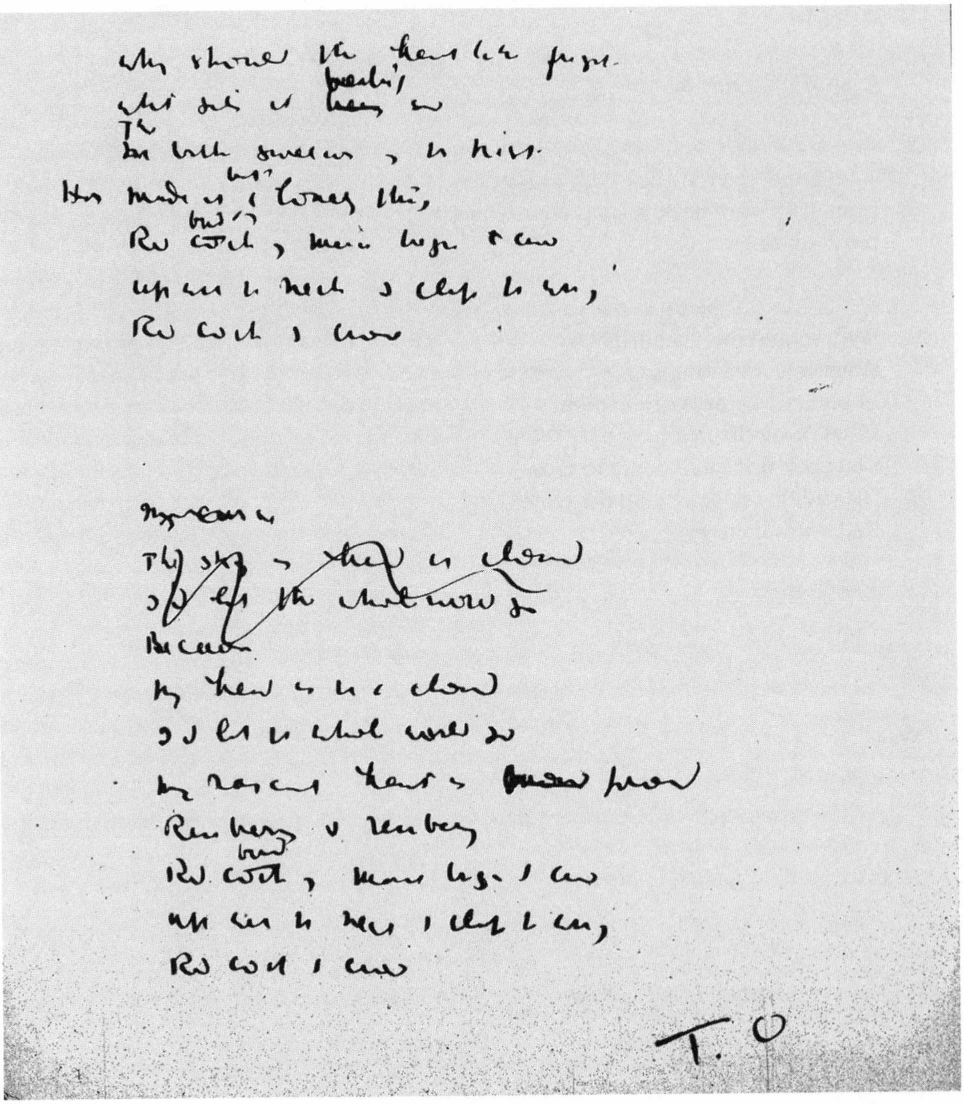
Why should the heart take fright
pulsing
What sets it beating so
The
The bitter sweetness of the night
but
Has made it a lonely thing
bird
Red cock of March begin to crow
Up with the neck & clap the wing
Red cock & crow

~~[illegible]~~
~~The sky is there in cloud~~
~~& I let the whole world go~~
Because
My head is in a cloud
& I'd let the whole world go
My rascal heart is ~~[illegible]~~ proud
Remembering & remembering
bird
Red cock of March begin to crow
Up with the neck & clap the wing,
Red cock & crow

T. O.

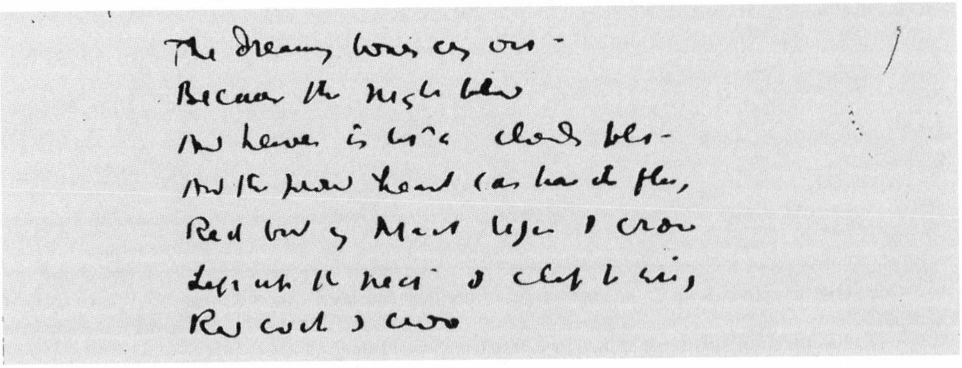
The dreaming bones cry out—
Because the night [illegible]
And heaven is in a cloud [illegible]—
And the proud heart can hardly fly,
Red bird of March begin to crow
Lift up the neck & clap the wing,
Red cock & crow

[NLI 8775(2), 2^{r} and 2^{v}]

[2^{r}]

Why should the heart take fright
beating
What sets it ~~being~~ so
The
~~In~~ bitter sweetness of the night
but
Has Made it ^ a lonely thing
bird
Red ~~cock~~ of March begin to crow
Up with the neck & clap the wing
Red cock & crow

~~My curse~~
The sky is hid in cloud
I'd let the whole world go
Because
My head is in a cloud
I d let the whole world go
My rascal heart is ~~prow~~ proud
Rem~~emb~~ering & remembering
bird
Red cock of March begin to crow
Up with the neck & clap the wing
Red cock & crow

T. O.

[2^{v}]

The dreaming bones cry out
Because the night blow
And heaven is but a cloudy blot
And the proud heart can have its fling
Red bird of March begin to crow
Lift up the neck & clap the wing
Red cock & crow

2^{r}, 1–7 Revised from NLI 8775(2), 1^{r}, and constituting a nearly complete draft of verse one of the First Musician's second song, *VPl* 101–107.

8–18 Constitute a draft of verse two of the First Musician's second song, *VPl* 112–118, incorporating NLI 13,583, 38^{r}, ll. 23–24.

lower right "T. O." for "Turn Over" (i.e., to 2^{v})?

2^{v}, 1–7 Constitute a draft of verse three of the First Musician's second song, *VPl* 123–129.

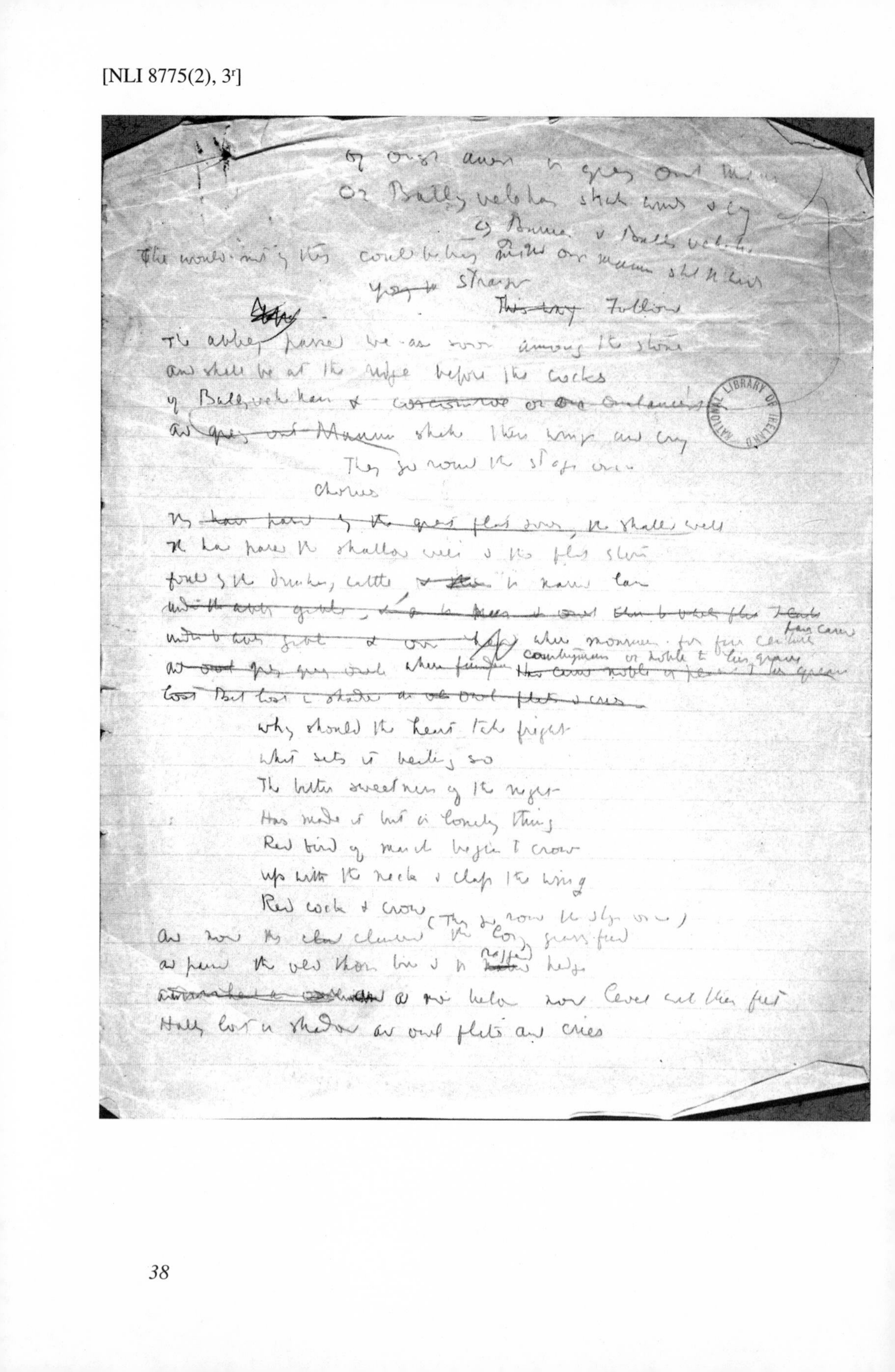

[NLI 8775(2), 3r]

[NLI 8775(2), 3r]

Of Ough Anish or grey Out Mana
Or Bally velehan shake winds & cry
of [*?Banna*] *& Bally vehehan*
or
might Ough Manna shake the wind
1 *They would not if they could betray*
~~*Young M Stranger*~~
[*?~~Young~~*] ~~*This way*~~ *Follow*
2 *The abbey passed we are soon among the stone*
3 *And shall be at the ridge before the cocks*
4 *of Ballyvehehan &* ~~*Corcomroe or Ouc Ouchanish*~~
5 ~~*And grey Out Manna*~~ *shake their wings and cry*
They go round the stage once
Chorus
6 ~~*They have passed by the great flat* [*?stone*]*, the shallow well.*~~
7 *They have passed the shallow well & the flat stone*
8 *fouled by the drinking cattle,* ~~*&* [*?through*]~~ *the narrow lane*
9 ~~*Under the abbey gable, & go to Man and Ouch*~~
~~*There the owl flits & cries*~~
have carried
10 ~~*Under the abbey gable & over head*~~ *Where mourners for five centuries*
Countryman or noble to his grave
11 ~~*And owl grey grey owls Where friend or Had carried noble or peasant to his grave*~~
12 ~~*lost But lost in shadow an ol owl flits & cries.*~~
13 *Why should the heart take fright*
14 *What sets it beating so*
15 *The bitter sweetness of the night*
16 *Has made it but a lonely thing*
17 *Red bird of March begin to crow*
18 *Up with the neck & clap the wing*
19 *Red cock & crow*
(They go round the stage once)
20 *And now they* [*?~~clim~~*] *climbed the long grassy field*
ragged
21 *And passed the old thorn tree & the* ~~*narrow*~~ *hedge*
22 ~~[*?Aughanish*] *head & Oughtmanna*~~ *And go below now level with their feet*
23 *Holly lost in shadow an owl flits and cries*

---

1 Cf. *VPl* 90, spoken by the Young Man.

2–5*sd* Anticipate *VPl* 91–95, spoken by the Stranger, and l. 95*sd*.

6–12 Anticipate, very roughly, *VPl* 96–100, spoken by the First Musician.

13–19 Cf. *VPl* 101–107, the first verse of the First Musician's second song, following drafts on NLI 8775(2), 1r and 2r.

19*sd*–23 Roughly equivalent to *VPl* 107*sd*–111, also spoken by the First Musician.

[NLI 8775(2), 4r]

[NLI 8775(2), 4r]

They go round the stage once

1 *They clamber among the stones before the green*
2 *above the ash, above briar & thorn*
3 ~~*And turn their eyes toward*~~ *one bows his head, & toward* [?] *turn their eyes*
4 *One on the other, & then turn away –*
5 *The dreaming bones cry out*
6 ~~*I d let the whole world go*~~ *Because the night winds blow*
7 ~~*My rascal heart is*~~ *proud* *The heaven is but a cloudy blot*
The extravagant heart ~~*has ca may ca*~~
8 ~~*Remembering and remembering*~~ ~~*And the proud*~~ *heart* ~~*can have its fling*~~
9 *Red bird of March begin to crow* *will have its fling*
10 *Up with the neck & clap the wing*
11 *Red cock & crow*

---

sd–4 The *VPl* coordinates are ll. 118*sd*–122, spoken by the First Musician; but the resemblance ends after the second line of the speech.

3 "one bows his" for "one bowing his" or "one bowing her"?

5–11 Cf. *VPl* 123–129, the third verse of the First Musician's second song. Yeats copies and cancels (at left) lines composed in NLI 13,583, 38r (ll. 23–24), and in NLI 8775(2), 2r; for these lines of the second verse he substitutes (at right) lines from the third verse, drawn and revised from NLI 8775(2), 2v.

[NLI 8775(2), 5r]

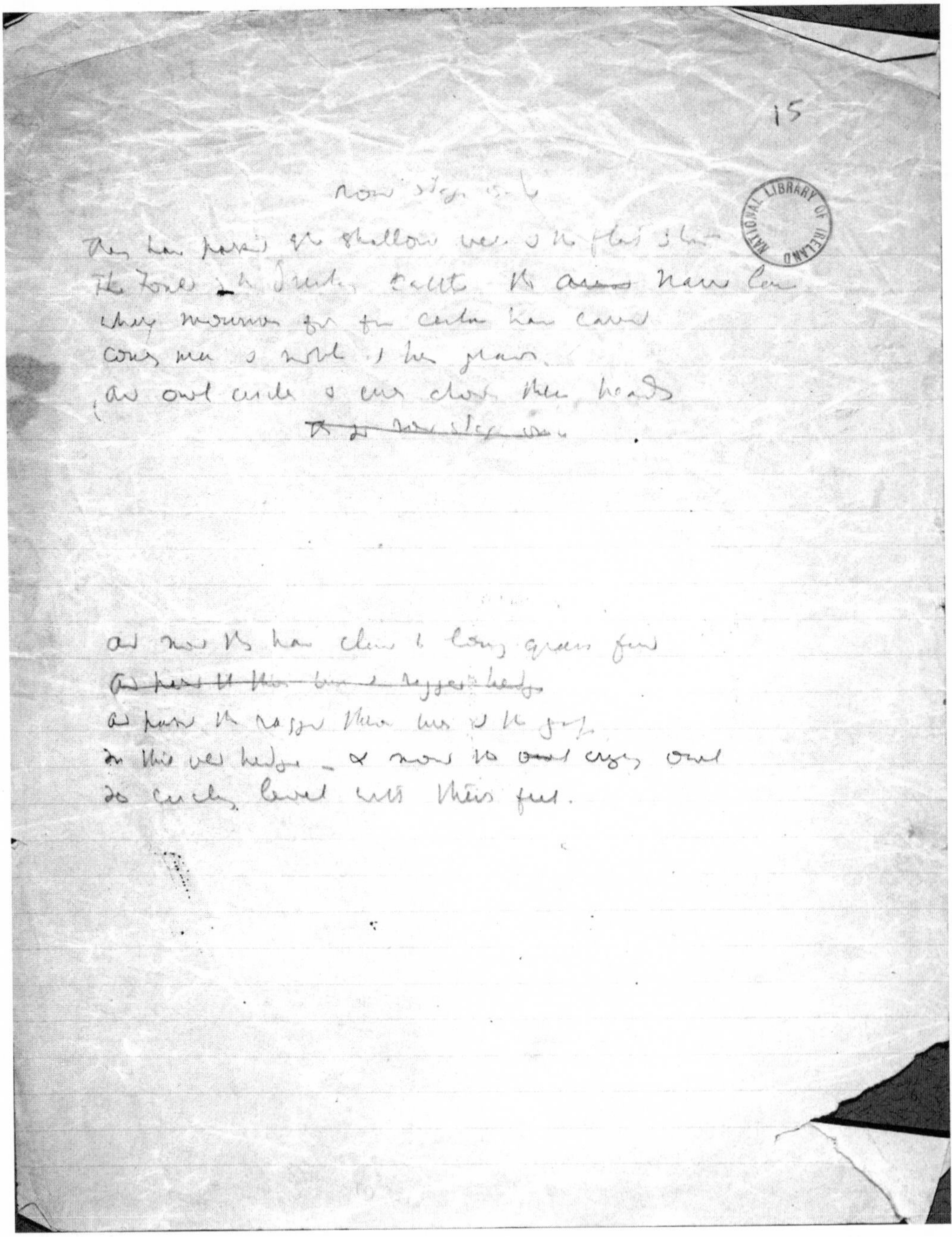

[NLI 8775(2), 5^{r}]

15

Round stage once

They have passed the shallow well & the flat stone
~~*The*~~ *Fouled by the drinking cattle the [?~~arrow~~] narrow lane*
Where mourners for five centuries have carried
Country man & noble to his grave
An owl circles & cries above their heads
~~*they go round stage once*~~

And now they have climbed [?through] long grass field
~~*And passed the thorn bound ragged hedge*~~
And passed the ragged thron trees & the gap
In this old hedge – & now the ~~*owl*~~ *crying owl*
Is circling level with their feet

Moved in 1967 from NLI 8775(1), this folio reworks passages heavily revised in NLI 8775(2), 3^{r}.

sd–5 Correspond to *VPl* 95*sd*–100; cf. NLI 8775(2), 3^{r}, ll. 6–12, spoken by the chorus (later the First Musician).

5*sd*–10 Correspond to *VPl* 107*sd*–111; cf. NLI 8775(2), 3^{r}, ll. 20–23, also spoken by the chorus (or the First Musician).

[Texas(A)]

At the grey round of the hill
A wandering aery music
Runs, runs & is suddenly
The
^Winds ~~blow~~ out of Clare-Galway or A wind that blows out
Carry it – suddenly it is still. of Galway

I have heard in the night air
Music of a lost kingdom
And taken in that snare And in that murderous snare
A man is crazed of a sudden We may be lost of a suden
In that sweet wandering snare

O what musician began
A wandering aery music
They dreamed that laughed in the sun
Dry bones that dream are bitter
They dream and darken our sun

Their crazy fingers play
Music of a lost kingdom
Our luck is withered away
And wheat in the wheat-ear withered
And the wind blows it away.

Inscribed in another hand (at lower right): "Composed Ely Place / ~~10~~ 9: vii: '17", this folio carries the first of two curtain songs for the musicians ("Songs for the unfolding and folding of the cloth"), *VPl* 283–302.

I. *The Dreaming of the Bones*

Photographs and Transcriptions of the Early Manuscripts (1917–1918)

C. Complete Verse Version from Mixed States, Harvard(A) (1917–1918)

Yeats made this composite manuscript with paste pot, scissors, and four kinds of paper. For the sake of analysis, the four papers, which also correspond to the four states of the text, are designated A, B, C, and D here and in the transcription notes. In sum, the procedure consisted of

(A) his laying out eighteen sheets, on which
(B) largely fair copies of the play's songs and surrounding set pieces were pasted in sequence, with
(C) an older draft of the dialogue and two loose slips to bridge holograph states B and C, with matching typed and handwritten insertions.
(D) In making a third such bridge (of 8^r) and in copying over (on 1a) the first page of the assembly, Yeats employed a fourth paper (D).

A was only used as backing to merge B and C fragments in an integrated state. As the physical evidence of Yeats's construction provides a fascinating picture of a whole play made of parts composed at different times, background shading has been applied to the transcription of the B state to differentiate it from the longer C state. Unfortunately, in pasting down most C fragments, initially extracted from an exercise book in which both sides of some leaves were used, Yeats rendered inaccessible part of the evidence of his composing process. See the introduction, part II, for a detailed gloss of Harvard(A). The manuscript's four states are correspondent with the following paper types given in the census: A, type 11; B, type 12; C, type 8; D, type 2.

(1)

The Dreaming of the Bones.

The stage is any bare ~~space~~ place in a room with a wall against it. A screen ~~with a pattern of a mountain & sky~~ ~~can stand~~ or a curtain with a pattern of mountain or sky upon it may be hung or stand against the wall, but the pattern must only symbolize or suggest. ~~Three musicians enter~~ A musician enters; he stands singing, while the others enter. As they sit down against the wall. ~~By the walls~~ They have carried in or found against the wall, a cloth, their instruments a drum a zither a flute. Or they have unfold the cloth as in the Hawks Well while the instruments are carried.

First Musician (singing)

Why does my heart beat so
Did not a shadow pass?
It passed by a woman's eyes.
Who can have trod in the grass?
What rogue is night wandering?
Have not old writers said
That dizzy dreams can spring
From the dry bones of the dead?
And many a night it seems
That all the valley fills
With those phantastic dreams,
They overflow the hills
So passionate is a shade
Like wine that fills to the top
A grey green cup of jade
Or maybe an agate cup

(speaking)

[Harvard(A), 1^{r}]

The Dreaming of the Bones
The stage is any bare ~~space~~ place in a room with a
wall against it. A screen ~~with a pattern of a mountain~~
~~& sky can stand~~ or a curtain with a pattern of
mountain and sky upon it may be hung or stand against
the wall, but the pattern must only symbolize or suggest –
A musician enters He
~~Three musicians enter; one~~ stands singing while ~~the~~ two
others enter. All three sit down against the wall.
~~By the wall a~~ They have carried in or found against the wall, a cloth
Their instruments a drum a zither a flute. Or they have
the
unfold ~~a~~ cloth as in the Hawks Well while the
while the instruments are carried.
First Musician (singing
Why does my heart beat so
Did not a shadow pass?
It passed by a moment ago.
Who can have trod in the grass?
What rogue is night wandering?
Have not old writers said
That dizzy dreams can spring
From the dry bones of the dead?
And many a night it seems
That all the valley fills
With those phantastic dreams
They over flow the hills
So passionate is a shade
Like wine that fills to the top
A grey green cup of jade
Or maybe an agate cup
(speaking)

---

sd Especially the rough second half of 1^{r} suggests why Yeats copied over the setting onto folio 1a, on paper type D, and revised as he did so, but only after assembling as a complete contiguous version of folios 1–24. The setting of 1a varies as follows: "(The stage . . . bare place . . . room close to the wall. A screen with a pattern of mountain & sky can stand against the wall, a curtain with a like pattern hangs upon it, but . . . suggest. One musician enters, and then two others take their places. Then all three . . . wall by their instruments which are already there – a Drum, a Zither and a Lute. Or they unfold a cloth as . . . Well, while the instruments are carried in.)" A direction at the First Musician's entrance: "(or all three Musicians, singing)".

1–16*sd* *variants in folio 1a:* 1 so] so? 2 shadow] shaddow 3 by] but 6 writers] writer's 7 spring] ~~spread~~ spring 8 dead?] dead 10 the] the ~~fi~~ 15 grey green] grey-green 16*sd* *lacking*.

2

The hour before dawn and the moon covered up
The little village of Abbey is covered up
The little narrow trodden way that runs
From the white road to the abbey of Corcomroe
Is covered up; and all about the hills
are like a circle of agate or of jade
Somewhere among grey rocks on the scarce grass
Birds cry, they cry their loneliness
Even the sunlight can be lonely here.

(3)

Even hot noon is lonely. I hear a footfall
A young man with a lanthorn comes this way
He seems an Aran fisher for he wears
The flannel bawneen & the cow hide shoe.
He stumbles wearily & prays while he stumbles.
A young man enters praying. in
Irish or in Latin.
Chorus
Once more the birds cry in their loneliness
But now they wheel about our heads & now
They have dropped on the grey stone to the north east
A young man & girl in the clothes & c
past time & wearing masks come in.

[Harvard(A), 2^{r} and 3^{r}]

[2^{r}]

2

[. . .]
1 The hour before dawn and the moon covered up
2 The little village of Abbey is covered up
3 The little narrow trodden way that runs
4 From the white road to the Abbey of Corcomroe
5 Is covered up; and all about the hills
6 Are like a circle of agate or of jade
7 Some where among grey rocks on the scarce grass
8 Birds cry, they cry their loneliness
9 Even the sun light can be lonely here.

[3^{r}]

(3)

1 Even hot noon is lonely. I hear a foot fal
2 A young man with a lanthorn comes this way
3 He seems an Arran fisher for he wears
4 The flannel bawneen & the cow hide shoe
5 He stumbles wearily & preys while he stumbles.
A young man enters preying in
Irish or in Latin.
Chorus
6 Once more the birds cry in their loneliness

([?2]

7 But now they wheel about our heads & now
8 They have dropped on that grey stone to the north east
A young man & girl in clothes of a
past time & wearing masks come in.

3^{r}, 7–8*sd* Taken from a draft state on paper type C, near the top of a page numbered “(2”?

[Harvard(A), 4r and 5r]

(4)

YOUNG MAN
(Raising his lantern)
Who is there? I cannot see what you are like,
Come to the light.

Young man
(Raising his lantern)
Who is there? I cannot see what you are like;
Come to the light

YOUNG MAN
I was in the postoffice, and if taken
I shall be put against a wall and shot.

Young Man
I was in the post-office, and if taken
I shall be put against a wall and shot

[Harvard(A), 4r and 5r]

[4r]

(4)

Stranger.
But what have you to fear
Young Man
And why have you come creeping through the dark
T (Girl blows out lanthorn)
The wind has blown my lanthorn out. Where are you
I saw a pair of heads against the ~~sy~~ sky
after you are in the right
And lost them ~~again; & yet you have spoken best~~
I should not be afraid in County Clare
~~There nothing English here – afraid or not~~
And should be or should not be have no choice

([?3]
~~I have For~~ I have to put myself into your hands.
now that my candle s out
Stranger
You have fought in Dublin

[5r]

YOUNG MAN
(Raising his lantern)
Who is there? I cannot see what you are like,
Come to the light
Young Man
(Raising his lantern)
Who is there? I cannot see what you are like;
Come to the light.

YOUNG MAN
I was in the postoffice, and if taken
I shall be put against a wall and shot.
Young Man
I was in the post-office, and if taken
I shall be put against a wall and shot

4r, 8–12 Taken from a draft state on paper type C, near the top of a page numbered "(3"?

Stranger

You know of some place, refuge, I have some place,
Or friend who will come to meet you.

Young man.

I am to lie
At daybreak on the mountain & keep watch
Until an Aran coracle puts in
At Muckanish or at the rocky shore
Under Finvara, but would break my neck
If I went stumbling there alone in the dark

Stranger

You know the pathways that the sheep tread out
And all the hiding places of the hills
And that they had better hiding places once

Young man

You'd say they had before English robbers
Cut down the trees, or set them upon fire
For fear their owners might find shelter there.
What is that sound?

Stranger.

An old hare [illegible]

He has been hiding on the road we came.

[illegible]

[Harvard(A), 6[r] and 7[r]]

[6[r]]

Stranger
You know of some place of refuge, have some plan,
Or friend who will come to meet you.
Young Man.
I am to lie
At day break on the mountain & keep watch
Until an Aran coracle puts in
At Muckenish or at the rocky shore
Under Kin varra, but would break my neck
If I went stumbling there alone in the dark
Stranger
You know the pathways that the sheep tread out
And all the hiding places of the hills
And that they had better hiding places once
Young Man
You d say they had better before English robbers
Cut down the trees, or set them upon fire
For fear their owners might find shelter there.
What is that sound?

[7[r]]

(5)

[. . .]
Stranger.
An old horse gone astray
He has been wandering on the road all night
Young Man
I took him for a man & horse
~~I took him for horseman, mounted~~ police
~~Are out upon the roads – men~~ of our race
~~It was against the grain to fire at~~ soldiers
~~Who are not of our race~~, but
Are out upon the roads – in ~~Dublin~~ the late rising
I think there was no man of us but hated
To fire at soldiers who but did their duty
And were not of our race, but when a man
Was born in Ireland of an Irish stock
When he takes part against us
[?] ...safe

7[r], 12 The cropped fragment ends in a lacunae, though a conjunction is made and the ellipsis filled with 8[r], ll. 1 and 4, typed and longhand versions of *VPl* 67b.

STRANGER

I will put you safe,

No living man shall set his eyes upon you.

I will not answer for the dead.

Stranger

I will put you safe

No living man shall set his eyes upon you;

I will not answer for the dead.

(4

Young Man.

The dead?

Stranger.

~~Yesterday, this hill~~

For certain ~~The [illegible]~~ days, the ~~[illegible]~~ stones where you must lie

And under the [illegible] ~~[illegible]~~ ?

Or I [illegible] ~~[illegible]~~

Have in the hours before the break of day

Been haunted.

Young Man.

But I was not born at midnight:

Stranger.

Many a man ~~that was~~ born in the full daylight

Can see them plain — ~~[illegible]~~

~~Or in the crowded [illegible]~~

— will pass them on the high road

Or in the crowded market place of the town

And never know that they have passed

Young Man

My grandam ~~[illegible]~~

[Harvard(A), 8[r] and 9[r]]

[8[r]]

STRANGER

I will put you safe,
No living man shall set his eyes upon you.
I will not answer for the dead.

Stranger

I will put you safe
No lining man shall set his eyes upon you;
I will not answer for the dead.

[9[r]]

(6)

[. . .]

(4

Young Man.

The dead?

Stranger.

~~For certain days that hill~~
For certain stones
~~The cert~~ days, the ~~hill~~ ^ where you must lie
~~And wait the Aran coracle to Muckanish~~ } ?
~~On the rock shore under the wood has been~~
Have
~~As~~ in the hour before the break of day
Been haunted.

Young Man.

But I was not born at midnight.

Stranger.

a man
Many ~~that were~~ born in the full daylight
plain
Can see them ^ – ~~pass them on the highroad maybe~~
~~Or in the crowded market~~
– will pass them on the high road
Or in the crowded market place of the town
And never know that they have passed

Young Man

dam
My grand~~m dam mother~~

9[r], 4–5 The brace and query mark at the end of these lines are in ink, with the rest of the leaf pasted onto 9[r]. The cancellations are in pencil, however, as nowhere else in this folio.

[Harvard(A), 10[r]]

[Harvard(A), 10r]

(7)

they did
would have it that penance every where (5
~~And living their old lives again in dream~~
Young Man.
through
And living ^ their old lives ~~again~~.
Stranger.
hang
In a dream. ~~whirl~~
Some for an old scruple must ~~hang~~ spitted
~~For an old scruple must~~ & &
Because of an
~~For ^ an old scruple must hang spitted~~
~~Upon the swaying branch~~
~~old~~ tops of lofty trees
Upon a swaying ~~branch under the moon~~
Some are consumed in fire, some withered up
~~By the cold North~~
By hail and sleet out of the wintry North
~~And some but live again their lives in a dream~~
And some but live through their old lives again
Young Man.
Well let them dream into what shape they please
And fill waste mountains with the invisible tumult
Of the fantastic conscience – I have no need to dread
They cannot put me into jail or shoot me
~~They cannot put me into jail or shoot me~~

And seeing that their blood s returned to [?fields] (6
That have for centuries drunk rebels blood
They would not if they could betray

19–21 A fragment from a draft on paper type C numbered "(6" and here pasted below page "(5" of that state.

[Harvard(A), 11r and 12r]

STRANGER

This pathway

leads to the ruined Abbey of Corcomroe

The Abbey passed we are soon among the stone

And shall be at the ridge before the cocks

Of Aughanish or Bailevlehan

Or grey Aughtmana shake their wings and cry.

(They go round the stage once)

Stranger

This pathway

Leads to the ruined Abbey of Corcomroe;

The abbey passed we are soon among the stone

And shall be at the ridge before the cocks

Of Aughanish or Bailevlehan

Or grey Aughtmana shake their wings & cry

(They go round the stage once)

3

Of Aughanish or Ballyvelehan

Or grey Aughtmana shake their wings and cry

(They go round the stage once)

First musician (speaking)

They've passed the shallow well and the flat stone

Fouled by the drinking cattle, the narrow lane

Where mourners for five centuries have carried

noble or peasant to his burial;

An owl is crying, out above their heads

(Singing)

Why should the heart take fright?

What sets it beating so?

The bitt bitter sweetness of the night

Has made it but a lonely thing

Red bird of March begin to crow

Up with the neck & clap the wing

Red cock and crow

(They go round the stage once)*.

[Harvard(A), 11^{r} and 12^{r}]

[11^{r}]

STRANGER

This pathway
leads to the ruined Abbey of Corcomroe
The Abbey passed we are soon among the stone
And shall be at the ridge before the cocks
Of Aughanish or Bailevlehan
Or grey Aughtmana shake their wings and cry.
(They go round the stage once)

Stranger

This pathway
Leads to the ruined Abbey of Corcomroe;
The Abbey passed we are soon among the stone
And shall be at the ridge before the cocks
Of Aughanish or Baile vlehan
Or grey Aughtmana shake their wings & cry
(They go round the stage once)

[12^{r}]

(8)

[. . .]

3

Of Aughanish or Bally velehan
or grey Augh mana shake their wings and cry
(They go round the stage once)

First Musician (speaking)

~~The've~~ passed the shallow well and the flat stone
Fouled by the drinking cattle, the narrow lane
Where mourners for five centuries have carried
Noble or pleasant to his burial:
An owl is crying out above their heads

(singing)

Why should the heart take fright?
What sets it beating so?
The ~~bitt~~ bitter sweetness of the night
Has made it bit a lonely thing
Red bird of March begin to crow
Up with the neck & clap the wing
Red cock and crow
(They go round the stage once) }.

12^{r}, 3 "The've" for "They've"?
12^{r}, 6 "pleasant" for "peasant"?

(9)

First musician (speaking)

And now they have climbed through the long grassy field
And passed the ragged thorn trees & the gap
In the ancient hedge; and the tomb nested owl
At the foot's level beats with a vague wing

(singing)

My head is in a cloud
I'd let the whole world go
My rascal heart is proud
Remembering and remembering
Red bird of March begin to crow
Up with the neck & clap the wing
Red cock & crow

[Harvard(A), 13r]

(9)

First Musician (speaking)

And now they have climbed through the long grassy field
And passed the ragged thorn trees & the gap
In the ancient hedge; and the tomb nested owl
At the foot s level beats with a vague wing

(singing)

My head is in a cloud
I d let the whole world go
My rascal heart is proud
Remembering and remembering
Red bird of March begin to crow
Up with the neck & clap the wing
Red cock & crow

(10)

(They go up more steps)

Young Man (Stranger)

They are among the stones above the ash

Above the briar and thorn and the scarce grass

Hidden amid the shadow far below them

The cat headed bird is crying out.

(singing)

The dreaming bones cry out

Because the night winds blow

And heaven is a cloudy blot

Calamity can have its fling

Red bird of March begin to crow

Up with the neck and clap the wing

Red cock and crow

The stranger

We are almost at the summit and can rest

The road is a faint shadow there; and there

The Abbey lies amid its broken tombs

In the old days we should have heard a bell

Calling the monks before day broke and prayers

And when the day had broken on the ridge

The crowing of its cocks.

Young Man

Is there no house

Famous for sanctity or architectural beauty

In Clare or Kerry or in all wide Connacht

The enemy has not unroofed.

Stranger.

Close to the altar

Broken by wind and frost and worn by time

[Harvard(A), 14^{r}]

[?w]
(10)

(They go round stage)
First Musician (speaking)
They are among the stones above the ash
Above the briar and thorn & the scarce grass
Hidden amid the shaddow far below them
The cat headed bird is crying out.
(singing)
The dreaming bones cry out
Because the night winds blow
And heaven 's a cloudy blot
Calamity can have its fling
Red Bird of March begin to crow
Up with the neck & clap the wing
Red cock & crow
The Stranger
We are almost at the summit & can rest
The road is a faint shadow there; & there
The Abbey lies amid its broken tomb
In the old days we should have heard a bell
Calling the monks before day broke to preyer
And when the day had broken on the ridge
The crowing of the cocks
Young Man
Is there no house
Famous for sanctity or architectural beausty
In Clare of Kerry or in all wide Connacht
The enemy has not unroofed.
Stranger.
Close to the altar
Broken by wind & frost & worn by time

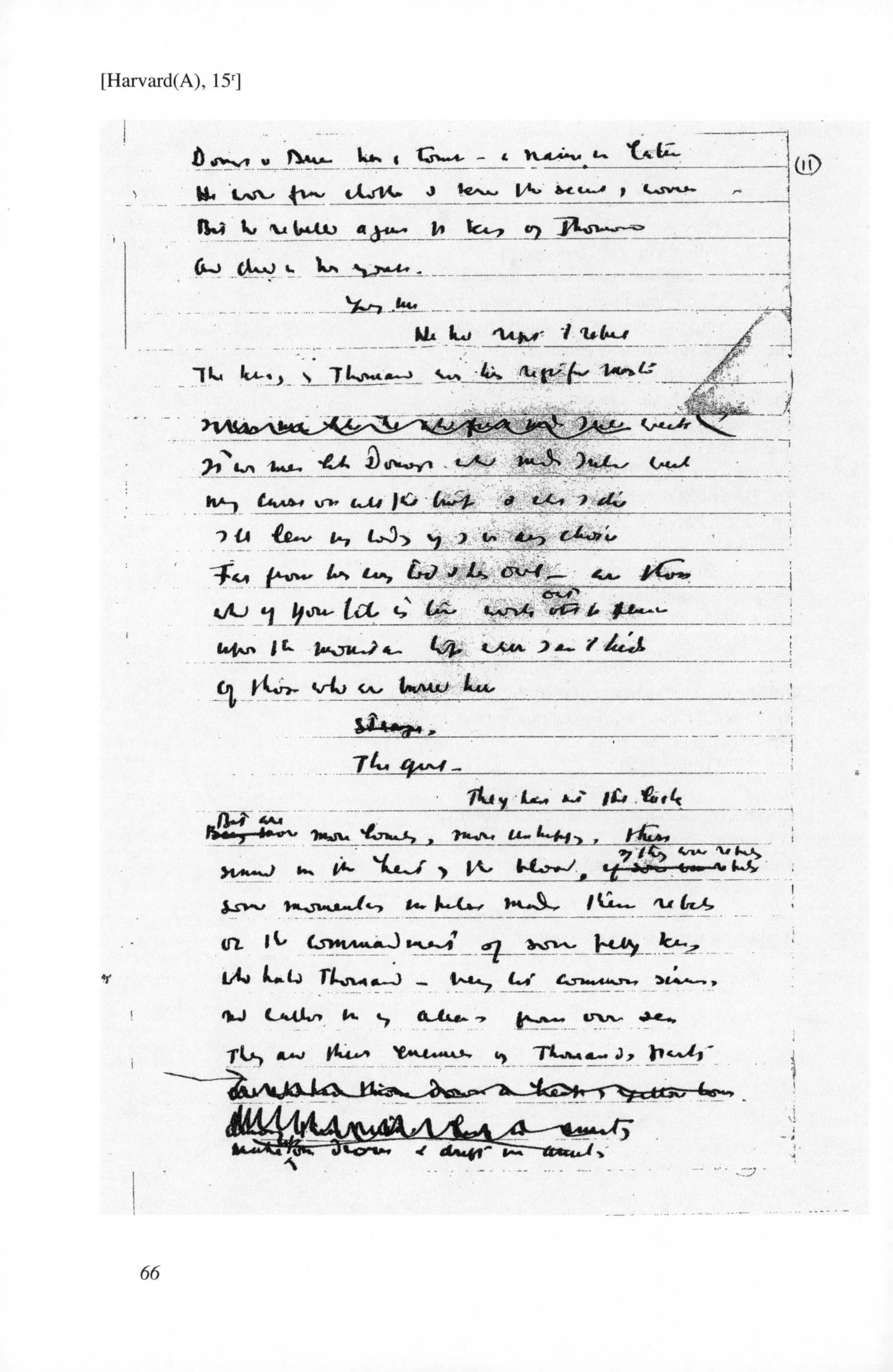

[Harvard(A), 15r]

[Harvard(A), 15r]

(11)

Donough & Brien has a tomb – a name in Latin
He wore fine cloth & knew the secrets of women
But he rebelled against the King of Thomond
And died in his youth.
Young Man.
He had right to rebel
The King of Thomond was his rightful master
(7
~~It was men like he who first made Ireland weak~~
It was men like Donough who made Ireland weak
My curse on all that troop & when I die
I ll leave my body if I ve any choice
Far from his ivy tod & his owl – are those
out
Who if your tale is true work ~~out~~ a penance
Upon the mountain where I am to hide
Of those who are buried here
~~Stranger.~~
The Girl –
They have not that luck
But are
~~Being more~~ lonely, more unhappy. These
If they were rebels
Sinned in the heat of the blood. ~~If some were rebels~~
Some momentary impulse made them rebels
Or the commandment of some petty king
Who hated Thomond – being but common sinners
No callers in of aliens from over sea
→They and their enemies of Thomonds party
~~All who have thrown down a heap of yellow bones~~
~~Among these ruins live in amity~~
up
Make ^ one drove & drift in amity

6–23 Constitute a virtually intact page of paper type C—numbered "(7"—pasted beneath the bottom edge of a draft fragment (on same paper type) bearing ll. 1–5.
21 The arrow indicates that revisions were to be inserted, now lost.

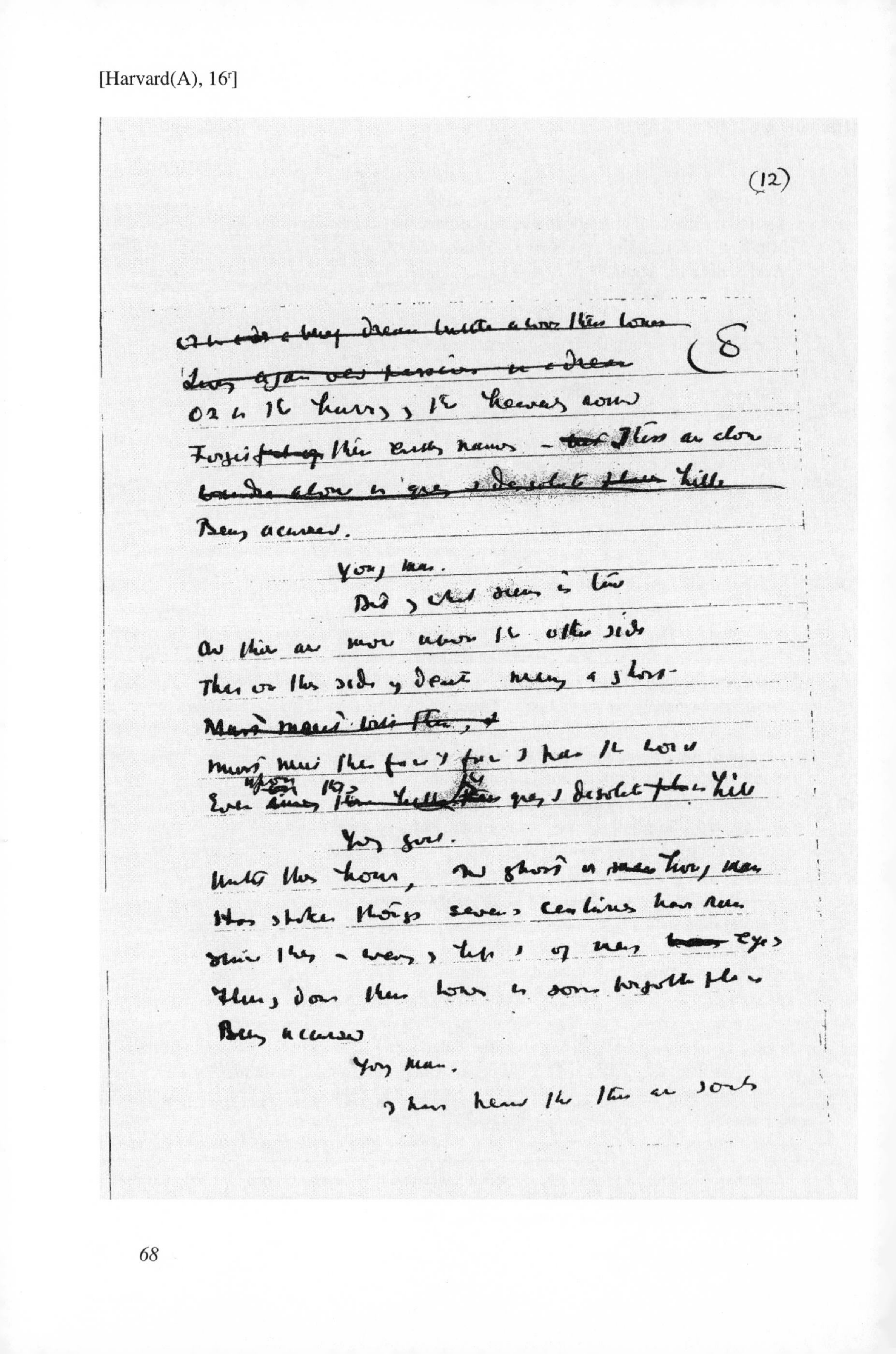

(12)

[Harvard(A), 16r]

(12)

1 ~~Or in a dr a brief dream battle above their bones~~
2 ~~Living again old passions in a dream~~ (8
3 Or in the hurry of the heavenly round
{T}
4 Forget~~ful of~~ their earthly names – ~~but~~{t}hese are alone
5 ~~Wander alone in grey & desolate places hills~~
6 Being acursed.
Young Man.
But if what seems is true
7 And there are more upon the other side
8 Than on this side of death many a ghost
9 ~~Must meet with them, &~~
10 Must meet them fact to face & pass the word
upon
~~on~~ this ~~that~~
11 Even ~~among~~ ~~these hills~~ ~~these~~ grey & desolate ~~place~~ hill
Young Girl.
12 Until this hour, no ghost or ~~man~~ living man
13 Has spoken though seven centuries have run
14 Since they – weary of life & of mens ~~bones~~ eyes
15 Fling down their bones in some forgotten place
16 Being accursed
Young Man.
I have heard that there are souls

1–16 Constitute an intact page of paper type C, numbered "(8".

(13)

who have seen after a monstrous fashion (9
Take on them after death a monstrous image
To drive the living [illegible] this man is for
crazy & be a [illegible] of the dead

Girl.

But their
wrong comes even in their middle life
and [illegible] now the [illegible] the image
of their first youth after it was in that youth
Their sin began.

Young Man.

I have heard of angry ghosts
who ~~[illegible]~~ wander in a ~~[illegible]~~ wilful solitude

Girl

These have no thoughts but love nor joy
~~[illegible]~~
But that upon the very passing [has called] the dream
And penance ripening to its height & hearts
~~And [illegible]~~ [and hearts are wrung] they gaze into one another
Being accursed.

[Harvard(A), 17r]

(13)

Who having sinned after a monstrous fashion (9
Take on there after death a monstrous image
To drive the living should they meet its face
Crazy & be a terror to the dead
Girl.
But these
Were comely even in their middle life
And carry now that they are dead the image
Of their first youth for it was in that youth
Their sin began.
Young Man.
I have heard of angry ghosts
Who ~~wanter~~ wander in ~~a wi~~l wilful soletude
Girl
These have no thought but love nor joy
~~But when that return or [?] again~~
that has called
But when their old passion ~~calls~~ the [?dream] ~~anew~~
And hearts are [?washed] away
~~Are the most racked~~ they gaze at one another
Being accursed.

1–15 Constitute an intact page of paper type C, numbered "(9".

(14)

But that upon the instant when their penance (10
Draws to its height — & when two hearts are wrung
Nearest to breaking, if the hearts of shadows break
~~[illegible]~~
Their eyes can meet each other in any pang
That is so bitter as this desolate glen
Being accursed.

Young Man

But what is this strange penance
That when their eyes have met can wring them most?

Girl

~~[illegible]~~ lips
Though eyes can meet their can never meet.

Young Man

~~[illegible] side by side~~
And yet it seems they wander side by side
But doubtless — you would say — that when lips meet
~~[illegible]~~
And have not living nerves it is no meeting.

Girl

Although they have no blood or living nerves (11
Who once lay warm & live the live long night
In one another's arms & know their part
In life being now but of the people of dreams
Is a dream's part, although they are but shadow

[Harvard(A), 18r]

(14)

(10

But that upon the instant when their penance
Draws to its height, & when two hearts are rung
nearest to breaking if hearts of shadows break
~~Being accursed his eyes can mix with hers~~
His eyes can mix with hers nor any pang
That is so bitter as that double glance
Being accursed.

Young Man

But what is this strange penance
That when their eyes have met can wring them most

Girl

~~Although~~ lips
Though eyes can meet their ^ can never meet

Young man.

~~And yet, you have said, they wander side by side~~
And yet it seems they wander side by side
But doubtless – you would say – that when lips meet
~~That [?] have no blood in t~~
And have not living nerves it is no meeting.

Girl

Although they have no blood [?or] living nerves (11
Who once lay warm & live the live long night
In one anothers [?~~life~~] arms & know their part
In life being now but of the people of dreams
Is a dream s part, although they are but shadow

1–15 Constitute a slightly cropped page of paper type C, numbered "(10" and followed by a smaller fragment excised from the top of the next page in the same draft state and numbered "(11".

2 "rung" for "wrung"?

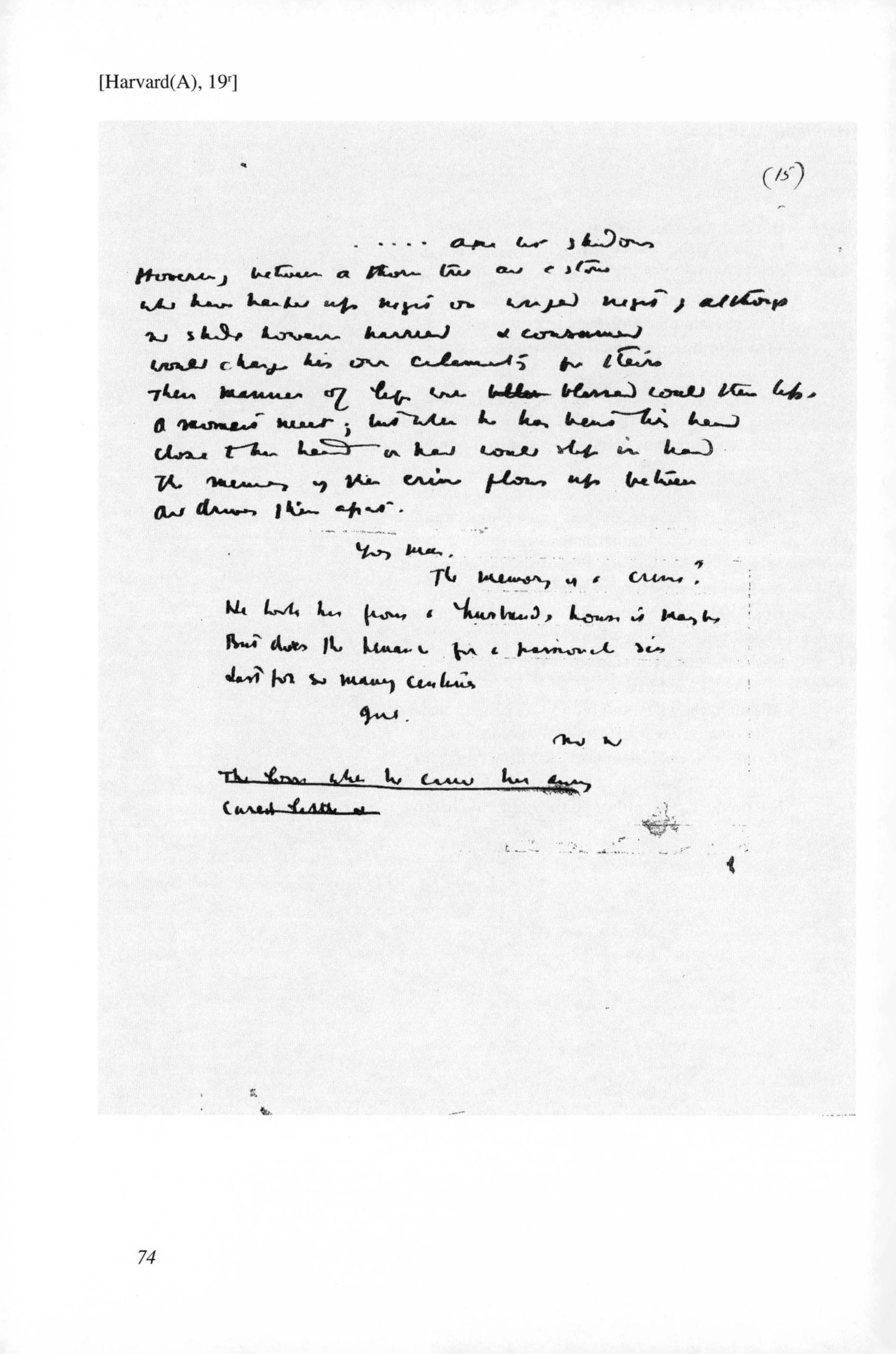

[Harvard(A), 19^{r}]

[Harvard(A), 19^{r}]

(15)

. . . . . are but shadows
Hovering between a thorn tree and a stone
Who have heaped up night on winged night; although
no shade however harried & consumed
would change his own calamity for theirs
Their manner of life were ~~bitter~~ blessed could their lips
A moment meet; but when he has bent his head
Close to her head or hand would slip in hand
The memory of their crime flows up between
And drives them apart

Young Man.

The memory of a crime?
He took her from a husband s house it may be
But does the penance for a passionate sin
Last for so many centuries

Girl.

No no
~~The lover when he carried her away~~
~~Cared little &~~

---

1 Carries on, after the ellipse, with a continuation of the Girl's speech from 18^{r}, l. 19.

1–10 Constitute an insert, on paper type B, between the paper C state on 18^{r} and the C state of 19^{r}, ll. 10b–15.

(16)

12

The man she chose, the man she was chosen by
Cared little and cared little ~~from whose~~ from whose house
They fled towards dawn amid the flight of arrows
Or that it was a husband and a king
And how, if that were all, should those lips find
On crowded road or on the unpeopled hill.
Helen herself had opened wide the doors
Where night by night she dreams herself awake
And gathers to her arms a dreaming man.

Young Man

What crime can stay so in the memory.
What crime can keep apart the lips of lovers
Wandering and alone.

Girl.

Her king and lover
Was overthrown in battle by her husband,
And for her sake and for his own, being blind
And bitter and bitterly in love, he brought
A foreign army from across the sea.

Young man.

You speak of Diarmuid and Dervorgilla
Who brought the Norman in.

[Harvard(A), 20r]

(16)

(12

The man she chose, the man she was chosen by
and cares little
Cared little ~~from whose~~ from whose house
They fled towards down amid the flight of arrows
Or that it was a husbands & a kings
And how if that were all should they lack friends
roads
On crowded ^ or on the unpeopled hill.
Helen her self had opened wide the door
Where night by night she dreams herself awake
And gathers to her arms a dreaming man.
Young Man
What crime can stay so in the memory.
What ~~cl~~ crime, can keep apart the lips of lovers
Wandering & alone.

Girl.
Her king & lover
Was overthrown in battle by her husband
And for her ~~sl~~ sake & for his own being blind
And bitter & bitterly in love he brought
A foreign army from across the sea
Young Man.
You speak of Dairmuid & Dervogilla
Who brought the Norman in.

13–18 Interpolated into the C state of the draft on paper type B. The cancellations indicated in pencil, through the heading "Young Man" and at diagonals through ll. 17 and 18, are evidently to be ignored, as they deliver to the text *VPl* 228–229.

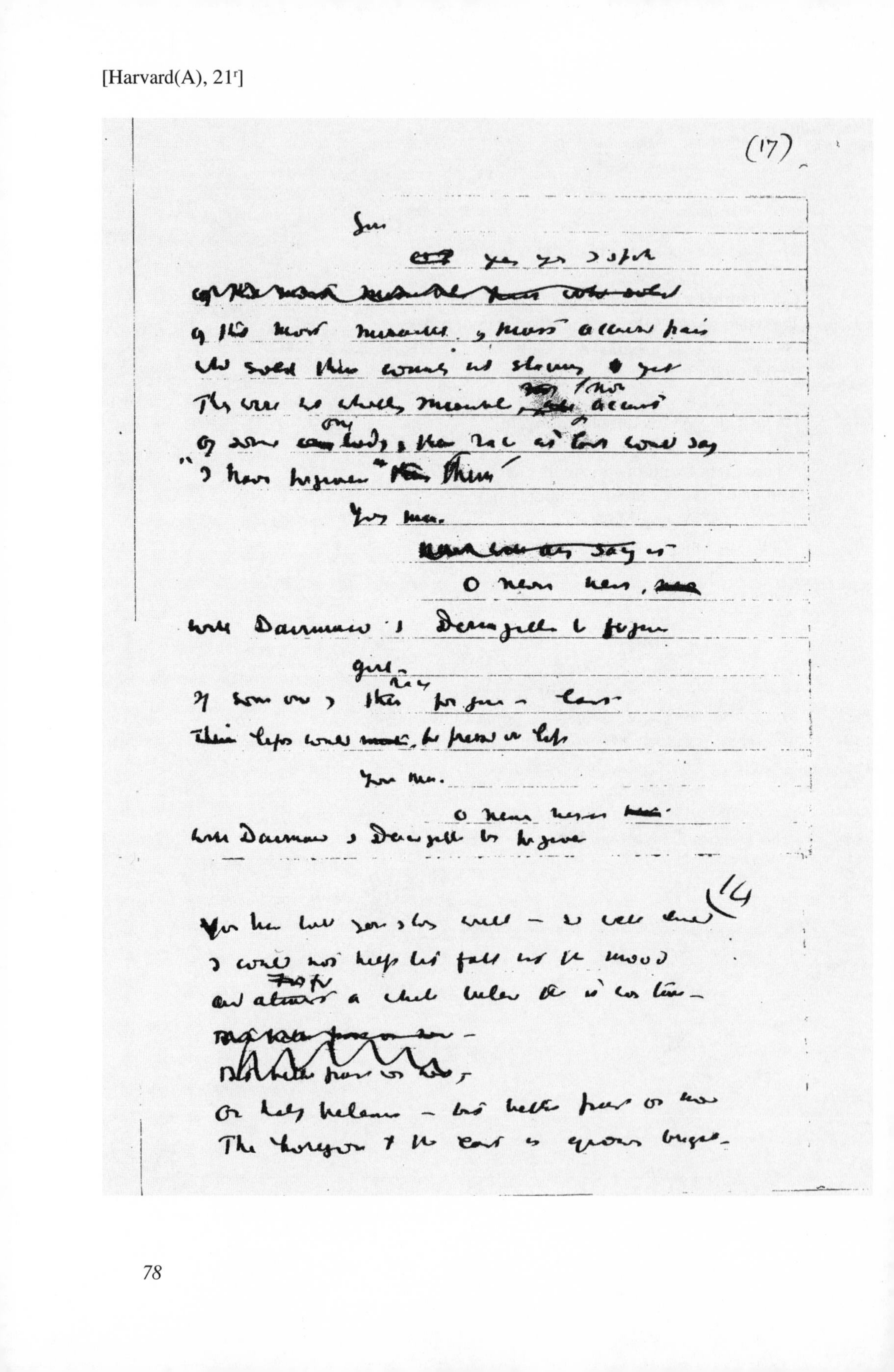

[Harvard(A), 21r]

[Harvard(A), 21[r]]

(17)

Girl
~~es [?]~~ Yes yes I spoke
~~Of that most miserable pair who sold~~
Of that most miserable, most accursed pair
Who sold their country into slavery, ~~&~~ yet
~~nor~~ nor
They were not wholly miserable, ~~all~~ ^ accurst
one
Of some ~~one body~~ of their race at last would say
"I have forgiven~~"~~ ~~them~~ them'
Young Man.
~~Never will any say it~~
O never never, ~~never~~
Will Dairmuid & Dervagilla be forgiven
Girl –
race
If some one of their forgive – last
~~Their~~ lips would ~~meet~~ be pressed on lips
Young Man.
O never never ~~never~~
Will Dairmuid & Dervogilla by forgiven

(14
You have told your story well – so well endeed
I could not help but fall into the mood
~~For~~ for
And ~~almost~~ a while believe that it was true –
~~But better push on now~~ –
~~But better push on now,~~ –
Or half believe – but better push on now
The horizon to the east is growing bright.

---

5 "Of" for "If"?

6 The first close quotation mark is canceled; when the quotation is then completed—after "them"—Yeats uses a simple inverted comma.

11–17 Constitutes a shorter fragment on paper type C and an abridgement to the B state following on folios 22–24.

[Harvard(A), 22r]

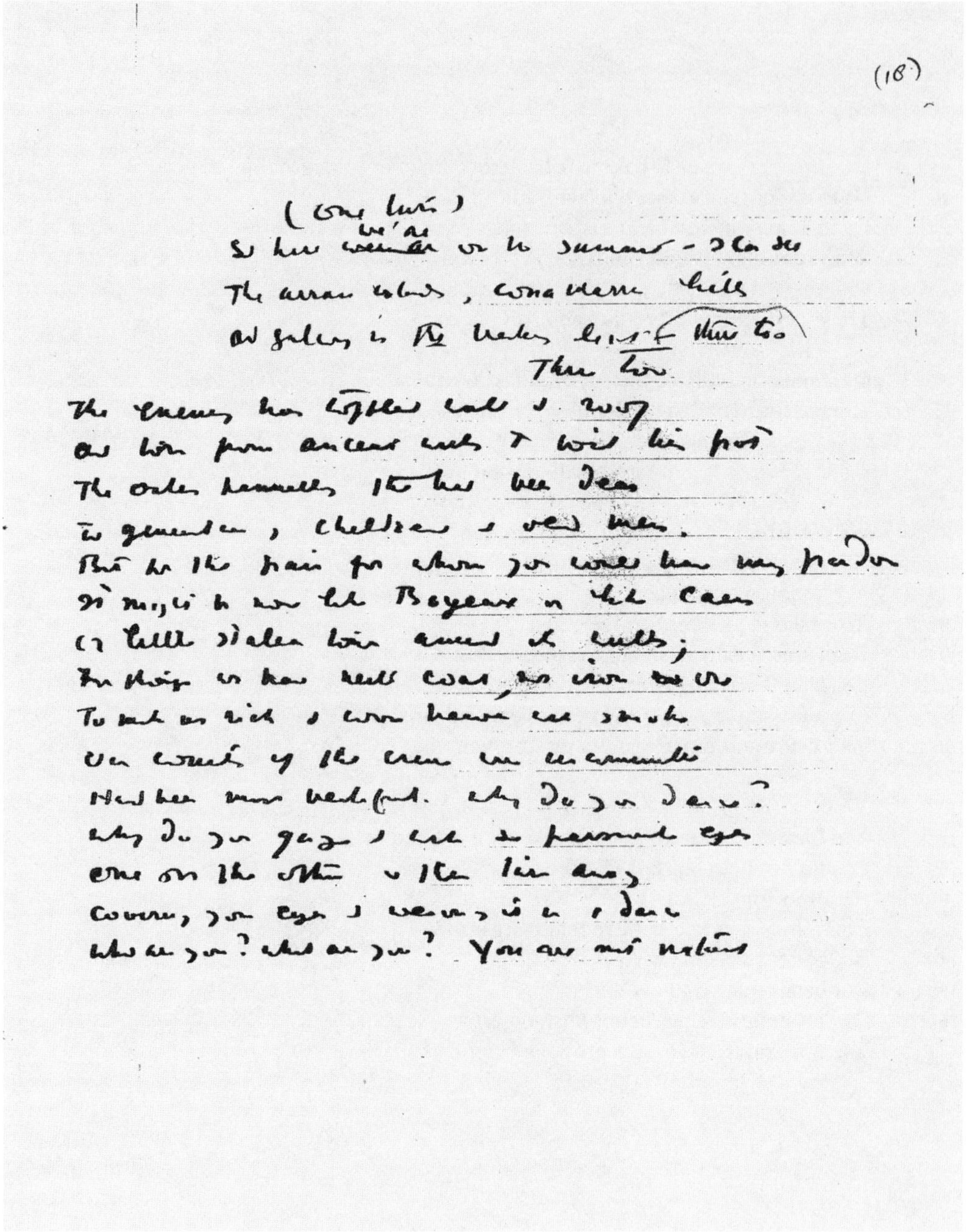

[Harvard(A), 22[r]]

(18)

(one turn)
we're
So here ~~were are~~ on the summit – I can see
The Arran Islands, Conamarra hills
And Galway in the breaking light – there too

There too
The enemy has toppled wall & roof
And torn from ancient walls to boil his pot
The oaken pannelling that had been dear
to generations of children & old men.
But for that pair for whom you would have my pardon
It might be now like Bayeux or like Caen
Or little Italian town amid its walls;
For though we have neither coal, not iron ~~or~~ ore
To make us rich & cover heaven with smoke
Our country if that crime were uncommitted
Had been most beautiful. Why do you dance?
Why do you gaze & with so passionate eyes
One on the other & then turn away
Covering your eyes & weaving it in a dance
Who are you? What are you? You are not natural

1*sd*–3 This fragment from the draft state borne on paper type C concludes with the words " – there too" and keys the interpolation of ll. 4–18 on paper type B.

(19)

Girl
seven hundred years our lips have never met
Young man
why do you look so strangely at one another
so strangely & so sweetly.
Girl.
seven hundred years
Young man
so strangely & so sweetly. all the ruin
all all their hands work is blown away
as though the mountain air had blown it away
Because their eyes have met. They cannot [illegible]
[illegible]
The dance is changing now. They have dropped their eyes
They have covered up their eyes as though their hearts
Had suddenly been broken. Never, never
shall Dermot & Dervorgilla be forgiven
[illegible]
[illegible]
[illegible]
[illegible]
[illegible]
[illegible]
[illegible] forgiven [illegible]
[illegible]
Music (singing)
At the grey round of the hill
Music of a lost kingdom
Runs, runs & is suddenly still
The winds [illegible] out of Clare-Galway
Carry it: suddenly it is still

[Harvard(A), 23^{r}]

(19)

Girl
Seven hundred years our lips have never met
Young Man
Why do you look so strangely at one another
So strangely and so sweetly.
Girl.
Seven hundred years
Young Man
So strangely and so sweetly. All the ruin
All all their handy work is blown away
As though the mountain air had blown it away
Because their eyes have met. They cannot hear
Being folded up & hidden in their dance
The dance is changing now. They have dropped their eyes
They have covered up their eyes as though their hearts
Had suddenly been broken. Never, never
Shall Dairmuid & Dervogilla be forgiven
They have drifted in a dance from rock to rock
They have raised their hands as though to snatch the sleep
That lingers always in the abyss of the sky
Though they can never reach it – A cloud floats up
And covers all the mountain head in a moment –
And now it lifts & they are swept away
forgiven
I had almost yeilded & ~~forgiven all~~ all
This is endeed a place of terrible temptation
Musicians (singing)
I
At the gray round of the hill
Music of a lost kingdom
Runs, runs & is suddenly still
The winds ~~of of~~ out of Clare-Galway
Carry it: suddenly it is still

I have heard in the night air
A wandering airy music
And moidered in that snare
A man is lost of a sudden
In that sweet wandering snare

What finger first began
Music of a lost kingdom
They dream that laughed in the sun
Dry bones that dream are bitter
They dream & darken our sun

crazy
Those dizzy fingers play
A wandering airy music
Our luck is withered away
As wheat in the wind's ear withers
And the wind blows it away

II

My heart ran wild when it heard
The curlew cry before dawn
And the eddying cat-headed bird
But now the night is gone
I have heard from far below
On sea-girt dunghills
The strong march birds a crow
Stretch neck & clap the wing
Red cocks & crow

W B Yeats
August 1917

[Harvard(A), 24^{r}]

I have heard in the night air
A wandering airy music
And moidered in that snare
A man is lost of a sudden
In that sweet wandering snare

What finger first began
music of a lost ~~kind~~ kingdom
They dream that laughed in the sun
Dry bones that dream are bitter
They dream & darken our sun

crazy
Those ~~crazy~~ fingers play
A wandering airy music
our luck is withered away
And wheat in the wheat ear withered
And the wind blows it away

II

My heart ran wild when it heard
The curley cry before dawn
And the eddying cat-headed bird
But now the night is gone
I have heard from far below
on sea-girt Aughanish
The strong March birds a crow
Stretch neck & clap the wing
Red cocks & crow
WB Yeats
August 1917

---

17 "curley" for "curlew"?

I. *The Dreaming of the Bones*

Transcription of NLI 8775(3) for the Complete Version (1918–1935)

With *apparatus criticus* of variants in NLI 8775(4), Texas(B), Harvard(B), Quinn, NLI 30,051, NLI 30,071, Texas(C), Emory, NLI 30,007, BL Add. MS 55879, Texas(E), BL Add. MS 55884, BL Add. MS 55891

[NLI 8775(3), 1r]

THE DREAMING OF THE BONES.

The stage is any bare place in a room with a wall against it. A screen with a pattern of mountain and sky can stand against it and a curtain with a like pattern hang upon it, but the pattern must only symbolize or suggest.

at L

Three MUSICIANS ENTER; one stands singing while the others enter. Then all three sit down against the wall by their instruments, which are already there - a drum, a zitha, and a flute. Or they unfold a cloth as in "The Hawk's Well", while the instruments are carried in.

---

dp PERSONS IN THE PLAY / Three Musicians *(their faces made up to resemble masks)* / A YOUNG MAN / A Stranger *(wearing a mask)* / A Young Girl *(wearing a mask)* // Time — 1916 *BL Add. MS 55879, Texas(E)* PERSONS OF *rev to* PERSONS IN *NLI 30,007*

sd room with a wall against it . . . stand against it and a . . . hang upon it, . . . suggest. ¶ . . . zitha *rev to* room with a wall beyond it . . . . can stand or hang against the wall, . . . suggest. ¶ . . . zither *NLI 8775(4)* room with a wall against it. A screen with . . . can stand . . . suggest. ¶ *rev to* room with a wall beyond it. A screen or curtain with . . . can hang or stand . . . suggest.¶ *Texas(B)* room with a wall against it . . . . stand against it and a . . . suggest. ¶ Three MUSICIANS enter, one stands . . . others enter. *rev to* room close to a wall. . . . stand against wall or a . . . suggest. ¶ One MUSICIAN enters, and then two others, the first stands . . . others take their places. *Harvard(B)* room close to a wall. . . . stand against wall or a curtain with . . . suggest. ¶ One MUSICIAN enters, and then two others, the first stands . . . others take their places. *Quinn* (. . . room close to a wall. . . . stand against the wall, or a curtain with . . . symbolise or suggest. One Musician enters, and then two others, the first stands singing while the other two take thier [*sic*] places. Then . . . by therr [*sic*] instruments, . . . Drum, a Zither, and a Lute. Or . . . as in the Hawk's Well, while . . .) *NLI 30,051* room close to the wall . . . the wall, or a curtain with . . . symbolise or suggest. One musician enters, and then two others, the first stands singing while the others take their places. Then . . . by their instruments, . . . drum, zither, and a flute. Or . . . as in 'The Hawk's Well,' while *Texas(C), Emory* room close to the wall. A screen, with . . . sky, can . . . the wall, or a curtain with . . . symbolise or suggest. One Musician enters and then two others ; the first stands singing, as in preceding plays, while the others take their places. Then . . . by their instruments, . . . drum, a zither, and a flute. Or . . . as in 'At the Hawk's Well', while *BL Add. MS 55879, Texas(E), NLI 30,007, BL Add. MSS 55884 and 55891*

Song [Song for the folding and unfolding of the cloth] *BL Add. MS 55879, Texas(E)*

Mere typographical and format differences, as between underscoring and italics in stage directions, are not normally reported in the *apparatus criticus*. Neither is the distinction between "&" and "and" in handwritten inscriptions. In NLI 8775(3), typed stage directions are in red; from this ribbon copy two carbon copies were prepared, with underscoring by hand (in red ink): NLI 8775(4) and Texas(B).

[NLI 8775(3), 1[r] continued]

FIRST MUSICIAN (singing)

Why does my heart beat so {?,}
Did not a shadow pass?
It passed but a moment ago.
Who can have trod in the grass?
What rogue is night-wandering?
Have not old writers said
That dizzy dreams can spring

From the dry bones of the dead {?;}
And many a night it seems
That all the valley fills
With those fantastic dreams.
They overflow the hills,

1*sd* FIRST MUSICIAN (singing) *rev to* FIRST MUSICIAN or all the Musicians (singing) *Harvard(B)* FIRST MUSICIAN — OR ALL THE MUSICIANS (singing) *Quinn* FIRST MUSICIAN (or all three musicians, singing) *NLI 30,051, Texas(C), Emory,* [Musicians,] *BL Add. MS 55879, Texas(E), NLI 30,007, BL Add. MSS 55884 and 55891*

1 so?] so. *NLI 30,051*

4 grass?] grass. *NLI 30,051*

5 night-wandering *NLI 30,051*

8 dead?] dead; *Harvard(B), Quinn*

11 dreams.] dreams; *Harvard(B), Quinn*

12 hills,] hills *NLI 30,051*

[NLI 8775(3), 2r]

So passionate is a shade,
Like wine that fills to the top
A grey-green cup of jade,
Or maybe an agate cup.
~~(the three musicians are now seated)~~

(speaking) The hour before dawn and the moon covered up {;,}

The little village of Abbey is covered up {;,}
The little narrow trodden way that runs
From the white road to the Abbey of Corcomroe
Is covered up; and all about the hills
Are like a circle of Agate or of Jade.
Great
Somewhere among ~~grey~~ rocks on the scarce grass
Birds cry, they cry their loneliness.
Even the sunlight can be lonely here

16*sd* The three Musicians are now seated by the drum, flute, and zither at the back of the stage. The First Musician speaks. *BL Add. MS 55879, Texas(E), NLI 30,007, BL Add. MSS 55884 and 55891*

17 up;] up. *NLI 8775(4), Texas(B), Texas(C), Emory* up: *Harvard(B)*

18 up;] up, *NLI 8775(4), Texas(B)*

22 Agate . . . Jade. *rev to* agate . . . jade. *NLI 30,007, BL Add. MS 55879, Texas(E), BL Add. MSS 55884 and 55891*

23 Great] great *NLI 8775(4), Harvard(B), Quinn, Texas(C), Emory, BL Add. MS 55879, Texas(E), NLI 30,007, BL Add. MSS 55884 and 55891* grey *Texas(B)*

24 loneliness.] lonliness. [*with sd*] (music to suggest / birds cry) *NLI 8775(4)*, [. . . a bird's cry] *Texas(B)*

25 here] here, *Harvard(B), Quinn, Texas(C), Emory, BL Add. MS 55879, Texas(E), NLI 30,007, BL Add. MSS 55884 and 55891*

---

24 Typist initially typed "lonliness." Then, following erasure on ribbon copy NLI 8775(3), "loneliness." is typed in same space as correction.

[NLI 8775(3), 2^{r} continued]

Even hot noon is lonely. I hear a footfall -
A young man with a lantern comes this way
He seems an Aran fisher, for he wears
The flannel bauneen and the cow-hide shoe.
He stumbles wearily, and stumbling prays.

from R

(A YOUNG MAN ENTERS, ^ **praying in Irish)**

~~**CHORUS**~~

Once more the birds cry in their loneliness,
But now they wheel about our heads, and now
They have dropped on the grey stone to the north-east.

(A YOUNG MAN and a YOUNG GIRL in the costume of a past time come in~~.~~ ~~They wear heroic masks)~~

L

27 way] way. *Harvard(B), Quinn, Texas(C), Emory, BL Add. MS 55879, Texas(E), NLI 30,007, BL Add. MSS 55884 and 55891*

29 bauneen] bawneen *Texas(C), Emory, BL Add. MS 55879, Texas(E), NLI 30,007, BL Add. MSS 55884 and 55891*

30*sd* bird music again [*added*] *NLI 8775(4), Texas(B)* young man enters, *rev to* Young Man enters, *BL Add. MS 55879, NLI 30,007* Young Man enters, *Texas(E), BL Add. MSS 55884 and 55891* CHORUS. *NLI 8775(4), Harvard(B), Quinn*

32 heads,] heads; *Texas(C), Emory, BL Add. MS 55879, Texas(E), NLI 30,007, BL Add. MSS 55884 and 55891*

33*sd* A man and a girl both in . . . time, come *Texas(C), Emory* A man and a girl, both in . . . time, come *rev to* A [*lacunae*], in . . . time, come *NLI 30,007* A stranger and a young girl, in . . . time, come *rev to* A Stranger and a Young Girl, in . . . time, come *BL Add. MS 55879* A Stranger and a Young Girl, in . . . time, come *Texas(E), BL Add. MSS 55884 and 55891* They wear heroic masks *NLI 8775(4) and all succeeding MSS*

[NLI 8775(3), 3r]

YOUNG MAN (in bauneen, raising his lantern)

34 **Who is there? I cannot see what you are like.**
35 ~~Come n~~ Come to the light.

STRANGER.

But what have you to fear?

YOUNG MAN.

36 **And why have you come creeping through the dark?**

(The GIRL blows out lantern.)

37 **The wind has blown my lantern out. Where are you?**
38 **I saw a pair of heads against the sky**
39 **And lost them after** { ; , } **but you are in the right,**
40 **I should not be afraid in County Clare.**
41 **And should be, or should not be have no choice,**
to
42 **I have ^ put myself into your hands,**
43 **Now that my candle's out.**

STRANGER.

You have fought in Dublin?

YOUNG MAN.

44 **I was in the Post Office, and if taken**
45 **I shall be put against a wall and shot.**

STRANGER.

46 **You know some place of refuge, have some plan**
47 **Or friend who will come to meet you?**

34*sd* in bauneen, *lacking Texas(C), Emory, BL Add. MS 55879, Texas(E), NLI 30,007, BL Add. MSS 55884 and 58891*

34 like.] like, *Harvard(B), Quinn, Texas(C), Emory* like, *rev to* like. *NLI 30,007*

35 Come closer to the light [*rev to* lanthorn]. *rev to* Come to the light. *NLI 8775(4)* Come closer to the light *Texas(B)*

36 dark?] dark. *Texas(C), Emory*

36*sd* girl *rev to* Girl *NLI 30,007* [*notation added:*] not after beat *rev to* drum beat to blow – no drum for return position *NLI 8775(4)*

39 right,] right *NLI 8775(4)* after, but . . . right *Texas(B), Texas(C), Emory* after, but . . . right; *Harvard(B), Quinn*

40 Clare.] Clare; *NLI 8775(4), Texas(C), Emory, BL Add. MS 55879, Texas(C), NLI 30,007, BL Add. MSS 55884 and 55891*

41 be, or] be or *NLI 8775(4)* be or . . . choice *Texas(B)* be or . . . choice, *Harvard(B), Quinn, Texas(C), Emory* be have *rev to* be, have *NLI 30,007* be, have *BL Add. MS 55879, Texas(E), BL Add. MSS 55884 and 55891*

42 have to] have *NLI 8775(4)*

[NLI 8775(3), 4r]

YOUNG MAN.

I am to lie
At daybreak on the mountain and keep watch
Coracle
Until an Aran ~~curricle~~ puts in
At Muckanish or at the rocky shore
Under Finvarra, but would break my neck
If I went stumbling there alone in the dark.

STRANGER.

We know the pathways that the sheep tread out,
And all the hiding-places of the hills,
And that they had better hiding-places once.

YOUNG MAN.

You'd say they had better before English robbers
Cut down the trees or set them up on fire
For fear their owners might find shelter there.
What is that sound?

STRANGER.

An old horse gone astray.
He has been wandering on the road all night.

YOUNG MAN.

I took him for a man and horse. Police
Are out upon the roads. In the late Rising
I think there was no man of us but hated
To fire at soldiers who but did their duty

---

49 curricle *Texas(B)* curricle *rev to* coracle *NLI 8775(4)* curricle *rev to* corricle *Harvard(B)* corricle *Quinn* coracle *NLI 30,051, Texas(C), Emory, BL Add. MS 55879, Texas(E), BL Add. MSS 55884 and 55891*

51 Finvarra,] Finvarra *NLI 8775(4), Texas(B)* Finvarra; *Harvard(B), Quinn* Finvarra *rev to* Finvarra, *Texas(C)* Kinvarra, *NLI 30,051* Finvarra, *rev to* Finvaragh, *NLI 30,007, BL Add. MS 55879* Finvaragh, *Texas(E), BL Add. MS 55891* Finvaragh, *rev to* Finvara *BL Add. MS 55884*

54 hiding-places] hiding places *NLI 30,051*

55 hiding-places] hiding places *NLI 30,051*

60 *sd added* (music suggests tread of / horse) *NLI 8775(4)* (Music to suggest tread of horse) *Texas(B)*

---

57 The syllables of "upon" are marked to close up spacing here and on the carbon copy NLI 8775(4) but not in the Texas(B) copy. The typographical error is also noted on Harvard(B).

[NLI 8775(3), 5[r]]

66 **And were not of our race, but when a man**
67 **Is born in Ireland and of Irish stock**
68 **When he takes part against us -**

STRANGER.

I will put you safe,
69 **No living man shall set his eyes upon you.**
70 **I will not answer for the dead.**

YOUNG MAN.

The dead?

STRANGER.

71 **For certain days the stones where you must lie**
72 **Have in the hour before the break of day**
73 **Been haunted.**

YOUNG MAN.

74 But **I was not born at midnight.**

STRANGER.

that was
75 **Many a man** ^ **born in the full daylight**
76 **Can see them plain, will pass them on the high-road**
77 **Or in the crowded market-place of the town,**
78 **And never know that they have passed.**

YOUNG MAN.

My Grandam
79 **Would have it they did penance everywhere**;
Some
80 **Or lived through their old lives again.**

---

67 stock] stock, *BL Add. MS 55879, Texas(E), NLI 30,007, BL Add. MSS 55884 and 55891*
69 you.] you; *BL Add. MS 55879, Texas(E), NLI 30,007, BL Add. MSS 55884 and 55891*
74 But I] I *Texas(B), Harvard(B), Quinn*
75 man that was born] man born *Texas(B), Harvard(B), Quinn, Texas(C), Emory*
79 everywhere;] everywhere *Texas(B), Harvard(B), Quinn, Texas(C), Emory*
80 Some / Or] Or *Texas(B), Harvard(B), Quinn, Texas(C), Emory*

---

74 Young Man's speech shifted right beginning with Harvard(B).
75 Massive textual lacunae in NLI 30,007 from this point to l. 163.
80 "Or" is not stricken though implicitly superseded by "Some" as in *VPl* 78.

[NLI 8775(3), 6r]

STRANGER.

In a dream;
And some for an old scruple must hang spitted
Upon the swaying tops of lofty trees {;}
Some are consumed in fire~~s~~, some withered up
By hail and sleet out of the wintry North,
And some but live through their old lives again.

YOUNG MAN.

Well, let them dream into what shape they please
And fill waste mountains with the invisible tumult
Of the fantastic conscience. I have no dread;
They cannot put me into jail or shoot me,
And seeing that their blood has returned to fields
That have grown red from drinking blood like mine,
They would not if they could betray.

STRANGER. This pathway
Runs to the ruined Abbey of Corcomroe; ~~this pathway?~~
The Abbey passed, we are soon among the stone
And shall be at the ridge before the cocks
Of Augenish or Balyvelehan
Or grey Aughtmana shake their wings and cry.

(They go round the stage once)
(half round – finish back to audience –

---

80 dream;] dream *Texas(B)*
82 trees;] trees. *Texas(B)*
83 fire,] fires, *Texas(B)*, *Harvard(B)*, *Quinn*
88 dread;] dread *NLI 8775(4)*, *Texas(B)* dread. *Harvard(B)*, *Quinn*
89 jail . . . me,] jail . . . me; [jail *circled but not emended*] *BL Add. MS 55879*, *Texas(E)* jail . . . me; *rev to* gaol . . . me; [*with inscription:* gaol / as in / earlier / plays] *BL Add. MSS 55884 and 55891*
90 And] And, *Harvard(B)*, *Quinn*
91 mine,] mine *Texas(B)*, *Texas(C)*, *Emory* They *rev to* That [*but queried in black ink*] *BL Add. MS 55879* That have grown *Texas(E)*, *BL Add. MSS 55884 and 55891*
93 Corcomroe;] Corcomroe? *NLI 8775(4)*, *Texas(B)* Corcomroe; this pathway *rev to* Comrcomroe this pathway; *Quinn*
96 Augenish or Balyvelehan] Aughanish or Bailevlehan *Texas(C)*, *Emory* Aughanish or Bailevelehan *BL Add. MS 55879*, *Texas(E)*, *BL Add. MSS 55884 and 55891*
97 Aughtmana] Aughmana *Texas(B)*, *Harvard(B)*, *Quinn*
97*sd* round *rev to* 1/2 [*followed by inscription in pencil:*] moving in time to the music / of drum *NLI 8775(4)* once *rev to* once moving to top of drum *Texas(B)*

Passage corresponding to NLI 8775(3), 6r, is missing from NLI 30,007.
97 "t" inscribed medially, as shown, in black ink; also in NLI 8775(4).
97*sd* Beneath the inscribed note (in pencil) is drawn a curvilinear arrow, indicating a clockwise rotation.

[NLI 8775(3), 7r]

FIRST MUSICIAN (speaking)

They've passed the shallow well and the flat stone
Fouled by the drinking cattle, the narrow lane
Where mourners for five centuries have carried
Noble or peasant to his burial.
An owl is crying out above their heads. – *action*
(singing) Why should the heart take fright?
What sets it beating so?
The bitter sweetness of the night
Has made it but a lonely thing.
Red bird of March, begin to crow,
Up with the neck and clap the wing,
Red cock, and crow.

(They go once round the stage.
The MUSICIAN speaks)

98*sd* speaking *rev to* speaking as they move *NLI 8775(4), Texas(B)*

101 burial.] burial; *BL Add. MS 55879, Texas(E), BL Add. MSS 55884 and 55891*

102*sd lacking NLI 8775(4), Texas(B), Harvard(B), Quinn, Texas(C), Emory, BL Add. MS 55879, Texas(E), BL Add. MSS 55884 and 55891*

103*sd* singing] Singing ¶ *BL Add. MS 55879, Texas(E), BL Add. MSS 55884 and 55891*

103 fright?] fright *Texas(B)*

107 crow. *rev to* crow! *BL Add. MS 55879* crow! *Texas(E), BL Add. MSS 55884 and 55891*

109 crow. *rev to* crow! *BL Add. MS 55879* crow! *Texas(E), BL Add. MSS 55884 and 55891*

109*sd* stage. The . . . speaks *rev to* stage to sound of drum. The . . . speaks as they move *NLI 8775(4), Texas(B) del* The MUSICIAN speaks *Harvard(B) lacking* The MUSICIAN speaks *Quinn* The first musician speaks. *Texas(C), Emory* The First Musician speaks. *BL Add. MS 55879, Texas(E), BL Add. MSS 55884 and 55891*

Passage corresponding to NLI 8775(3), 7r, is missing from NLI 30,007.

109*sd* At right, a faint curvilinear arrow is drawn in pencil, beside a nearly indecipherable notation, perhaps "contrary circle."

[NLI 8775(3), 7^{r} continued]

And now they have climbed through the long grassy field
And passed the ragged thorn trees and the gap
In the ancient hedge; and the tomb-nested owl
At the foot's level beats with a vague wing.
(singing) **My head is in a cloud;**
I'd let the whole world go {; ,}
My rascal heart is proud,
Remembering and remembering.
Red bird of March, begin to crow,
Up with the neck and clap the wing
Red cock and crow.

---

111 thorn trees] thorn-trees *BL Add. MS 55879, Texas(E), BL Add. MSS 55884 and 55891*

114*sd* singing] Singing ¶ *BL Add. MS 55879, Texas(E), BL Add. MSS 55884 and 55891*

114 cloud;] cloud *Texas(B)*

115 go;] go. *NLI 8775(4), Texas(B)* go, *rev to* go. *Texas(C)* go. *Emory*

116 proud,] proud *NLI 8775(4), Texas(C), Emory, BL Add. MS 55879, Texas(E), BL Add. MSS 55884 and 55891*

118 crow. *rev to* crow! *BL Add. MS 55879* crow! *Texas(E), BL Add. MSS 55884 and 55891*

119 wing *rev to* wing, *Harvard(B)* wing, *Quinn, BL Add. MS 55879, Texas(E), BL Add. MSS 55884 and 55891*

120 cock *rev to* cock, *Harvard(B)* cock, *Quinn* cock, and crow. *rev to* cock, and crow! *BL Add. MS 55879* cock, and crow! *Texas(E), BL Add. MSS 55884 and 55891*

Passage corresponding to NLI 8775(3), 7^{r}, is missing from NLI 30,007.

[NLI 8775(3), 8[r]]

quick circle – right round.

(They go round the stage once. look up L.
The MUSICIAN speaks)

They are among the stones above the ash
Above the briar and thorn and the scarce grass;
Hidden amid the shadow far below them
The cat-headed bird is crying out.

(singing) The dreaming bones cry out
Because the night winds blow
And heaven's a cloudy blot; .
Calamity can have its fling.
Red bird of March begin to crow,
Up with the neck and clap the wing,
Red cock and crow.

121*sd* *lacking* quick . . . L. *all MSS save NLI 8775(3)* once. The . . . speaks *rev to* once to sound of drum. The . . . speaks as they move *NLI 8775(4), Texas(B)* once. The MUSICIAN speaks) *rev to* once) ¶ (Speaking) *Harvard(B)* (They go once round the stage) ¶ (speaking) *Quinn* They go once round the stage. The first musician speaks.) *Texas(E)* They go round the stage. The first musician speaks.) *Emory* The MUSICIAN] The First Musician *BL Add. MS 55879, Texas(E), BL Add. MSS 55884 and 55891*

121 ash *rev to* ash, *Harvard(B)* ash, *Quinn, BL Add. MS 55879, Texas(E), BL Add. MSS 55884 and 55891*

122 grass;] grass *NLI 8775(4), Texas(B)* grass *rev to* grass. *Harvard(B)* grass. *Quinn*

123 them *rev to* them, *Harvard(B)* them *Quinn*

125 out *rev to* out, *Texas(B)*

125sd singing] Singing ¶ *BL Add. MS 55879, Texas(E), BL Add. MSS 55884 and 55891*

127 blot.] blot; *NLI 8775(4), Texas(B), Harvard(B), Quinn, Texas(C), Emory*

129 March begin *rev to* March, begin *Harvard(B)* March, begin *Quinn* March, begin to crow, *rev to* March, begin to crow! *BL Add. MS 55879* March, . . . crow! *Texas(E), BL Add. MSS 55884 and 55891*

130 wing,] wing *NLI 8775(4), Texas(B), Texas(C), Emory* wing *rev to* wing, *Harvard(B)*

131 cock *rev to* cock, *Harvard(B)* cock, *Quinn* cock, and crow. *rev to* cock, and crow! *BL Add. MS 55879, Texas(E), BL Add. MSS 55884 and 55891*

Passage corresponding to NLI 8775(3), 8[r], is missing from NLI 30,007.

[NLI 8775(3), 8[r] continued]

STRANGER.

We're almost at the summit and can rest
The road is a faint shadow there; and there
The abbey lies amid its broken tombs . *(pointing to left)*
In the old days we should have heard a bell
Calling the monks before day broke to prayer;
And when the day has broken on the ridge,
The crowing of its cocks.

YOUNG MAN.

Is there no house
sanctity
Famous for ~~sanctuary~~ or architectural beauty

---

132 rest *rev to* rest, *NLI 8775(4)* rest. *Harvard(B), Quinn, Texas(C), Emory, BL Add. MS 55879, Texas(E), BL Add. MSS 55884 and 55891*

133 there; and] there and *NLI 8775(4), Texas(B)* there and *rev to* there, and *Harvard(B)* there, and *Quinn*

134 abbey] Abbey *BL Add. MS 55879, Texas(E), BL Add. MSS 55884 and 55891*

134*sd* *lacking all MSS save NLI 8775(3) and NLI 8775(4)*

136 monks . . . broke to prayer. *rev to* monks, . . . broke, to prayer; *NLI 8775(4)* prayer *Texas(B)* prayer *rev to* prayer, *Harvard(B)* prayer, *Quinn* prayer;] pray; *Texas(C), Emory, BL Add. MS 55879, Texas(E), BL Add. MSS 55884 and 55891*

137 has *rev to* had *BL Add. MS 55879* had *Texas(E), BL Add. MSS 55884 and 55891*

139 Famous for sanctuary or architectural beauty *rev to* Famous for architectural beauty or sanctity *rev to* Once famous for its sanctity or beauty *rev* to Famous for sanctity or architectural beauty *NLI 8775(4)* Famous for sanctuary or architectural beauty *rev to* Once famous for its sanctity or beauty *Texas(B)*

Passage corresponding to NLI 8775(3), 8[r], is missing from NLI 30,007.

[NLI 8775(3), 9r]

In Clare or Kerry, or in all wide Connaught
The enemy has not unroofed?

STRANGER.

Close to the altar
Broken by wind and frost and worn by time
Donnogh O'Brien has a tomb, a name in Latin.
He wore fine clothes and knew the secrets of women,
But he rebelled against the King of Thomond
And died in his youth.

YOUNG MAN.

And why should he rebel?
The King of Thomond was his rightful master.
It was men like Donnogh who made Ireland weak -
My curse on all that troop, and when I die
I'll leave my body, if I have any choice,
Far from his ivy tod and his owl; have those
Who, if your tale is true, work out a penance
Upon the mountain-top where I am to hide,
Come from the Abbey graveyard {?}

~~**THE GIRL**~~**.** Stranger

They have not that luck,
⊙ **But are more lonely, those that are buried there,**
Warred in the heat of the blood; if they were rebels

---

140 Connaught] Connacht *Texas(C), Emory* Connaught, *BL Add. MS 55879* [*circled*], *Texas(E)* Connacht, *BL Add. MSS 55884 and 55891*

142 and worn by time *rev to* or the ivy tendril *NLI 8775(4)* [*but revision canceled*], *Texas(B)*

143 Donnogh *rev to* Donogh *Harvard(B)* Donogh *Texas(C), Emory, BL Add. MS 55879, Texas(E), BL Add. MS 55891* Donogh *rev to* Donough *BL Add. MS 55884*

144 women,] women *Texas(C), Emory*

148 Donnogh *NLI 8775(4), Texas(B), Quinn* Donogh *rev to* Donough *BL Add. MS 55884*

151 owl; have *rev to* owl. Have *Harvard(B)* owl. Have *Quinn* ivy tod . . . owl: have *rev to* ivy-tod . . . owl. Have *BL Add. MS 55879* ivy-tod . . . owl. Have *Texas(E), BL Add. MSS 55884 and 55891*

153 hide,] hide *NLI 30,071*

154 graveyard?] graveyard. *NLI 8775(4), Texas(B)* come . . . grave yard *NLI 30,071*

154 Stranger [*no other MS follows this state*] GIRL . . . luck,] luck *NLI 30,071* THE GIRL] YOUNG GIRL *BL Add. MS 55879, Texas(E), BL Add. MSS 55884 and 55891*

155 lonely. those . . . there,] lonely, those . . . there, *NLI 8775(4), Texas(B), Harvard(B), Quinn, Texas(C), Emory* lonely, Those . . . there, *NLI 30,071* lonely; those . . . there *BL Add. MS 55879, Texas(E), BL Add. MSS 55884 and 55891*

156 blood;] blood *NLI 30, 071*

Passage corresponding to NLI 8775(3), 9r, is missing from NLI 30,007. "Stranger" (at l. 154 in pencil) is not in Yeats's handwriting.

[NLI 8775(3), 10r]

Some momentary impulse made them rebels
Or the commandment of some petty king
Who hated Thomond{. B / , b}eing but common sinners,
No callers in of the aliens from oversea,
They and their enemies of Thomond's party
Mix in a brief dream battle above their bones
~~or~~
and/ **Or make one drove; ~~and~~ drift in amity;**
Or in the hurry of the heavenly round
Forget their earthly names{. T / , t}hese are alone
Being accursed.

YOUNG MAN.

But
~~And~~ if what seems is true
And there are more upon the other side

---

157 rebels] rebels, *BL Add. MS 55879, Texas(E), BL Add. MSS 55884 and 55891*

159 Thomond. Being] Thomond, being *Texas(B)* Thomond; being *Harvard(B)* Thomond; being . . . sinners, *rev to* Tomond; being . . . sinners. *Quinn*

160 oversea,] oversea *Texas(B), Texas(C), Emory* callers in] callers-in *BL Add. MS 55879, Texas(E), BL Add. MSS 55884 and 55891*

162 bones *rev to* bones, *NLI 8775(4)* bones, *Texas(C), Emory* dream battle . . . bones; *rev to* dream-battle . . . bones *BL Add. MS 55879* dream-battle . . . bones *Texas(E), BL Add. MSS 55884 and 55891*

163 drove; and . . . amity,] drove and . . . enmity, *rev to* drove and . . . amity, *NLI 8775(4)* drove and . . . enmity, *Texas(B)* drove and . . . amity, *Harvard(B), Quinn* drove or . . . amity, *Texas(C), Emory* drove; or . . . amity; *BL Add. MS 55879, Texas(E), NLI 30,007, BL Add. MSS 55884 and 55891*

165 alone *rev to* alone, *NLI 8775(4), Harvard(B), NLI 30,007* [*with stricken query:* ? as on p. 140] names, these *Texas(B)* alone, *Quinn, BL Add. MS 55879, Texas(E), NLI 30,007, BL Add. MSS 55884 and 55891*

166 But] And *Texas(B), Harvard(B), Quinn, Texas(C), Emory*

---

163 "amity" is a retyped correction for the erased "enmity" on ribbon copy NLI 8775(3). At this point, the massive lacunae in NLI 30,007 ends and the text resumes.

[NLI 8775(3), 10r continued]

And there are more upon the other side
Than on this side of death, many a ghost
Must meet them fac~~e to~~ face and pass the word
Even upon this grey and desolate hill.

~~YOUNG GIRL~~. *Stranger*
Until this hour no ghost or living man
Has spoken though seven centuries have run
Since they, weary of life and of men's eyes,
Flung down their bones in some forgotten place
Being accursed.

YOUNG MAN.
I have heard that there are souls
Who, having sinned after a monstrous fashion
Take on them, being dead, a monstrous image

---

171 YOUNG GIRL *rev to* Stranger *unique to NLI 8775(3)*

172 spoken *rev to* spoken, *Harvard(B), BL Add. MS 55879, NLI 30,007* spoken, *Quinn, Texas(E), BL Add. MSS 55884 and 55891*

174 place *rev to* place, *NLI 8775(4), Harvard(B),* [*with note:* Cf. p. 140] *NLI 30,007* place, *Quinn, Texas(C), Emory, BL Add. MS 55879, Texas(E), BL Add. MSS 55884 and 55891*

176 fashion *rev to* fashion, *Harvard(B)* fashion, *Quinn, BL Add. MS 55879, Texas(E), NLI 30,007, BL Add. MSS 55884 and 55891*

177 them, being dead,] them being dead . . . [*Yeats's ellipsis*] *NLI 30,071*

---

171 "Stranger" (in pencil) is not in Yeats's handwriting.

[NLI 8775(3), 11[r]]

To drive the living, should they meet its face,
Crazy, and be a terror to the dead.

~~YOUNG GIRL~~. *Stranger*
But these
Were comely even in their middle life
And carry, now that they are dead, the image
Of their first youth, for it was in that youth
Their sin began.

YOUNG MAN.
I have heard of angry ghosts
Who wander in a wilful solitude.

~~THE GIRL~~. *Stranger*
These have no~~t~~ thought but love; nor joy.
But that upon the instant when their penance
Draws to its height and when two hearts are wrung
Nearest to breaking, if hearts of shadows break {; .}
His eyes can mix with hers, nor any pang
That is so bitter as that double glance
Being accursed.

YOUNG MAN.
But what is this strange penance —
That when their eyes have met can wring them most?

~~THE GIRL~~. *Stranger*
Though eyes can meet, their lips can never meet.

---

179 YOUNG GIRL *rev to* Stranger *unique to NLI 8775(3)*
180 life *rev to* life, *Harvard(B)* life *Quinn*
185 THE GIRL *rev to* Stranger *unique to NLI 8775(3)* THE GIRL] YOUNG GIRL *BL Add. MS 55879, Texas(E), NLI 30,007, BL Add. MSS 55884 and 55891* love;] love *Texas(B)* love *rev to* love, *Harvard(B)* love, *Quinn* love; not joy *rev to* nor any joy [*with marginal note:* short line? / nor any joy?] *NLI 30,007* nor any joy *BL Add. MS 55879, Texas(E), BL Add. MSS 55884 and 55891*
187 height *rev to* height, *NLI 30,007, BL Add. MS 55879* height, *Texas(E), BL Add. MSS 55884 and 55891*
188 break,] break. *Texas(B), Harvard(B), Quinn*
189 hers,] hers; *Texas(C), Emory, NLI 30,007, Texas(E), BL Add. MSS 55879 and 55884 and 55891*
190 glance *rev to* glance, *NLI 8775(4), Harvard(B)* glance, *Quinn, Texas(C), Emory, BL Add. MS 55879, Texas(E), NLI 30,007, BL Add. MSS 55884 and 55891*
194 THE GIRL *rev to* Stranger *unique to NLI 8775(3)* THE GIRL] YOUNG GIRL *BL Add. MS 55879, Texas(E), NLI 30,007, BL Add. MSS 55884 and 55891*

179, 185, 194 “Stranger” (in pencil) is not in Yeats’s handwriting.

[NLI 8775(3), 12^{r}]

YOUNG MAN.

195 **And yet it seems they wander side by side.**
196 **But doubtless you would say that when lips meet**
197 **And have not living nerves, it is no meeting.**

~~THE GIRL~~. *Stranger*

198 **Although they have no blood, or living nerves**
199 **Who once lay warm and live the live-long night**
200 **In one another's arms, and know their part**
201 **In life, being now but of the people of dreams,**
202 **Is a dream's part; although they are but shadows,**
203 **Hovering between a thorn tree and a stone,**
204 **Who have heaped up night on winged night; although**
205 **No shade however harried and consumed**
206 **Would change his own calamity for theirs,**
207 **Their manner of life were blessed could their lips**
208 **A moment meet; but when he has bent his head**
209 **Close to her head, or hand would slip in hand,**
210 **The memory of their crime flows up between**
211 **And drives them apart.**

YOUNG MAN.

The memory of a crime -
212 **He took her from a husband's house it may be,**
213 **But does the penance for a passionate sin**
214 **Last for so many centuries?**

---

197 THE GIRL *rev to* Stranger *unique to NLI 8775(3)* THE GIRL] YOUNG GIRL *BL Add. MS 55879, Texas(E), NLI 30,007, BL Add. MSS 55884 and 55891*

198 blood,] blood *NLI 8775(4), Texas(B), Harvard(B), Quinn, Texas(C), Emory* nerves *rev to* nerves, *NLI 8775(4)* nerves, *BL Add. MS 55879, Texas(E), NLI 30,007, BL Add. MSS 55884 and 55891*

200 arms,] arms *Texas(E)* arms *rev to* arms; *Harvard(B)* arms; *Quinn*

203 stone,] stone *NLI 8775(4), Texas(B), Harvard(B), Quinn, Texas(C), Emory* thorn tree *rev to* thorn-tree *NLI 30,007* thorn-tree *BL Add. MS 55879, Texas(E), BL Add. MSS 55884 and 55891*

204 winged *rev to* wingéd *NLI 30,007* wingéd *BL Add. MS 55879, Texas(E), BL Add. MSS 55884 and 55891*

209 head, or . . . hand,] head or . . . hand *Texas(B), Harvard(B), Quinn, Texas(C), Emory*

211 crime – *rev to* crime? *NLI 8775(4)*

212 house *rev to* house, *NLI 30,007* [*with canceled query mark*] house, *BL Add. MS 55879, Texas(E), BL Add. MSS 55884 and 55891*

---

197 "Stranger" (in pencil) is not in Yeats's handwriting.

[NLI 8775(3), 13[r]]

~~THE GIRL~~. *Stranger*

No, no,
The man she chose, the man she was chosen by
Cared little and cares little from whose house
They fled towards dawn amid the flights of arrows
Or that it was a husband's and a king's;
And how, if that were all, could she lack friends
On crowded roads or on the unpeopled hill?
Helen herself had opened wide the door
Where night by night she dreams herself awake
And gathers to her breast a dreaming man.

YOUNG MAN.

What crime can stay so in the memory?
What crime can keep apart the lips of lovers
Wandering and alone?

~~THE GIRL~~. *Stranger*

Her king and lover
Was overthrown in battle by her husband,
And for her sake and for his own, being blind
And bitter and bitterly in love, he brought
A foreign army from across the sea.

YOUNG MAN.

You speak of Dermot and of Dervogilla
Who brought the Norman in?

---

214 THE GIRL *rev to* Stranger *unique to NLI 8775(3)* THE GIRL] YOUNG GIRL *BL Add. MS 55879, Texas(E), NLI 30,007, BL Add. MSS 55884 and 55891* No, no,] No, no; *BL Add. MS 55879, Texas(E), NLI 30,007, BL Add. MSS 55884 and 55891*

215 by *rev to* by, *Harvard(B), NLI 30,007* by, *Quinn, BL Add. MS 55879, Texas(E), BL Add. MSS 55884 and 55891*

217 arrows *rev to* arrows, *Harvard(B)* arrows, *Quinn*

218 king's;] kings *Texas(B)*

219 how, if . . . all, could . . . friends] how if . . . all could . . . friends *Texas(B), Harvard(B), Quinn, Texas(C), Emory* friends, *BL Add. MS 55879, Texas(E), NLI 30,007, BL Add. MSS 55884 and 55891*

226 THE GIRL *rev to* Stranger *unique to NLI 8775(3)*

227 husband,] husband *Texas(B), Texas(C), Emory*

228 own,] own *Texas(B)*

231 Dervogilla] Dervorgilla *Texas(C), Emory, Texas(E)* Dervorgilla *rev to* Dervagilla *NLI 30,007, BL Add. MS 55891* Dermot and Dervagilla *rev to* Diarmuid and Dervorgilla *BL Add. MS 55884*

214, 226 "Stranger" (in pencil) is not in Yeats's handwriting.

[NLI 8775(3), 14r]

~~THE GIRL~~. *Stranger*

Yes, yes I spoke
233 **Of that most miserable, most accursed pair**
234 **Who sold their country into slavery, and yet**
235 **They were not wholly miserable and accursed**
236 **If somebody of their race at last would say;**
237 **'I have forgiven them'.**

YOUNG MAN.

Shall **Oh, never, never**
238 **~~Will~~ Dermot and Dervogilla be forgiven.**

~~THE GIRL~~. *Stranger*

239 **If someone of their race forgave at last**
240 **Lip would be pressed on lip.**

---

232 THE GIRL *rev to* Stranger *unique to NLI 8775(3)* THE GIRL] YOUNG GIRL *BL Add. MS 55879, Texas(E), NLI 30,007, BL Add. MSS 55884 and 55891* Yes, yes] Yes, yes, *BL Add. MS 55879, Texas(E), NLI 30,007, BL Add. MSS 55884 and 55891*

234 slavery, *rev to* slavery; *NLI 30,007* slavery *BL Add. MS 55879, Texas(E), BL Add. MSS 55884 and 55891*

235 accursed *rev to* accursed, *Harvard(B)* accursed, *Quinn*

236 say *rev to* say, *NLI 8775(4)* say *Texas(B), Harvard(B), Quinn* say: *Texas(C), Emory* say: *rev to* say, *NLI 30,007* say, *BL Add. MS 55879, Texas(E), BL Add. MSS 55884 and 55891*

237 'I . . . them'.] I . . . them. *Texas(B)* I . . . them. *rev to* 'I . . . them.' *Harvard(B)* 'I . . . them.' *Texas(C), Emory* 'I . . . forgotten them'. *rev to* 'I . . . forgiven them'. *NLI 30,007* [YOUNG MAN] Oh, *rev to* O, *NLI 30,007* O, *BL Add. MS 55879, Texas(E), BL Add. MSS 55884 and 55891*

238 Shall] Will *Texas(B), Harvard(B), Quinn* Will . . . Dervorgilla *Texas(C), Emory* Shall . . . Dervorgilla *rev to* Shall . . . Dervagilla *NLI 30,007, BL Add. MS 55879* Dervagilla *BL Add. MS 55891* Dermot and Dervagilla *rev to* Diarmuid and Dervorgilla *BL Add. MS 55884*

239 THE GIRL *rev to* Stranger *unique to NLI 8775(3)* THE GIRL] YOUNG GIRL *BL Add. MS 55879, Texas(E), NLI 30,007, BL Add. MSS 55884 and 55891*

232, 239 "Stranger" (in pencil) is not in Yeats's handwriting.

[NLI 8775(3), 14^{r} continued]

YOUNG MAN.

Shall **Oh, never, never**
241 **Will Dermot and Dervogilla be forgiven.**
242 **You have told your story well, so well indeed**
243 **I could not help but fall into the mood**
244 **And for a while believe that it was true,**
245 **Or half believe{;,} but better push on now.**
246 **The horizon to the East is growing bright.**
(They go once round stage) *1 slow 3 quick*
The Musicians play
247 **So here we're on the summit. I can see**
248 **The Aran Islands, Connemara Hills,** *(looks out over audience*

---

240 Oh, *rev to* O, NLI 30,007 O, *BL Add. MS 55879, Texas(E), BL Add. MSS 55884 and 55891*

241 Shall] Will *Texas(B), Harvard(B), Quinn* Will . . . Dervorgilla *Texas(C), Emory* Shall . . . Dervorgilla *rev to* Shall . . . Dervagilla *NLI 30,007, BL Add. MS 55879* Dervagilla *BL Add. MS 55891* Dermot and Dervagilla *rev to* Diarmuid and Dervorgilla *BL Add. MS 55884*

244 true,] true *NLI 8775(4), Texas(B), Harvard(B), Quinn, Texas(C), Emory, NLI 30,007, BL Add. MS 55891* true *rev to* true, *BL Add. MSS 55879 and 55884*

245 believe;] believe, *NLI 8775(4), Texas(B), Harvard(B), Quinn, Texas(C), Emory*

246 East *rev to* east *NLI 30,007* east *BL Add. MSS 55884 and 55891*

246*sd* They go once round stage *rev to* They go half round stage music suggests / a dance *NLI 8775(4)* stage *rev to* stage music may / suggest dance *Texas(B)* They . . . stage *Harvard(B), Quinn, Texas(C), Emory* They go round stage once. The Musicians play. *BL Add. MS 55879, Texas(E), NLI 30,007, BL Add. MSS 55884 and 55891* 1 slow 3 quick [*in pencil*] *unique to NLI 8775(3)*

248*sd* *lacking Texas(B), Harvard(B), Quinn, Texas(C), Emory, BL Add. MS 55879, Texas(E), NLI 30,007, BL Add. MSS 55884 and 55891*

[NLI 8775(3), 15r]

And Galway in the breaking light; there too
The enemy has toppled roof and gable;
And torn the panelling from ancient rooms;
What generations of old men had known
Like their own hands, and children wondered at,
Has boiled a troøoper's porridge. That town had lain,
But for the pair that you would have me pardon,
Amid its gables and its battlements
Like any old admired Italian town;
For though we have neither coal nor iron ore,
To make us wealthy and corrupt the air *The*
Our country if that crime were uncommitted ~~*young*~~ *Girl*
Had been most beautiful. ~~Why do you dance?~~ *Seven hundred years*

250 The . . . toppled wall and roof *Texas(B), Harvard(B), Quinn, Texas(C), Emory* gable; *rev to* gable, *NLI 30,007, BL Add. MS 55879* gable, *Texas(E), BL Add. MSS 55884 and 55891*

251 And torn from ancient walls to boil his pot *Texas(B), Harvard(B), Quinn, Texas(C), Emory*

252 The oaken panelling that had been dear *Texas(B), Harvard(B), Quinn, Texas(C), Emory*

253 To generations of children and old men. *Texas(B), Harvard(B), Quinn, Texas(C), Emory*

254 *lacking Texas(B), Harvard(B), Quinn, Texas(C), Emory*

255–261*sd* through this / speech dance / Music / growing in / intensity *Texas(E) only* [*though, clearly, also inscribed beneath the paste-over on NLI 8775(4)*]

255 But for that pair for whom you would have my pardon *Texas(B), Harvard(B), Quinn, Texas(C), Emory* pardon, *BL Add. MS 55879, Texas(E), NLI 30,007, BL Add. MSS 55884 and 55891*

256 It might be now like Bayeux or like Caen *Texas(B), Harvard(B), Quinn, Texas(C), Emory*

257 Or little Italian town amid its walls *Texas(B),* [*rev to* walls;] *Harvard(B),* [walls;] *Quinn,* [*walls*] *Texas(C) and Emory*

258 For though we have neither coal nor iron ore *Texas(B), Harvard(B), Quinn, Texas(C), Emory* coal, nor *BL Add. MS 55879, Texas(E), NLI 30,007, BL Add. MSS 55884 and 55891*

259 To make us rich and win heaven with smoke [win *rev to* cover] *Texas(B),* [win *rev to* cover . . . smoke,] *Harvard(B),* [cover . . . smoke,] *Quinn,* [cover . . . smoke] *Texas(C) and Emory* air, *BL Add. MS 55879, Texas(E), NLI 30,007, BL Add. MSS 55884 and 55891*

260 country if . . . uncommitted *rev to* country, if . . . uncommitted, *Harvard(B)* country, if . . . uncommitted, *Quinn, BL Add. MS 55879, Texas(E), NLI 30,007, BL Add. MSS 55884 and 55891* country, . . . if uncommitted *Texas(C), Emory*

261 The Girl[.] Seven hundred years (turning) *NLI 8775(4)*

249–259 Yeats inserted substantial textual revisions at this point by means of a typed passage that was pasted onto 15r. This procedure was also followed in NLI 8775(4). These eleven new and reworked lines superseded ten lines of the earlier state, which are indentical to those found in Texas(B). Handwritten corrections generally relate to the 1931 Abbey Theatre production of the play, anticipating revisions that had yet to be implemented in copy for *The Collected Plays* (1934).

[NLI 8775(3), 15[r] continued]

Young Man (turning)
262 **Why do you gaze and with so passionate eyes**
263 **One on the other; and then turn away**
weave
264 **~~Covering your eyes and~~** ~~weaving~~ **~~it in a dan~~ce,**
265 **Who are you? What are you? You are not natural.**
(comes back to L.)

~~THE GIRL~~. *Stranger*
266 **Seven hundred years our lips have never met.**

YOUNG MAN.
267 **Why do you look so strangely at one another,**
268 **So strangely and so sweetly?**

~~THE GIRL~~. *Stranger*
269 **Seven hundred years.**

262*sd* *NLI 8775(3) and NLI 8775(4) only*

262 gaze and . . . eyes *rev to* gaze, and . . . eyes, *Harvard(B), Quinn, BL Add. MS 55879, Texas(E), NLI 30,007, BL Add. MSS 55884 and 55891*

263 other and . . . away *NLI 8775(4), Texas(B),* [*rev to* away,] *Harvard(B)* away *Quinn, BL Add. MS 55879, Texas(E), NLI 30,007, BL Add. MSS 55884 and 55891*

264 weaving . . . dance, *rev to* weaving . . . dance? *Harvard(B)* weaving . . . dance? *Quinn* weave . . . dance, *Texas(C), Emory* eyes, . . . weave . . . dance? *BL Add. MS 55879, Texas(E), NLI 30,007, BL Add. MSS 55884 and 55891*

265 What . . . You] what . . . you *Texas(C), Emory, BL Add. MS 55879, Texas(E), NLI 30,007, BL Add. MSS 55884 and 55891*

265*sd* *lacking all MSS save NLI 8775(3) and NLI 8775(4)*

266 THE GIRL *rev to* Stranger *unique to NLI 8775(3)* THE GIRL] YOUNG GIRL *BL Add. MS 55879, Texas(E), NLI 30,007, BL Add. MSS 55884 and 55891*

269 THE GIRL *rev to* Stranger *unique to NLI 8775(3)* THE GIRL] YOUNG GIRL *BL Add. MS 55879, Texas(E), NLI 30,007, BL Add. MSS 55884 and 55891*

266, 269 "Stranger" (in pencil) is not in Yeats's handwriting.

[NLI 8775(3), 16r]

YOUNG MAN.

So strangely and so sweetly. All the ruin,
All, all their handiwork is blown away
As though the mountain air had blown it away
Because their eyes have met. They cannot hear,
Being folded up and hidden in their dance.
The dance is changing now. They have dropped their eyes,
They have covered up their eyes as though their hearts
(He takes a step nearer, but
Had suddenly been broken - Never, never *falls back*
Shall Dermot and Dervogilla be forgiven. *again*
They have drifted in the dance from rock to rock
They have raised their hands as though to snatch the sleep
That lingers always in the abyss of the sky

277sd del NLI 8775(4) lacking on all other MSS

277 Never,] never, *Texas(C), Emory, BL Add. MS 55879, Texas(E), NLI 30,007, BL Add. MSS 55884 and 55891*

278 Dervorgilla [forgiven *rev to* forgiven.] *Texas(C)* Dervorgilla *Emory* Dervorgilla *rev to* Dervagilla *NLI 30,007, BL Add. MS 55879* Dervagilla *Texas(E), BL Add. MS 55891* Dermot and Dervagilla *rev to* Diarmuid and Dervorgilla *BL Add. MS 55884*

279 rock *rev to* rock, *Harvard(B)* rock, *Quinn* rock *rev to* rock. *Texas(C)* rock. *Emory, BL Add. MS 55879, Texas(E), NLI 30,007, BL Add. MSS 55884 and 55891*

281 sky *rev to* sky, *Harvard(B)* sky, *Quinn*

[NLI 8775(3), 16r continued]

(goes nearer)
Though they can never reach it. ^ **A cloud floats up**
~~*(They go out L*~~
And covers all the mountain head in a moment.
And now it lifts and they are swept away.
I had almost yielded and forgiven it all -
I leave this
~~**This is indeed a**~~ **place of terrible temptation.**
(The Stranger & the Young Girl go out) *Exit L.*

(The MUSICIANS begin unfolding and folding a black cloth. The FIRST MUSICIAN comes forward to the front of the stage, at the centre. He holds the cloth before him. The other two come one on either side and unfold it. They afterwards fold it up in the same way. When it is unfolded, the YOUNG MAN has left the stage).

282*sd* *lacking on all other MSS*

283 mountain head in a moment; *rev to* mountain-head in a moment; *NLI 30,007* mountain-head in a moment; *BL Add. MS 55879, Texas(E), NLI 30,007, BL Add. MSS 55884 and 55891*

283*sd* (Girl & Stranger go out R.) [*in black ink*] *NLI 8775(4)* *lacking on all other MSS*

284*sd* Stranger & Young Girl go out. *del NLI 8775(4)* *lacking Texas(B), Harvard(B), Quinn, Texas(C), Emory* The Stranger and the Young Girl go out. *BL Add. MS 55879, Texas(E), NLI 30,007, BL Add. MSS 55884 and 55891*

286 This is indeed a place of terrible temptation *rev to* A place of terrible temptation – a dreadful place – [*in black ink*] *rev to* A place of terrible temptation, a dreadful place. [*in pencil*] *NLI 8775(4)* This is indeed a place of terrible temptation. *Texas(B), Harvard(B), Quinn, Texas(C), Emory* This is indeed a place of terrible temptation. *rev to* [*lacunae*] temptation and a terrible place. *rev to* [*lacunae*] the temptation and the place *NLI 30,007* Terrible the temptation and the place. *rev to* Terrible . . . place! *BL Add. MS 55879* Terrible . . . place! *Texas(E), BL Add. MS 55891* Terrible . . . place. *BL Add. MS 55884*

286*sd* Exit L. *lacking on all MSS but NLI 8775(3) and NLI 8775(4)* MAN has left] MAN leaves *BL Add. MS 55879, Texas(E), NLI 30,007, BL Add. MSS 55884 and 55891*

[NLI 8775(3), 17r]

THE MUSICIAN (singing)

At the grey round of the hill
Music of a lost kingdom
Runs, runs and is suddenly still
The winds out of Clare - Galway
Carry it: suddenly it is still.

I have heard in the night air ~~*Young Man*~~
A wandering airy music ~~*could sing*~~
And moidered in that snare ~~*alternate*~~
A man is lost of a sudden, ~~*verses.*~~
In that sweet wandering snare.

What finger first began
Music of a lost kingdom?
They dream that laughed in the sun.
Dry bones that dream are bitter,
They dream and darken our sun.

Those crazy fingers play
A wandering airy music;
Our luck is withered away,
And wheat in the wheat-ear withered,
And the wind blows it away.

---

287 MUSICIAN] MUSICIANS *Texas(C), Emory, BL Add. MS 55879, Texas(E), NLI 30,007, BL Add. MSS 55884 and 55891* 1 [*centered, above line*] *NLI 8774 (4), Texas(B)* I [*centered, above line*] *Harvard(B)* I. *Quinn* I *Texas(C), Emory, BL Add. MS 55879, Texas(E), NLI 30,007, BL Add. MSS 55884 and 55891*

289 sill *rev to* still; *Texas(B), Harvard(B)* still; *Quinn* still. *Texas(C), Emory, BL Add. MS 55879, Texas(E), NLI 30,007, BL Add. MSS 55884 and 55891*

293 music *rev to* music, *Texas(B), Harvard(B)* music, *Quinn* music; *Texas(C), Emory, BL Add. MS 55879, Texas(E), NLI 30,007, BL Add. MSS 55884 and 55891*

295 sudden,] sudden *NLI 8775(4), Harvard(B), Quinn*

298 kingdom?] kingdom *NLI 8775(4)* kingdom *rev to* kingdom; *Texas(B)* kingdom *rev to* kingdom. *Harvard(B)* kingdom. *Quinn, Texas(C), Emory*

299 sun. *rev to* sun: *Texas(B)*

300 bitter *rev to* bitter; *Texas(B), Harvard(B)* bitter; *Quinn*

301–302 [*no space*] *rev to* [*space between stanzas*] *NLI 30,007*

[NLI 8775(3), 18[r]]

My heart ran wild when it heard
The curlew cry before dawn
And the eddying cat-headed bird;
But now the night is gone.
I have heard from far below
The strong March birds a-crow,
Stretch neck and clap the wing,
Red cocks, and crow.

W.B. YEATS.
August 1917.

307 2 [*centered, above line*] *NLI 8775(4), Texas(B)* II [*centered, above line*] *Harvard(B)* II. *Quinn, NLI 30,007, BL Add. MSS 55884 and 55891* II *Texas(C), Emory, BL Add. MS 55879, Texas(E)*

312 a-crow, *rev to* a-crow. *NLI 30,007, BL Add. MS 55879* a-crow. *Texas(E), BL Add. MSS 55884 and 55891*

314 cocks,] cock, *NLI 8775(4)* crow. *rev to* crow! *BL Add. MS 55879* crow! *Texas(E), BL Add. MSS 55884 and 55891* THE END [*inscribed below*] *NLI 30,007, BL Add. MS 55879* THE END [*below*] *Texas(E), BL Add. MSS 55884 and 55891* W.B. YEATS / August 1917. *rev to* W.B. YEATS. *Harvard(B)* W. B. YEATS. *Quinn* W. B. YEATS. *lacking Texas(C), Emory, NLI 30,007, BL Add. MS 55879, Texas(E), BL Add. MSS 55884 and 55891*

II. *Calvary*

Photographs and Transcriptions of the Early Manuscripts (1918–1919)

A. "The Road to Calvary"—First Two Drafts, NLI 30,361

NLI 30,361, folio 27^{v}

"Poems seem to disturb the spirits—once at Gogarty's when I was reading out my *Calvary* and came to the description of the entrance of Lazarus, the door burst open as if by the blast of wind where there could be no wind, and the family ghost had a night of great activity. From all which you will see that I am still of opinion that only two topics can be of the least interest to a serious and studious mind—sex and the dead." (*Letters* 729–730.)

[NLI 30,361, 1^r and 1^v]

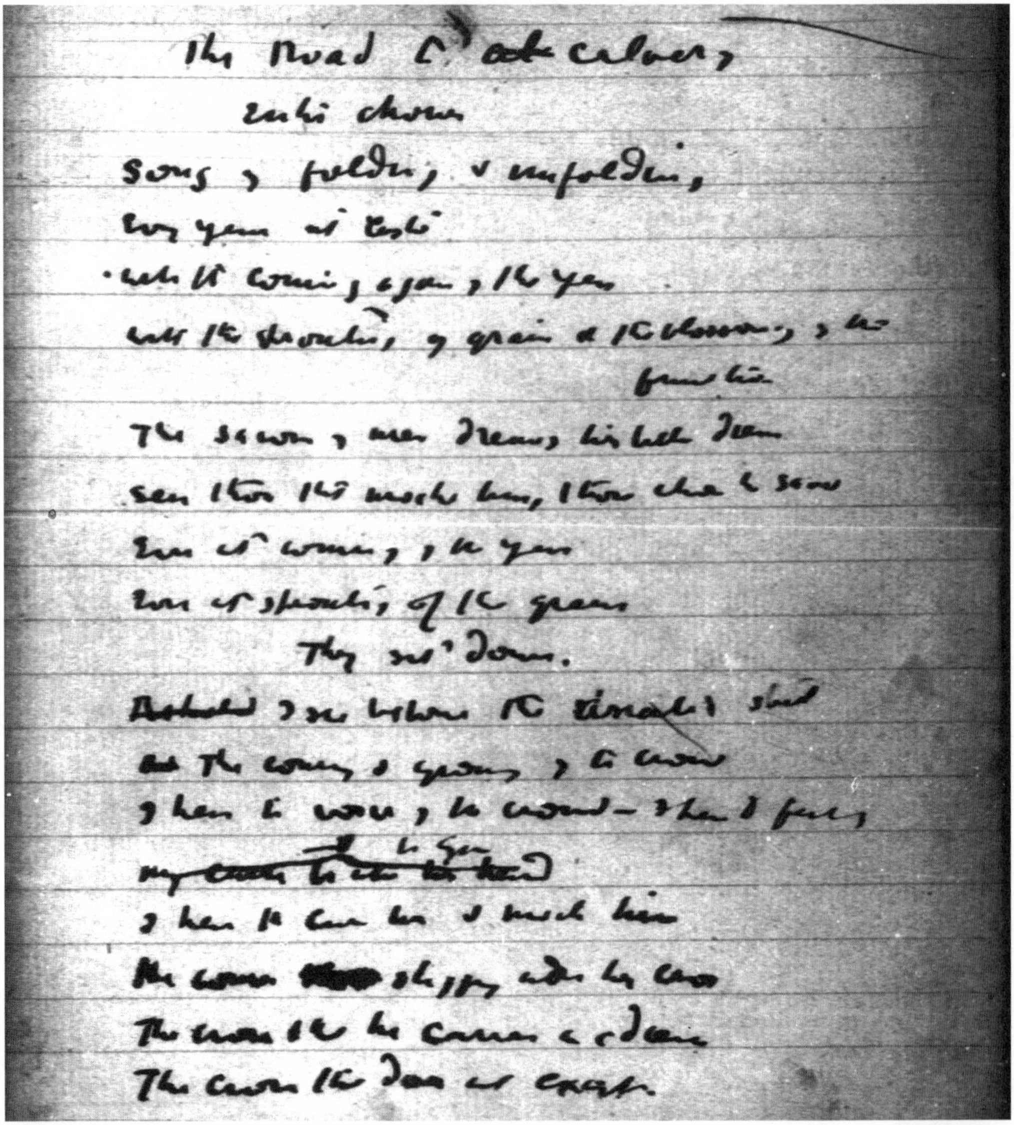

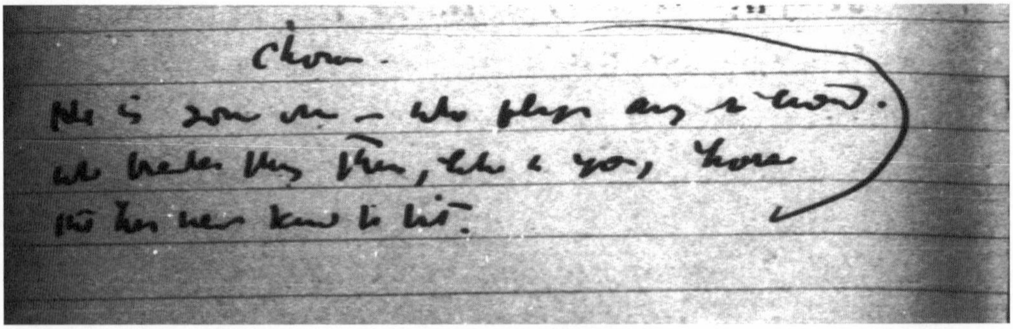

[NLI 30,361, 1r and 1v]

[1r]

The Road to ~~Al~~ Calvery

Enter Chorus

Song of folding & unfolding

Every year at Easter
With the coming again of the year
With the sprouting of grain & the blossoming of the
fruit trees
The savior of men dreams his bitter dream
Sees those that mocked him, those chosen he saved
Even at coming of the year
Even at sprouting of the grain

They sit down. { A }
~~Behold~~ I see before the { [?si] } siatic street
~~And~~ The coming & growing of the crowd
I hear the voice of the crowd – I heard feeling
[~~?~~] be given
~~My curse be upon his head~~
I hear them curse him & mock him
He comes ~~there~~ staggering under his cross
The cross that he carries in a dream
The cross that does not exist.

[1v]

Chorus

He is gone on – who plays among the crowd
Who breaks through them, like a young horse
That has never known the bit.

1v, 1–3 Partially inscribed on right with arrow indicating insertion just after 2r, l. 4.

[NLI 30,361, 2r]

[NLI 30,361, 2^{r}]

(Enter Christ with Chorus)

Chorus
I hear the voice of the crowd I hear them mock him
Who shall [?say] we may see our god
"Work a miracle now" "Set ~~thy~~ your self free"
"did you not make the world. Are you not god"
Chorus
" ⟶ Lazerus
I am he that you raised from the dead
I am Lazeras.

Christ.
You at any rate have not come to mock me.

~~Lazerus~~
~~I have~~
~~You~~ You owe to me your life.

Lazerus
I owe to you my life.

Christ.
You do not mock me

Lazerus
I come to ask of you your death

Christ.
My death.

4/5 Arrow indicates insertion of speech from 1^{v}.

[NLI 30,361, 3r]

[NLI 30,361, 3^{r}]

Lazerus

I dreaded your love always – I never could touch it
We were of your own followers, alone of your kin
I was never alone because of that love
I had hidden in the world – all was that love.
Then I died – ~~& you came~~ You were away at
The time – as I died I thought – this much can I
do & his love not hinder me – I can die &
Then you came & opened the door of the tomb
& brought me to life.

Christ

Nothing lives but through my love.

Lazerus

Was I not at peace being dead,
& you took from me my death – give me
Your death – that I may escape you.

Christ

~~I die for all the people~~ & ~~all~~ those die shall rise
again through me

Lazerus

Then it is true
~~Do not die because Christ Christ~~ ~~Is it true~~ that

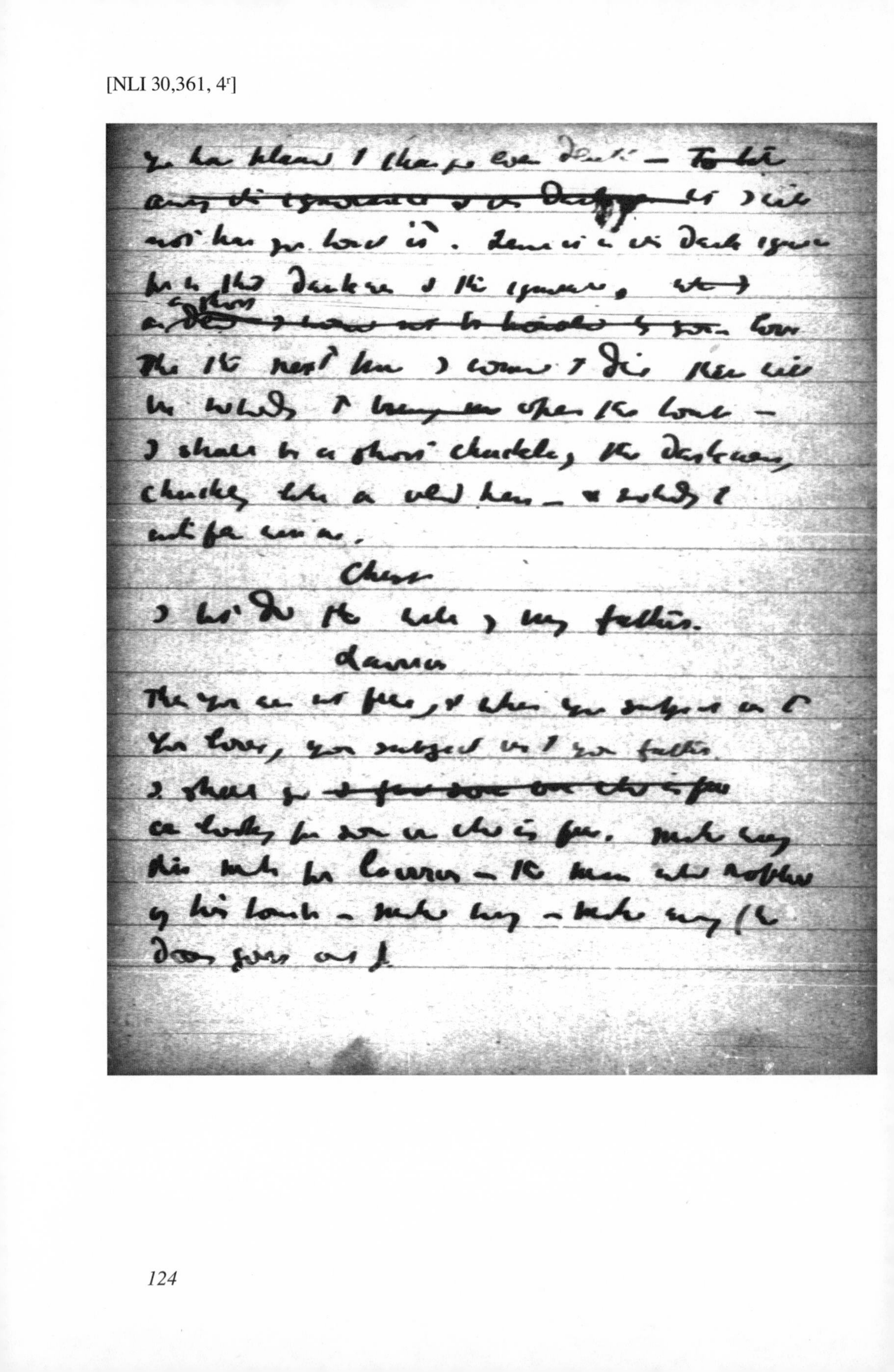

[NLI 30,361, 4^{r}]

[NLI 30,361, 4^{r}]

You have planned to change even death – ~~To take~~
~~Away its ignorance & its darkness~~ but I will
not have you touch it. Leave it in its dark ignorance
For in that darkness & that ignorance. ~~When I~~
 a ghost
~~am dead – I would not be troubled by your~~ love
Then the next time I come to die there will
Be nobody to ~~bring me~~ open the tomb –
I shall be a ghost chuckling the darkness,
Chuckling like an old hen – & nobody to
interfere with me.

Christ
I but do the will of my father.

Lazerus
Then you are not free, & when you subject us to
Your love, you subject us to your father.
I shall go ~~& find some one who is free~~
And looking for some one who is free. Make way
this [?much] for lazerus – the man whos robbed
of his tomb – make way – make way (he
~~does~~ goes out)

8 "chuckling the darkness" for "chuckling in the darkness"?

[NLI 30,361, 5r]

[NLI 30,361, 5^{r}]

Chorus.
Now come the holy women – [?Martha] & all
The married – ~~& [?]~~ They gather about him & they
Kiss his feeet. Now they cry out their love

Chorus.
Your love is every[?thing] to us Master – it is
In our love – without it we would die

2 voice[?s]
We are nothing & you made us alone

Christ
At the touch of your lips upon my feet
This day of my death grows sweet to me
Again. You know being simple of heart
That the soul of man is nothing without
the love of god. Why do you suddenly
fly from the street ~~& leave~~ as though in dred

Judas.
I am he, ~~God most high~~, that ~~betrayed~~
~~You~~ sold you for forty peices of silver

Christ.

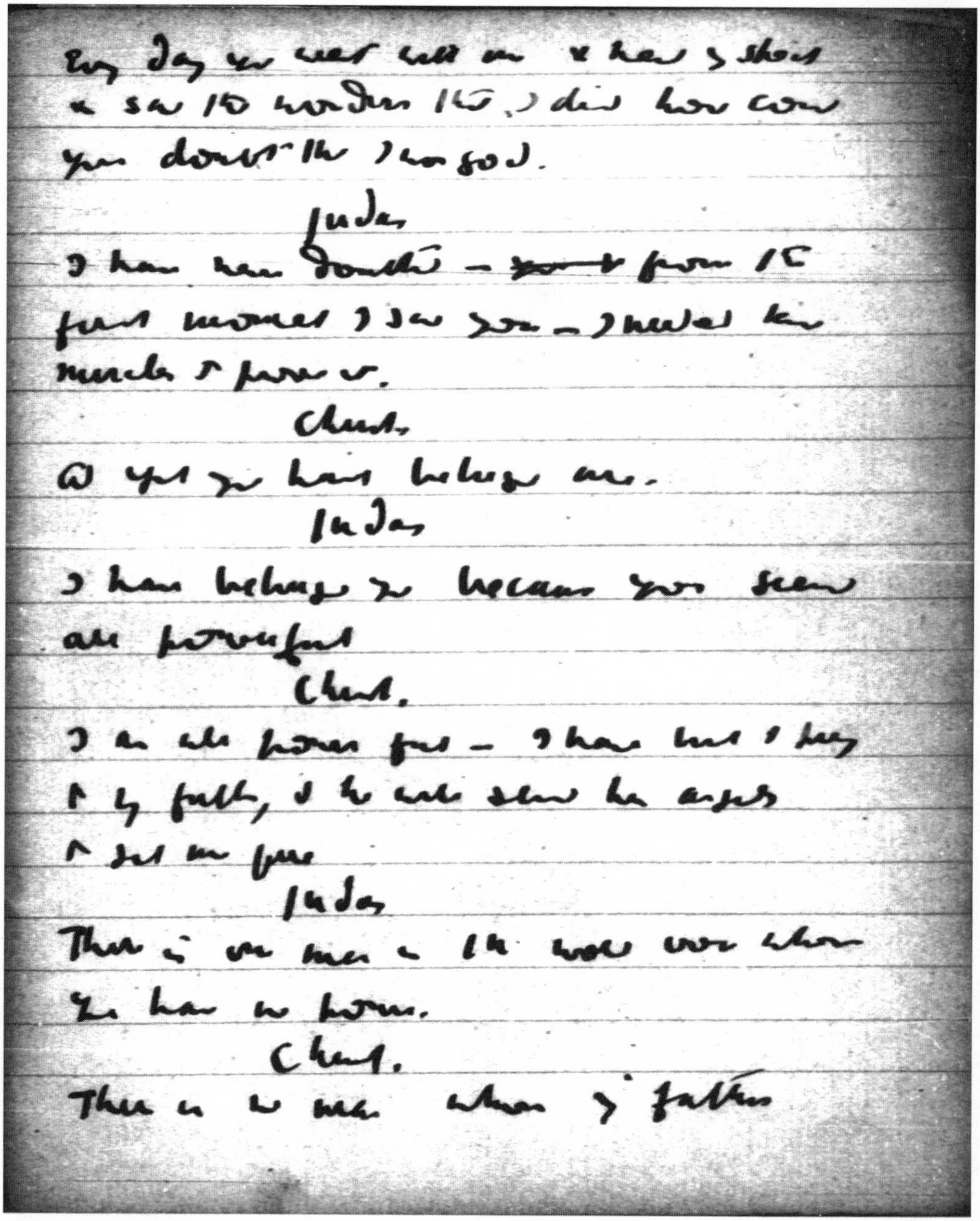

[NLI 30,361, 6^{r}]

Every day you went with me & heard my speech
& saw the wonders that I did how could
You doubt that I was god.

Judas

I have never doubted – ~~you f~~ from the
first moment I saw you – I needed know
miracles to prove it.

Christ.

And yet you have betrayed me.

Judas

I have betrayed you because you seemed
all powerful

Christ.

I am all power ful – I have but to pray
to my father, & he will send his angels
to set me free

Judas

There is no man in the world over whom
you have no power.

Christ.

There is no man whom my father

---

5 "know" for "no"?

[NLI 30,361, 7r]

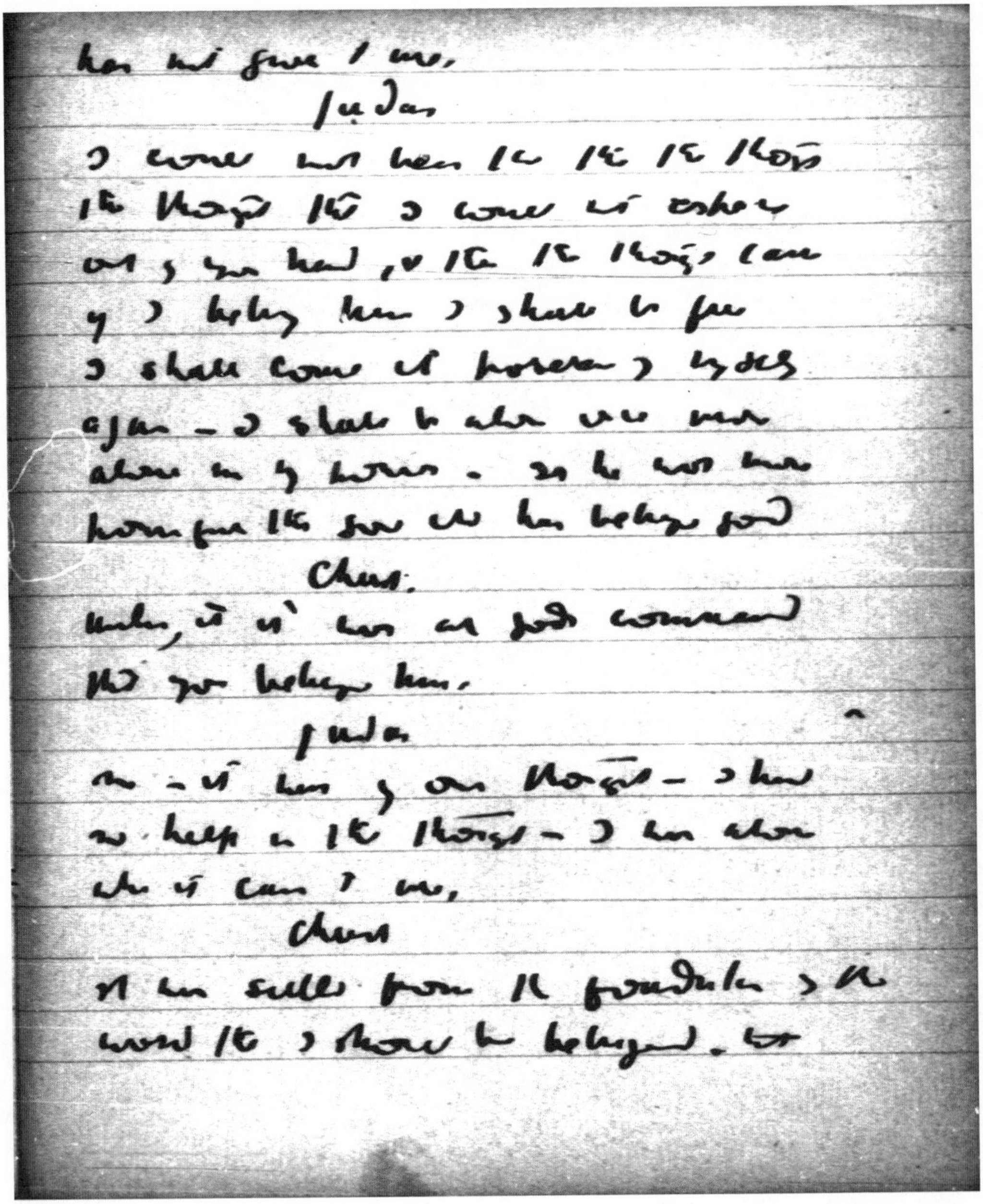

[NLI 30,361, 7r]

has not given to me.

Judas

I could not bear that the the thought
The thought that I would not escape
Out of your hand, & then the thought came
if I betray him I shall be free
I shall come into possession of myself
again – I shall be alone once more
alone in my powers. Is he not more
powerful this god who has betrayed god

Christ.

Unless, it it was as gods command
That you betrayed him.

Judas

No – it was my own thought – I had
no help in the thought – I was alone
when it came to me.

Christ

It was settled from the foundation of the
world that I should be betrayed. ~~but~~

[NLI 30,361, 8^r and 8^v]

[NLI 30,361, 8r and 8v]

[8r]

Judas

~~But~~ Yes that some man should betray
O I had thought of all that but not
[~~?~~] in such a village
I Judas, born on such a day, &
by such a woman, ~~Judas~~ not that I
& no other should go to the high priest
& chuckling to himself, as people chuckle
When they are alone – & for exactly so many
peices of silver, should make my contract
& that I should do the deed, not with
a nod, or a word, or by sending a
message but with a kiss upon your cheek
I betrayed you Christ I & no other
& now you cannot even save me.

Christ

Go from me.

{F / (}irst Roman Soldier

no he must stay – he has to set up the cross

Second Soldier

We have driven up all the others – they
Are too persistant, they are always wanting something.

[8v]

The second Adam is a tale
That some idle mocker tells
For all his rages

[?We]

8v, 4 Possibly canceled.

[NLI 30,361, 9^r and 9^v]

[NLI 30,361, 9r and 9v]

[9r]

Third Soldier
With only us & Judas here you will be [?calm]
& die in peace

Christ. (whose arms are now spread out
on the cross)
Who are you who ask nothing of God.

First Soldier
We are the gamblers – presently we are going
to throw the dice for your cloak & your
tunic.

Second Soldier
But it does who wins it, ~~we~~ for we are
~~god~~ good gamblers – he who loses to day
will win to morrow.

Third Soldier
We are content with what ever happens
so long as we do not know what is going
to happen – are we not your best
worshippers god, who ask nothing of ~~your will~~
your power or your love.

[9v]

We are the mockers – call out. Call out aloud
~~Call to your father now – complain aloud~~
Lift up your voice to him
That Master climbs
That he may send three chariots [?by]
~~It is certain he will see them~~ on a cloud
claim
To ~~guide~~ his true begotten son, or split
This ancient
~~This Even this~~ – mountain rock
And leave all the mockers
And who is not ~~now~~ mocking now, into the [?~~spi~~] pit

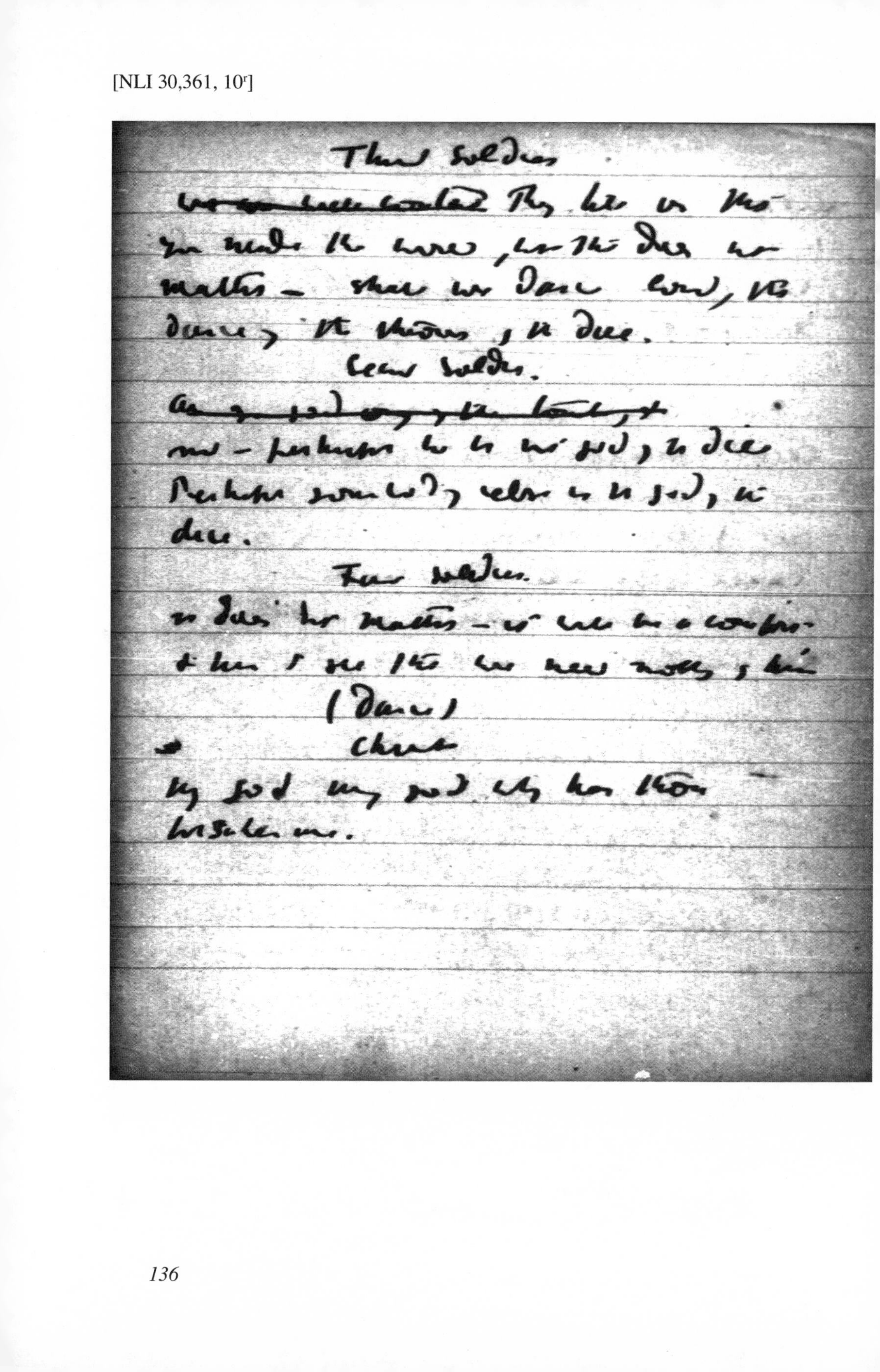

[NLI 30,361, 10^r]

[NLI 30,361, 10[r]]

Third Soldier
~~We are well content~~ They tell us that
You made the world, but that does not
Matter – shall we dance lord, the
dance of the throwers of the dice.

Second Soldier.
~~As your god crying by the touch, [?sl]~~
no – perhaps he is not god of the dice
Perhaps somebody else is the god of the
dice.

First Soldier.
It does not matter – it will be a comfort
To him to see that we need nothing of him.

(dance)

Christ
~~[?]~~
My god my god why has thou
forsaken me.

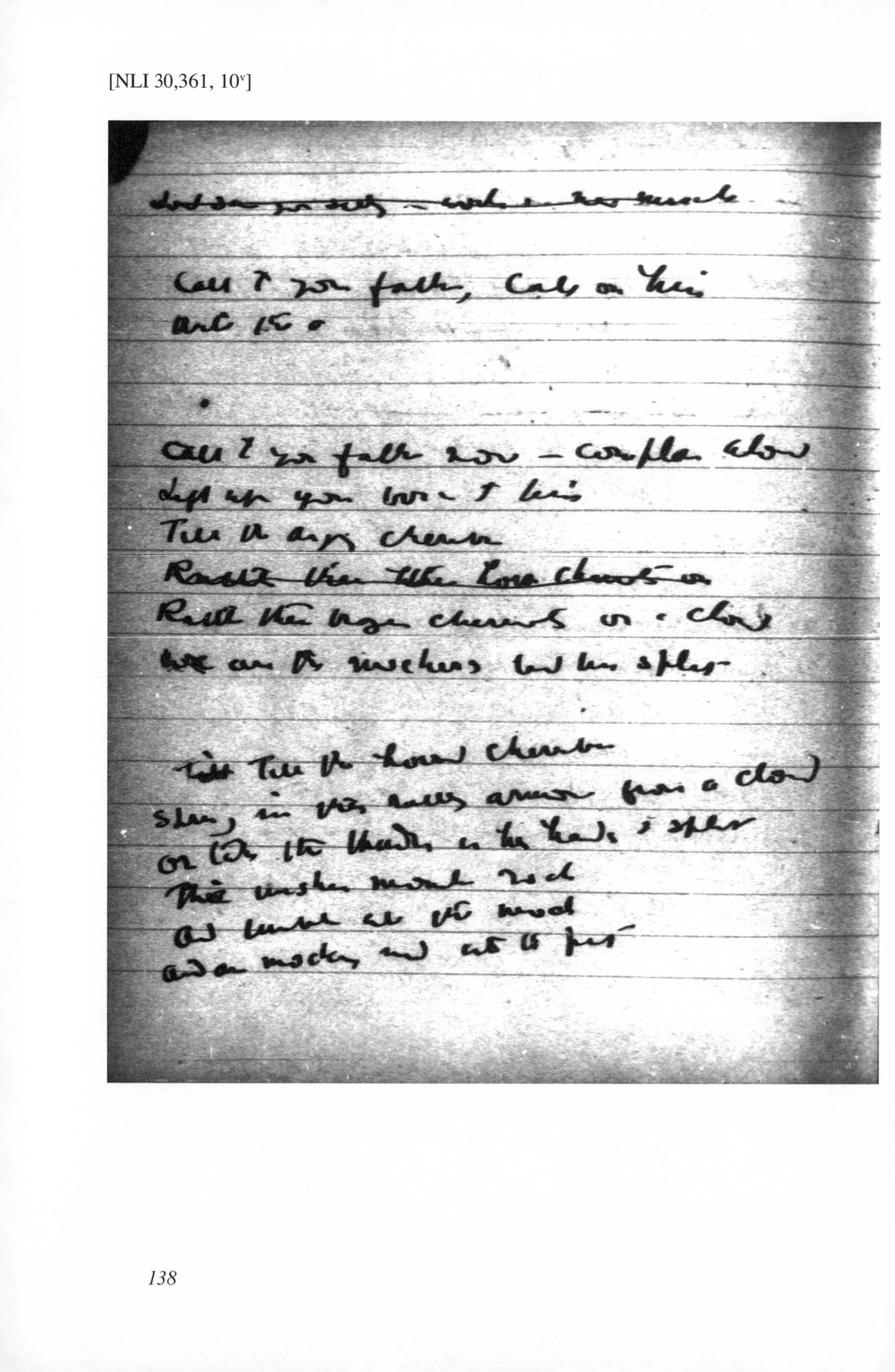

[NLI 30,361, 10^{v}]

~~Lord save your self – work a new miracle~~

Call to your father, Call on him
Art [?thou] [?o]

Call to your father now, complain aloud
Lift up your voice to him
Till the angry cherubs
~~Rattle their [?horse] chariots on~~
Rattle their brazen chariots on a cloud
We are the mockers bid him split

~~Till~~ Till the horsed cherubs
Spring in their rattling around from a cloud
Or take the thunder in his hands & split
Th{e/is} [?unshaken] mountain rock
And tumble all the mockers
And all mocking now into the pit

1–15 Appear to be spoken by the chorus; while responding to Christ's plaint on 10^{r}, ll. 11–12, the lines here return to the figures of the mockers and the bitted colt of 1^{r}, 1^{v}, and 2^{r}. Thus, this choral passage marks the end of the draft. At the same time, it faces the choral prelude of draft two on folio 11^{r}.

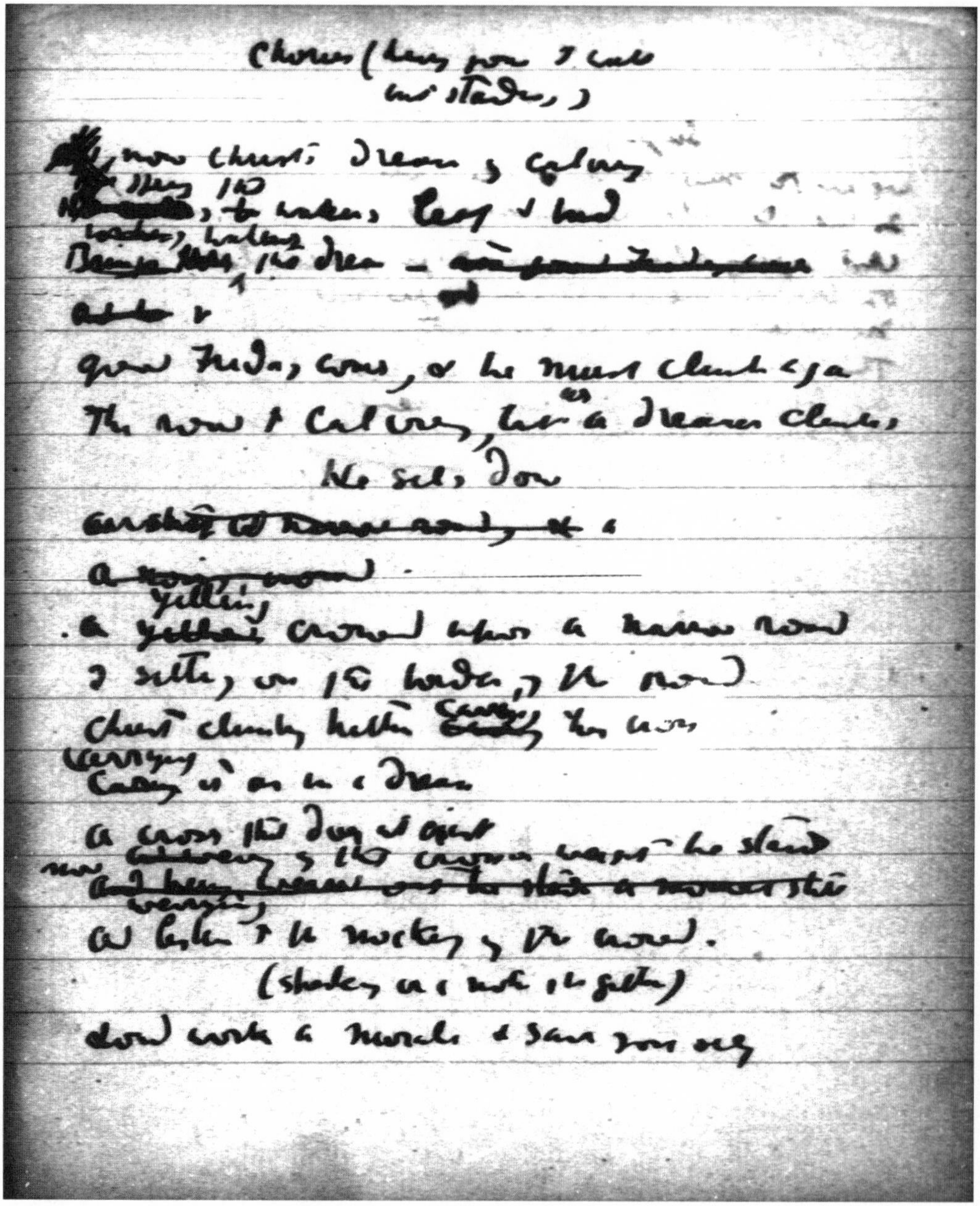

[NLI 30,361, 11^{r}]

Chorus (having gone to the wall
but standing)

1 ~~And~~ now Christs dream of Calvary
~~The~~ spring that
2 ~~That [?wakens],~~ ~~t~~ wakens, leaf & bud
~~wakens~~ wakens
3 ~~Brings him~~ ^ the dream – ~~[?at] good Friday comes~~
~~and~~
4 ~~And he~~ [?]
5 Good Friday comes, & he must climb again
as
6 The road to Calvary, but a dreamer climbs.

7 He sits down

8 ~~a steep & narrow road, &~~ a
9 ~~a noisy crowd~~
yelling
10 a ~~yellow~~ crowd upon a narrow road
11 & sitting on the border of the road
carrying
12 Christ climbing hither ~~carrying~~ his cross
Carrying
13 ~~Caring~~ it as in a dream
14 A cross that does not exist
15 ~~And we~~ary of that crosses weight he stands
now
16 ~~And being wearied out he stands a moment still~~
wearying
17 And listens to the mocking of the crowd.

(Speaking on a note to the gathering)

18 Lord work a miracle & save your self

The second draft begins with this folio.

[NLI 30,361, 11v]

[NLI 30,361, 11^{v}]

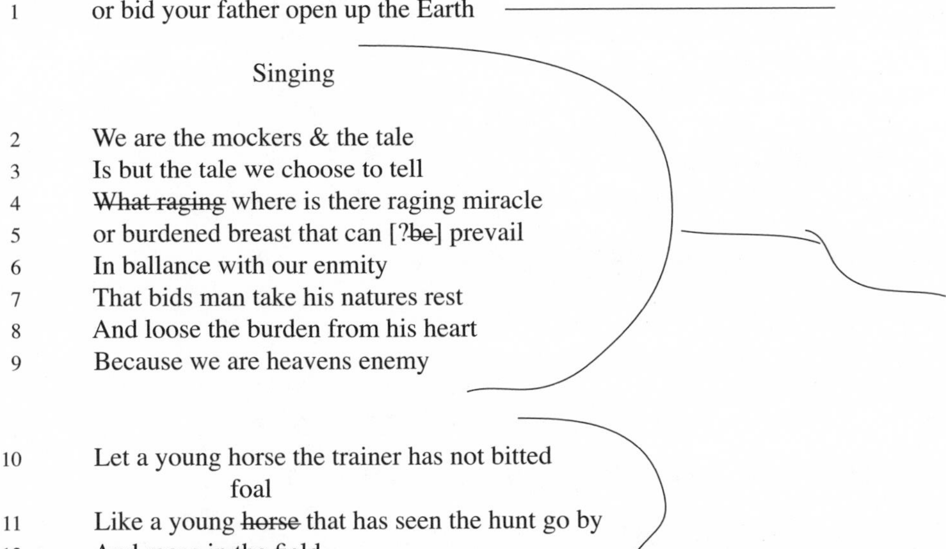

or bid your father open up the Earth

Singing

We are the mockers & the tale
Is but the tale we choose to tell
~~What raging~~ where is there raging miracle
or burdened breast that can [?~~be~~] prevail
In ballance with our enmity
That bids man take his natures rest
And loose the burden from his heart
Because we are heavens enemy

Let a young horse the trainer has not bitted
foal
Like a young ~~horse~~ that has seen the hunt go by
And races in the field.

---

1 Revises 12^{r}, l. 1, with a faint drawn line leading to the right margin and to that point on the facing page.
2–9 Partially inscribed on right with arrow leading to an interpolation on 12^{r} between 9 and 10.
10–12 Partially inscribed on right with a corresponding arrow leading to a substitution on 12^{r}, ll. 12–14.

[NLI 30,361, 12r]

[NLI 30,361, 12[r]]

1 Or bid your father split the earth in two
2 ~~A[?chasm] in the earth will open at your word~~
up
open ~~for~~ the heavens
3 And swallow us all – ~~or heaven itself will~~ open
chariots
4 ~~and charots~~ & horses come in the air.
5 And chariots wheel upon the clouds of heaven
Until the
6 ~~And the horse~~ chariots wheel upon the clouds.
7 ~~Call out, call out,~~
Call out
8 Call out ~~aloud~~ – your father is asleep
9 or he would never let his son be mocked

Then again in his natural voice
10 ~~But a young man throws the crowd aside~~
11 Who is this that shoulders through the crowd
~~has~~ has not yet been bitted
12 Like a young horse, that ~~never had been bitted~~
13 or like a ~~fool~~ foal that has seen the hunters pass
14 And races in the field.

Lazerus.
He raised me up
15 I am the man that died & I was raised up
16 I am called Lazerus

Christ.
[?You're] not Curst
17 ~~Considering that I raised you from the dead~~ dead
18 ~~You will not mock at me,~~ buried & raised up
19 Because you died, ~~&~~ were ~~raised up again~~
20 You will not mock at me.

9 Song from 11[v], ll. 2–9, is inserted here by arrow.
12–14 Superseded by 11[v], ll. 10–12, as indicated by arrow.

[NLI 30,361, 12v]

[NLI 30,361, 12^{v}]

Lazerus.

1 ~~For four whole days~~
For four whole days
2 I had been dead, & I was lying still
3 in an old comfortable cave up
4 When you came upon the mountainside
5 And dragged me to the light

Christ.

I called your name
6 Lazerus come out, I said, & came out
7 Bound hand & foot, your face bound up in a cloth.

Lazerus.

8 You took my death give me your death instead

Christ

9 I gave you life.

Lazerus

But death is what I ask
10 Alive I never could escape your love
11 And when I sickened ~~to my [?]~~ towards my death I thought
12 I ll to the desert or chuckle in a whole
13 A ghost a solitary thing & then

1–8 Bracketed to indicate substitution for 13^{r}, ll. 1–11.

6 "& [you] came out" for sense?

12 "whole" for "hole"?

13 Line leading off to indicate how the sequence of ll. 9–13 follows 13^{r}, ll. 12–15, and anticipates 14^{r}.

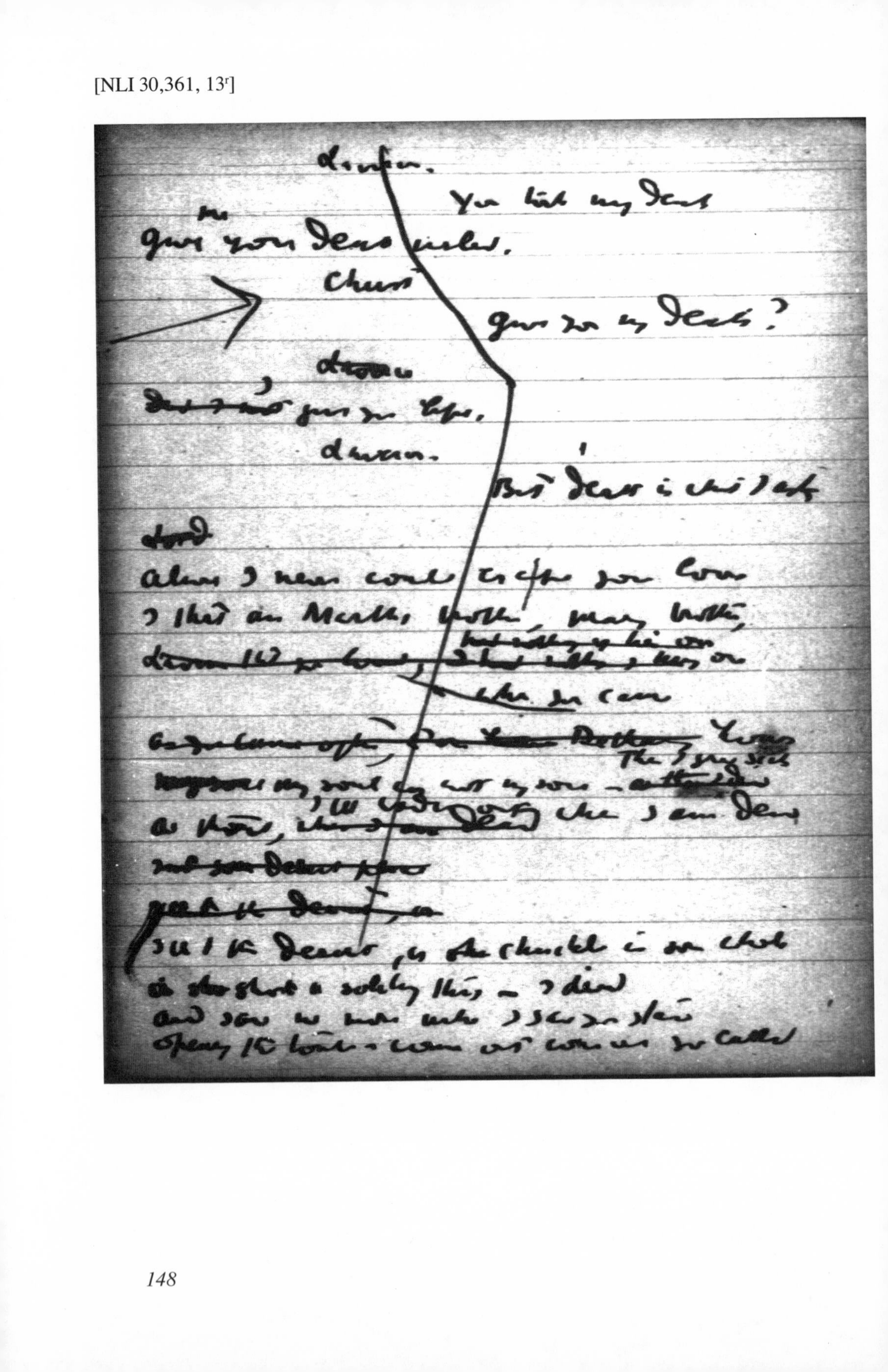

[NLI 30,361, 13[r]]

[NLI 30,361, 13[r]]

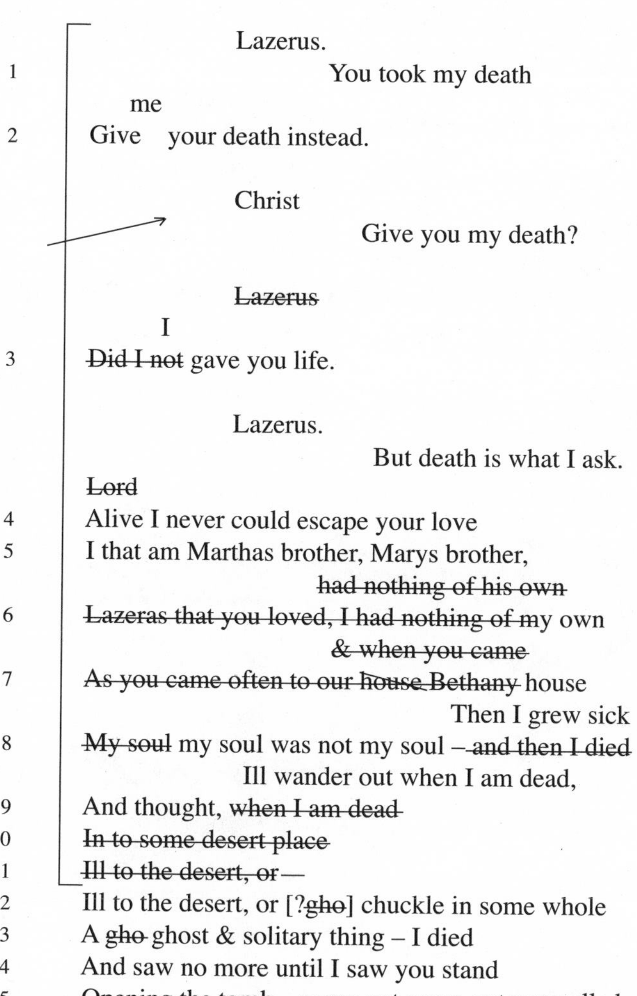

Lazerus.

1 You took my death

me

2 Give your death instead.

Christ

Give you my death?

~~Lazerus~~

I

3 ~~Did I not~~ gave you life.

Lazerus.

But death is what I ask.

~~Lord~~

4 Alive I never could escape your love

5 I that am Marthas brother, Marys brother,

~~had nothing of his own~~

6 ~~Lazeras that you loved, I had nothing of m~~y own

~~& when you came~~

7 ~~As you came often to our ~~house~~ Bethany~~ house

Then I grew sick

8 ~~My soul~~ my soul was not my soul – ~~and then I died~~

Ill wander out when I am dead,

9 And thought, ~~when I am dead~~

10 ~~In to some desert place~~

11 ~~Ill to the desert, or –~~

12 Ill to the desert, or [?~~gho~~] chuckle in some whole

13 A ~~gho~~ ghost & solitary thing – I died

14 And saw no more until I saw you stand

15 Opening the tomb – come out come out you called

---

2 Arrow indicates insertion of bracketed material from 12[v], ll. 1–8.

15 Followed by interpolation of 12[v], ll. 9–13.

[NLI 30,361, 14^r]

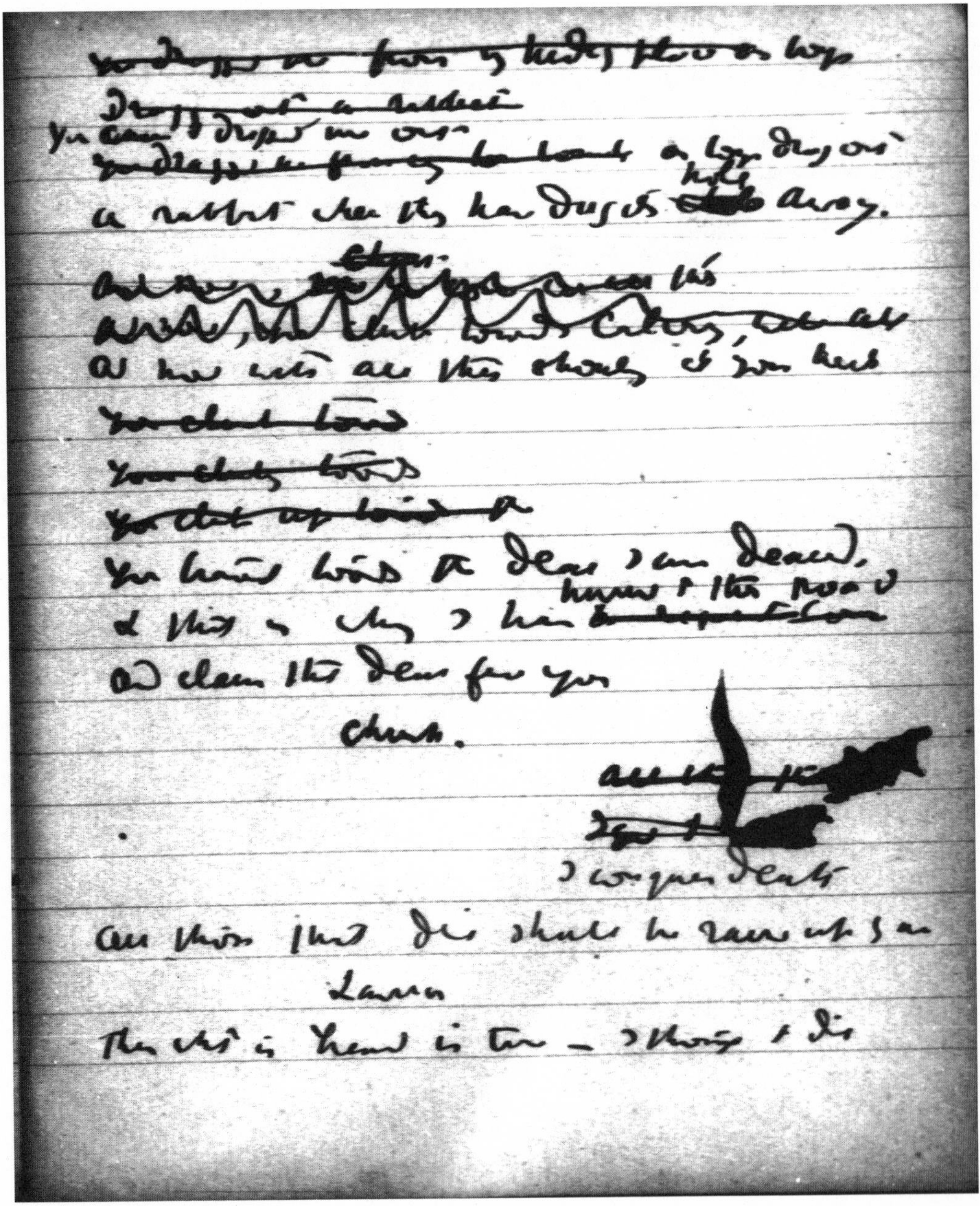

[NLI 30,361, 14r]

1 ~~You dragged me from my hiding place as~~ boys
2 ~~Dragg out a rabbit~~
3 You came & dragged me out
4 ~~You dragged me from my ho tomb~~ as boys drag out
hole
5 A rabbit when they have dug its ~~whole~~ away.

~~Christ~~
6 And now, ~~now you come with all~~ this
7 ~~And now, you climb towards Calvary, with all~~
8 And now with all this shouting at your heels
~~You climb towards~~
~~Your climbing towards~~
~~You climb up towards the~~
9 You travel towards the death I am denied.
hurried to this road
10 & that is why I have ~~a right to come~~
11 And claim that death from you

Christ.
~~All those that [?death]~~
~~I go to [?death]~~
I conquer death
12 All those that die shall be raised up by me

Lazerus
13 Then what is heard is true – I thought to die

[NLI 30,361, 15r]

[NLI 30,361, 15[r]]

I thought to die
When my allotted years ran out again
And that being gone you could not hinder it
~~But now you will take~~
But now you will quench the solitude of death
~~And will with your own light that corner~~
~~And full with your~~
That you may full with your own light that corner
Where I had thought I might lie safe for ever.

Christ
I do my fathers will.

Lazerus.
~~And not your own~~
~~And I was free four days – four days being~~ dead
And not your own
~~You are not~~
~~And those that love~~
And not your own
And I was free four days – four days being dead
Climb up to ~~Calvry~~ Calvary ~~but do not gaze~~
turn your eyes
From Lazerus that cannot find a tomb –
Although he search the world – make way
~~For Lazerus that has the world to search~~

---

6 "will" for "fill"?
7 "full" for "fill"?
8 "full" for "fill"?

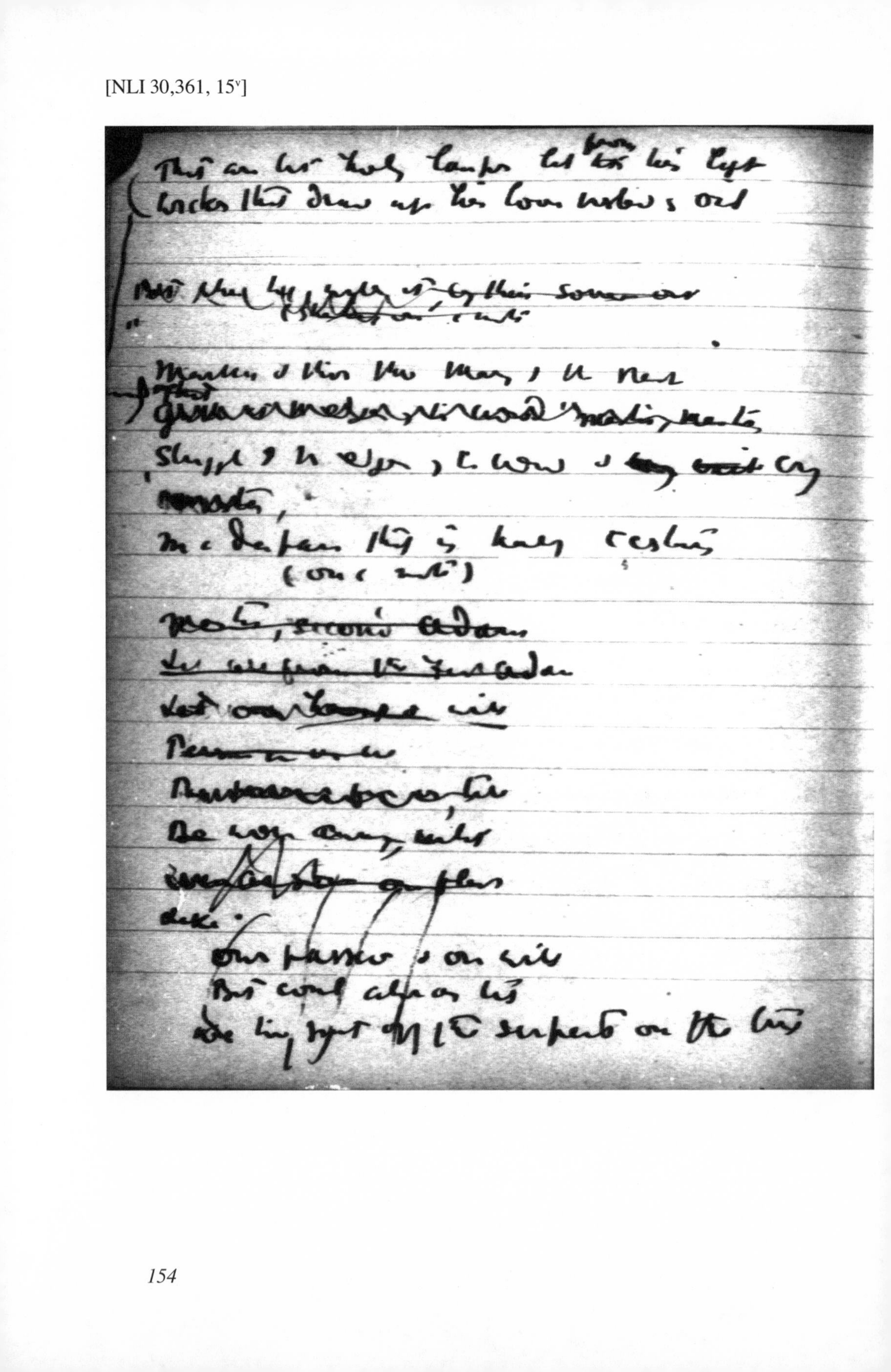

[NLI 30,361, 15v]

[NLI 30,361, 15v]

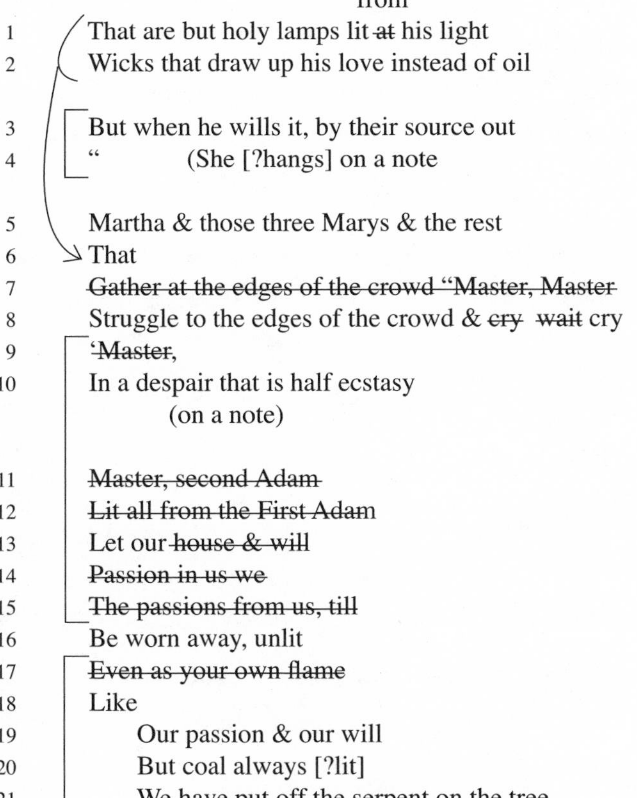

from
That are but holy lamps lit ~~at~~ his light
Wicks that draw up his love instead of oil

But when he wills it, by their source out
"   (She [?hangs] on a note

Martha & those three Marys & the rest
That
~~Gather at the edges of the crowd "Master, Master~~
Struggle to the edges of the crowd & ~~cry~~ ~~wait~~ cry
~~'Master,~~
In a despair that is half ecstasy
(on a note)

~~Master, second Adam~~
~~Lit all from the First Adam~~
Let our ~~house & will~~
~~Passion in us we~~
~~The passions from us, till~~
Be worn away, unlit
~~Even as your own flame~~
Like
Our passion & our will
But coal always [?lit]
We have put off the serpent on the tree.

1–2 Supersede canceled lines 6–7, as indicated by bracketing and arrows. The oil and wick metaphor anticipates Yeats's use later on, in the same manuscript notebook, when he composes "Solomon and the Witch" in NLI 30,361, on folios 30v and 31v. See note below on the exit sequence of *Calvary* in this second draft.

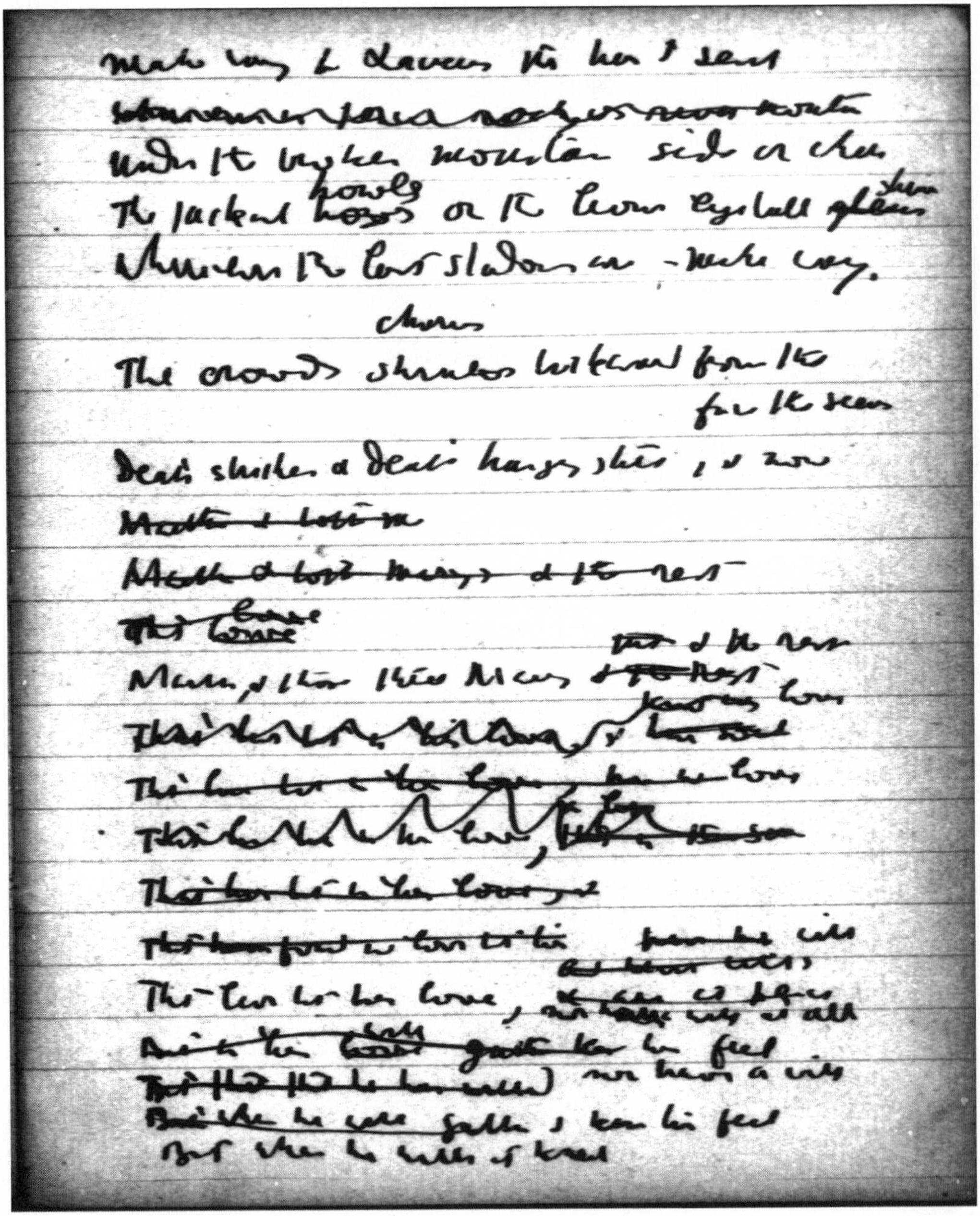

[NLI 30,361, 16r]

[NLI 30,361, 16r]

1 Make way for Lazerus that has to send
2 ~~Where ever in peace rock, or river mountain~~
3 Under the broken mountain side or where
howls shines
4 The jackal ~~howls~~ or the lions eyeball ~~gleams~~
5 Where ever the lost shadows are – make way.

Chorus
6 The crowd shrinks backward from the
face that seems
7 Death stricken & death hungry still, & now
8 ~~Martha & both M~~
9 ~~Martha & both Marys & the rest~~
~~love~~
10 ~~That lowe~~
~~that~~ & the rest
11 Martha, & those three Marys ~~& the rest~~
~~know his love~~
12 ~~That live but in his love, & his soul~~
13 ~~That live but in his love, have no~~ love
~~& love~~
14 ~~That live but in his love, that in their soul~~
15 ~~That live but in his love, &~~
16 ~~That have found no love but his~~ ~~from his~~ will
~~And never wills~~
17 That live but his love, ~~& are at peace~~
nor have a will at all
will
18 ~~But in his love gather kiss~~ his feet
nor have a will
19 ~~But that that he has willed~~
20 ~~But when he will gather~~ & kiss his feet
21 But when he wills it kneel

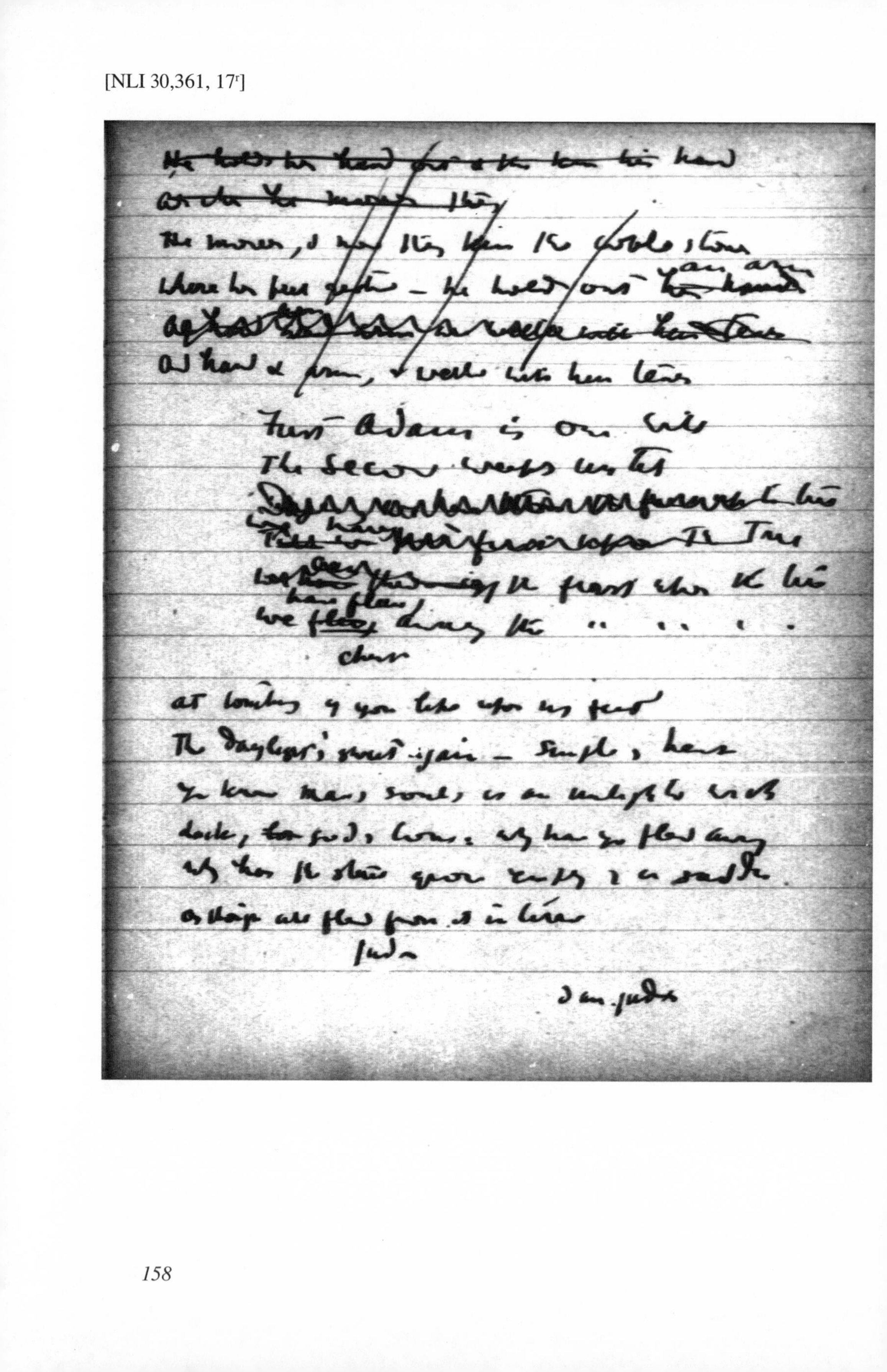

[NLI 30,361, 17r]

[NLI 30,361, 17[r]]

~~He holds his hand out & they kiss his hand~~
~~And when he moves they~~
He moves, & now they kiss the coble stones
an arm
Where his feet rested – he holds out ~~his hands~~
~~arm~~
~~A hand and arm was wetted with their tears~~
And hand & arm, & wetted with their tears

First Adam is our will
The Second weeps until
~~[?Dying] we have thrown the fruit upon the tree~~
We have
~~Till we put fruit upon The~~ Tree
can
We ~~have~~ thrown off the fruit upon the tree
have flung
We ~~fling~~ away the " " " "

Christ
At touching of your lips upon my feet
The daylights sweet again – simple of heart
You know mans souls as an unlighted wick
Lacking ~~lov~~ gods love: why have you fled away
Why has the street grown empty of a sudden
As though all fled from it in terror

Judas
I am Judas

13 Four ditto marks repeat the words "fruit upon the tree" from l. 12.

[NLI 30,361, 18r]

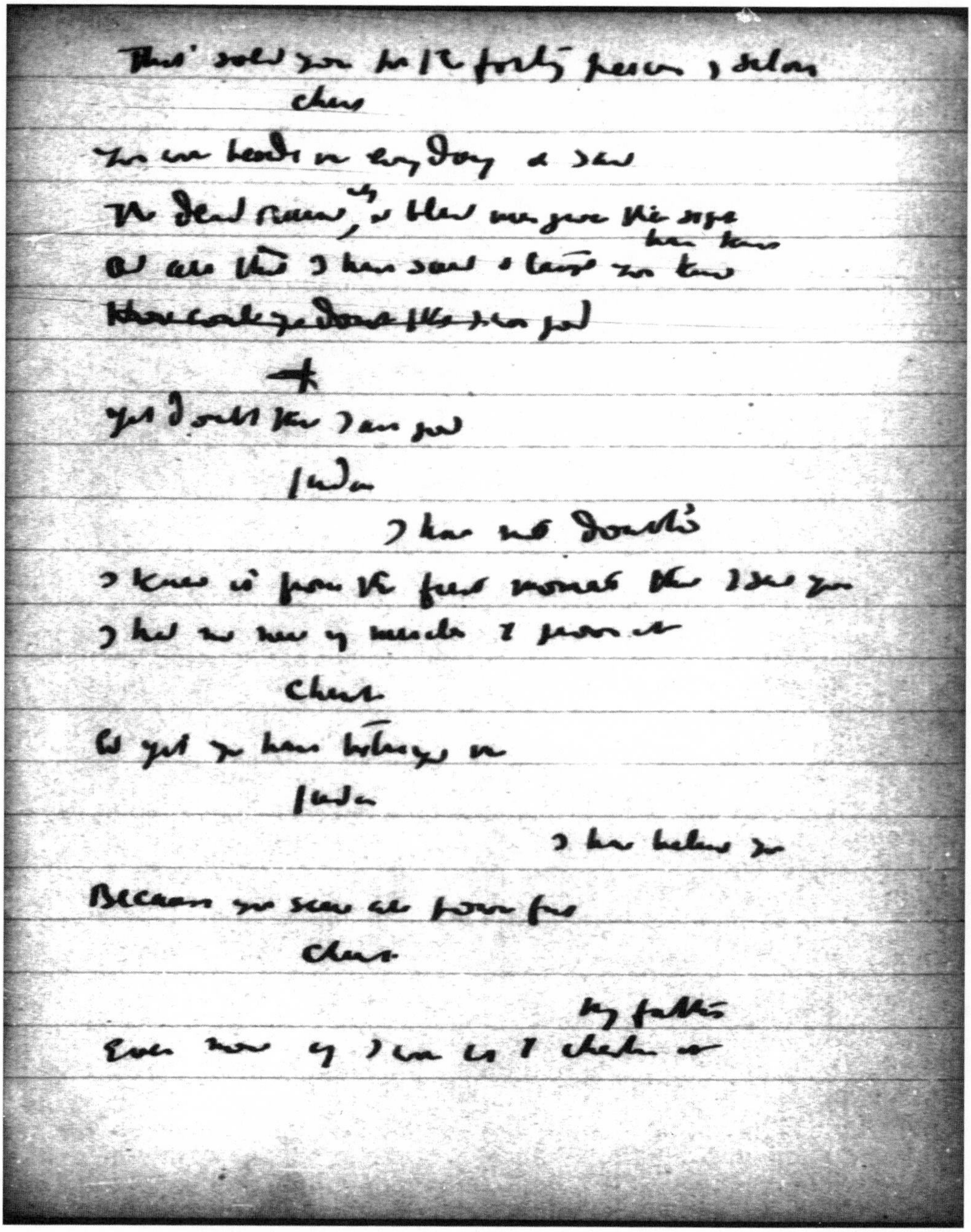

Tho' sold you for the forty pieces of silver

Christ

You were beside me every day & saw

The dead raised up, & blind men given their sight

And all that I have said & taught you know

~~Where could you doubt that I am god~~

+

Yet doubt that I am god

Judas

I have not doubted

I knew it from the first moment that I saw you

I had no need of miracles to prove it

Christ

And yet you have betrayed me

Judas

I have betrayed you

Because you seemed all powerful

Christ

My father

Even now if I were but to whisper it

[NLI 30,361, 18[r]]

1 That sold you for the forty peices of silver.

Christ

2 You were beside me every day & saw

up

3 The dead raised, & blind men given their sight

have known

4 And all that I have said & taught you knew

5 ~~How could you doubt that I~~ was god

~~J~~

6 Yet doubt that I am god

Judas

I have not doubted

7 I knew it from the first moment that I saw you

8 I had no need of miracles to prove it

Christ

9 And yet you betrayed me

Judas

I have betrayed you

10 Because you seemed all powerful.

Christ

My father

11 Even now if I were but to whisper it

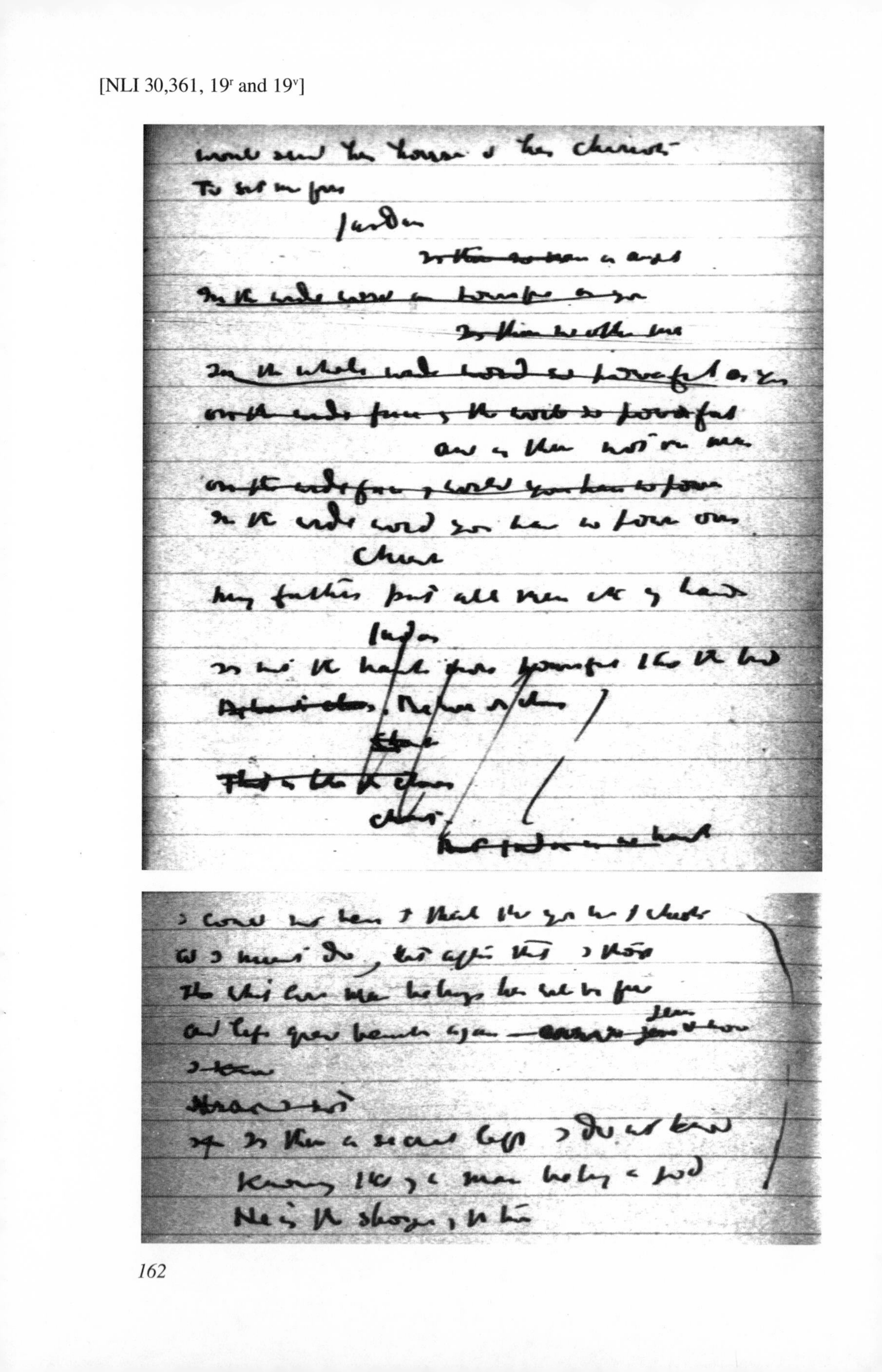

[NLI 30,361, 19^{r} and 19^{v}]

[NLI 30,361, 19r and 19v]

[19r]

1 Would send his horses & his chariots
2 To set me free

Judas

~~Is there no man~~ or angel
3 ~~In the wide world as powerful as you~~
~~Is there no other man~~
4 ~~In the whole wide world so powerful as you~~
5 ~~On the wide face of the world so powerful~~
And is there not one man
6 ~~On the wide face of world you have no power~~
7 In the wide world you have no power over

Christ

8 My father put all men in my hands

Judas

9 Is not the hawk more powerful than the birds
10 ~~[?Between] – its claws~~ [?Between] its claws

~~Christ~~

11 ~~That is [?between] its claws~~

Christ.

~~But Judas is no hawk~~

[19v]

1 I could not bear to think that you have to whisper
2 And I must die, but after that I thought
3 ~~The~~ What ever man betrays him will be free
Jesus
4 And life grew bearable again – ~~come in Jesus & now~~
5 ~~I knew~~
{H}
6 ~~{I}ave I not~~
7 ~~If~~ Is there a secret left I do not know
8 Knowing that if a man betray a god
9 He is the stronger of the two.

19v, 1–7 Lines bracketed for insertion at 20r, ll. 2–11.
1 "have [but] to whisper" for sense?

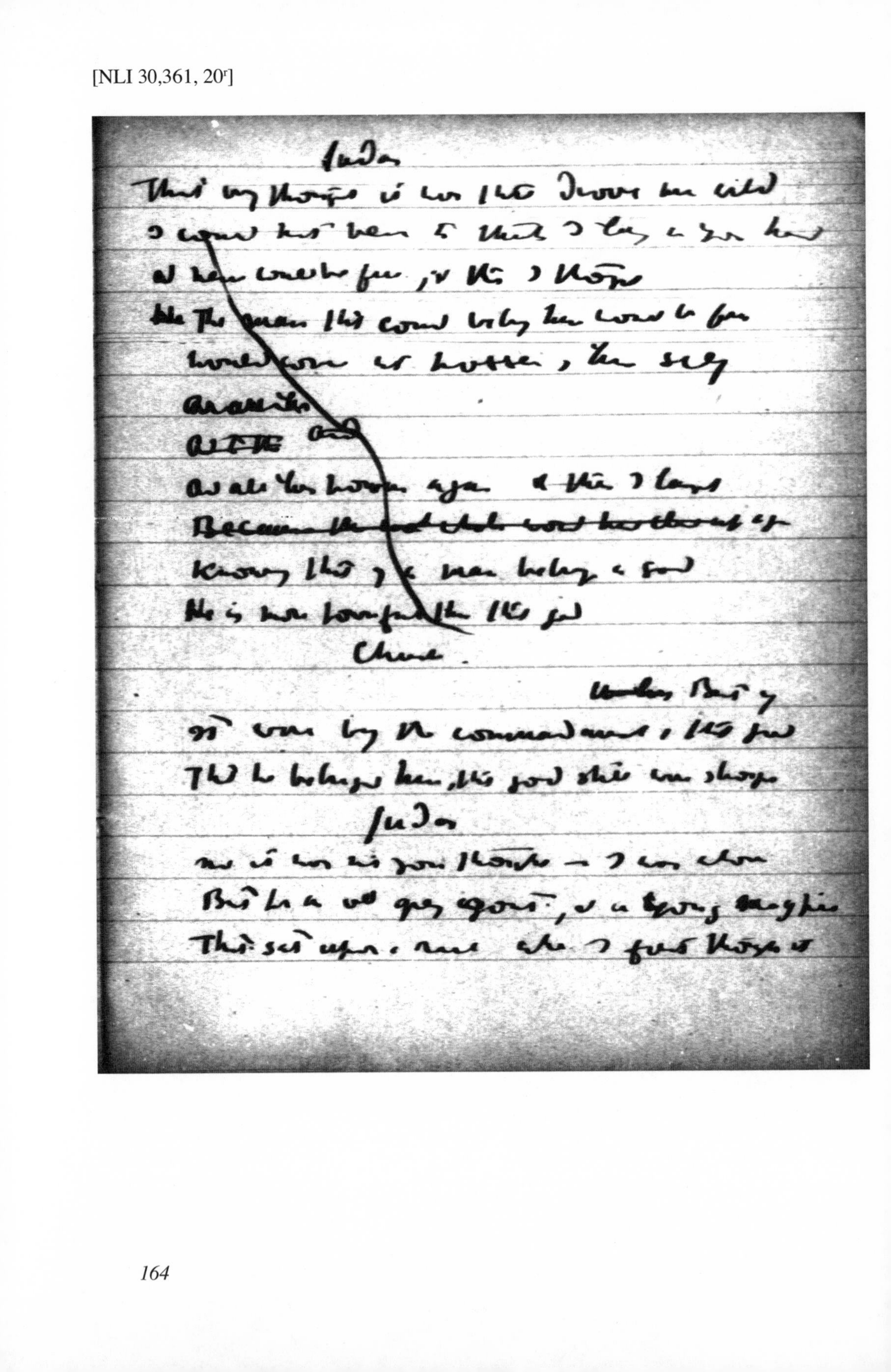

[NLI 30,361, 20r]

[NLI 30,361, 20r]

Judas

That very thought it was that drove me wild
I could not bear to think I lay in your hand
And never would be free, & that I thought
~~He~~ The man that could betray him would be free
Would come into possession of him self
~~And all his~~
~~And to the~~ And
And all his power again & then I laughed
~~Because the worl whole world had closed up~~ again
Know that if a man betray a god
He is more powerful than that god

Christ.

~~Unless~~ But if
It were by the commandment of that god
That he betrayed him, that god still were stronger

Judas

No it was not your thought – I was alone
But for an old grey goat, & a young magpie
That sat upon a rail when I first thought it

[NLI 30,361, 21[r]]

[NLI 30,361, 21^{r}]

Christ

on the hour
But my betrayal was decreed ~~the day~~
When the foundations of the world were laid

Judas
~~Yes – yes~~ –
~~I had thought of that~~ –
Yes – yes – that you would be betrayed by someone
I had thought of that – but not that I should do it
I the man Judas born on such a day
In such a village, such & such for parents
~~Not that I d go with such a coat~~
~~Nor that I do drest out of~~
Nor that I do, with my old coat upon me
To the high priest & chuckle to myself
As people chuckle when alone, & that I do it
For forty peices & no more no less
or a sent message
And neither with a nod, or look, ~~or message sent~~
But with a kiss upon your cheek – I did it
I Judas & no other man & now
me
You cannot even save ~~my soul.~~

Christ.

[illegible]

The Roman Soldiers

[illegible]

Second soldier

We [illegible] keep the [illegible] — They are [illegible]

They are always carrying something

Third soldier

~~[illegible]~~

[illegible]

~~[illegible]~~

[illegible] is peace

There is no one but ourselves [illegible] here

Christ

And who are you that ask your God for nothing

1 Soldier

We are the gamblers & when you are dead

We'll settle who is to have that cloak of yours

By throwing dice.

2 soldier

[NLI 30,361, 22r]

Christ

1 Go – go from me

First Roman Soldier

2 Now he must stay – He must hold up the cross

Second soldier

3 We ll keep the rest away – They are too persistent
4 They are always wanting something.

Third soldier

5 ~~With nobody but us & Judas here~~
~~[?]~~ ~~no one here~~
6 ~~By Judas & our selves you will die~~
~~Yet can~~ die in peace
7 There is no one but ourselves & Judas here.

Christ

8 And who are you that ask your god for nothing

{S}
1 {R}oldier

9 We are the gamblers & when you are dead
10 Well settle who is to have that cloak of yours
11 By throwing dice.

2 soldier

[NLI 30,361, 23r]

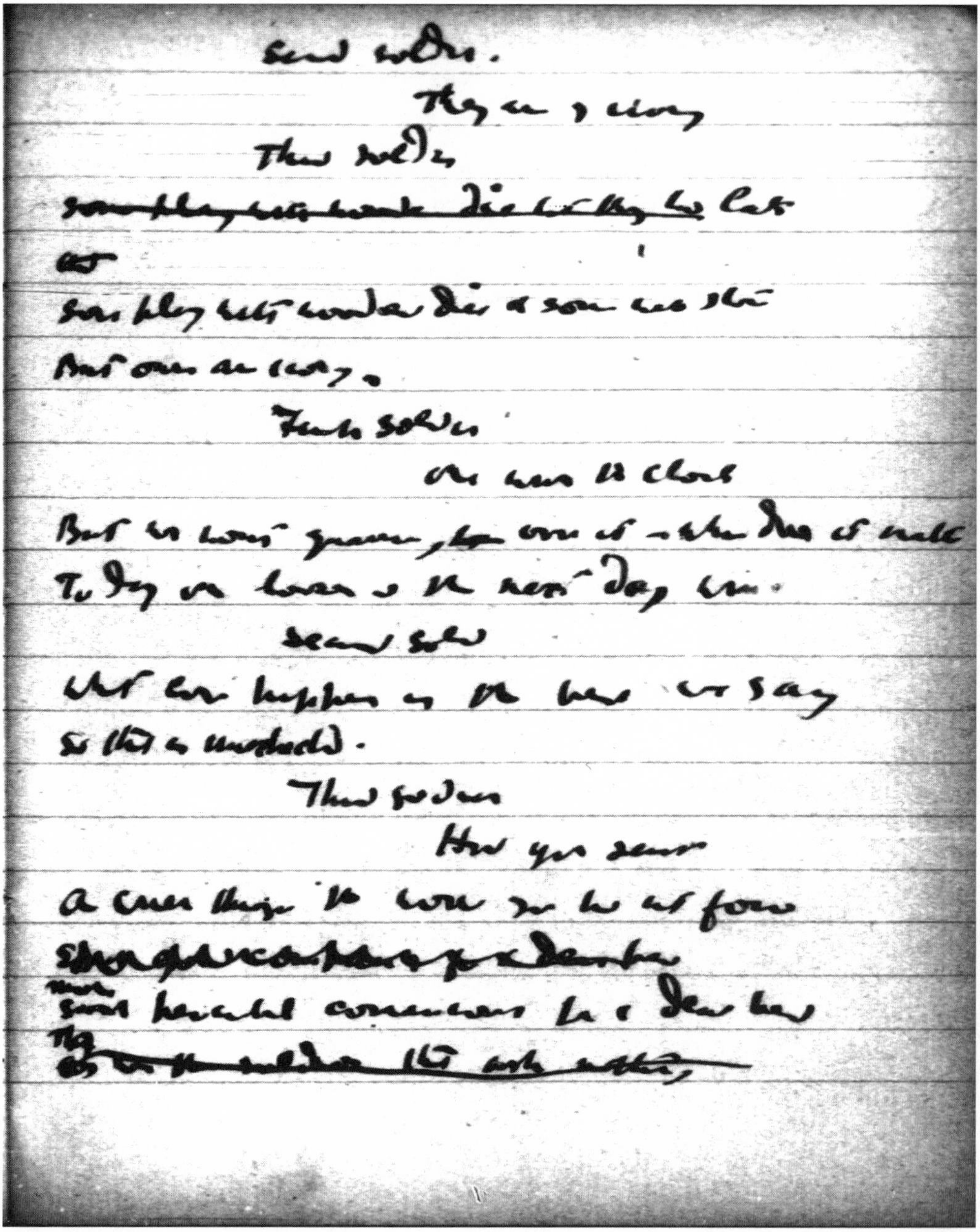

[NLI 30,361, 23^{r}]

Second soldier.
They are of ivory

Third Soldier
~~Some play with wooden dice but they don't last~~
~~And~~
Some play with wooden dice & some with stone
But ours are ivory.

First Soldier
One wins the cloak
But we wont quarrel, [~~?~~] over it – what does it matter
To day one loses & the next day wins.

Second Soldier
What ever happens is the best we say
So that is unexpected.

Third Soldier
Had you sent
A crier through the world you had not found
~~Even good companions for a death bed~~
More
~~Good~~ peaceable companions for a death bed
~~Than~~
~~As are these soldiers that ask nothing~~

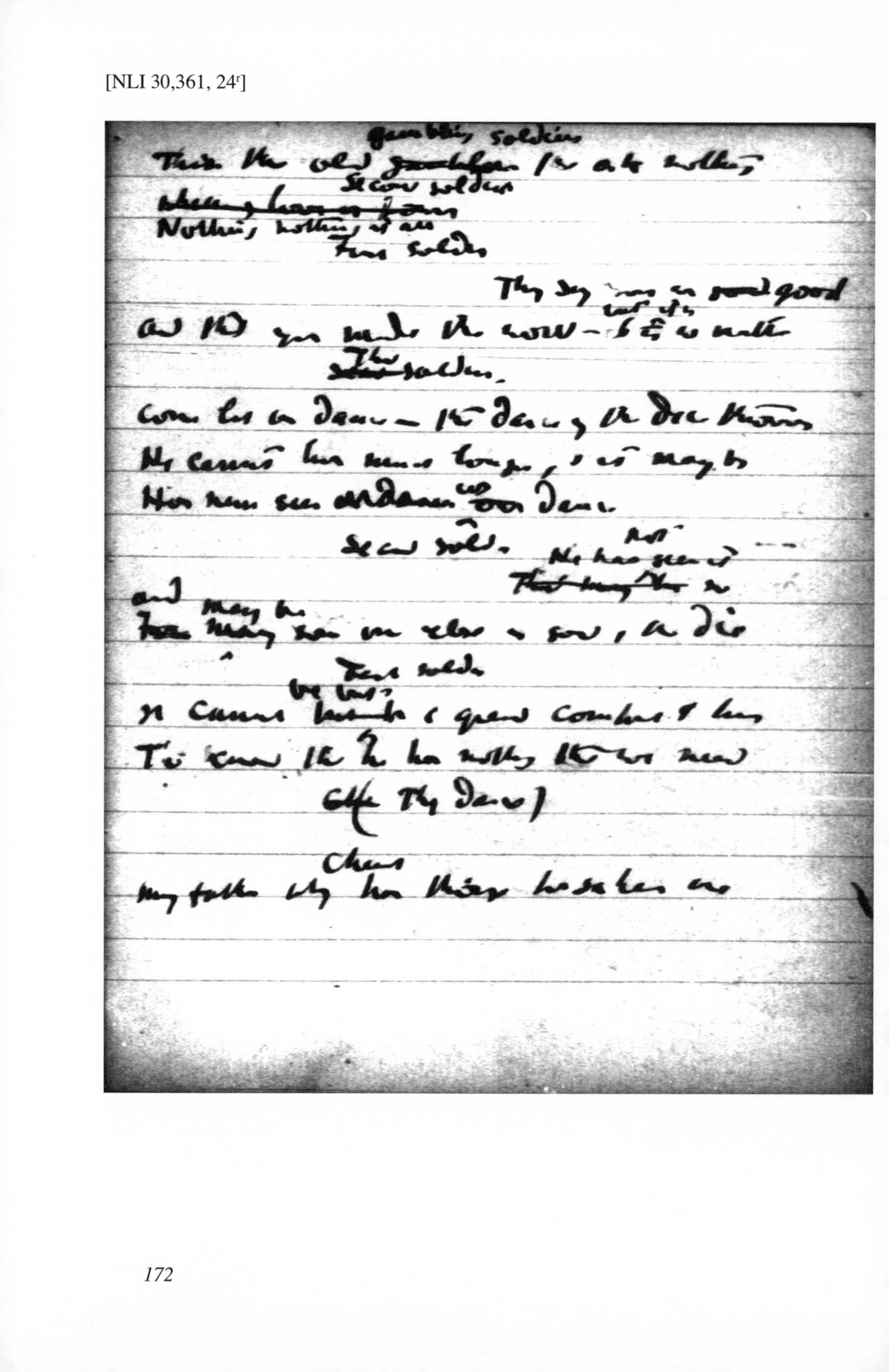

[NLI 30,361, 24r]

[NLI 30,361, 24[r]]

gambling soldiers
1 Than these old ~~gamblers~~ that ask nothing

Second Soldier
2 ~~Whether I have a power~~
3 Nothing nothing at all

First Soldier
They say you are ~~god~~ good
but it is
4 And that you made the world – ~~it is~~ no matter
Third
~~Second~~ Soldier.
5 Come let us dance—the dance of the dice throwers
6 He cannot live much longer, & it may be
us
7 Has never seen ~~us dance~~ ~~our~~ dance
^

Second Soldier not
He has ^ seen it
~~This may be so~~
8 And may be
9 ~~For~~ ~~may~~ some one else is god of the dice
^

First Soldier
be but
10 It cannot ~~but~~ ^ ~~be~~ a great comfort to him
11 To know that he has nothing that we need

~~Chr~~ (They dance)

Christ
12 My father why has though forsaken me

---

12 "though" for "thou"?

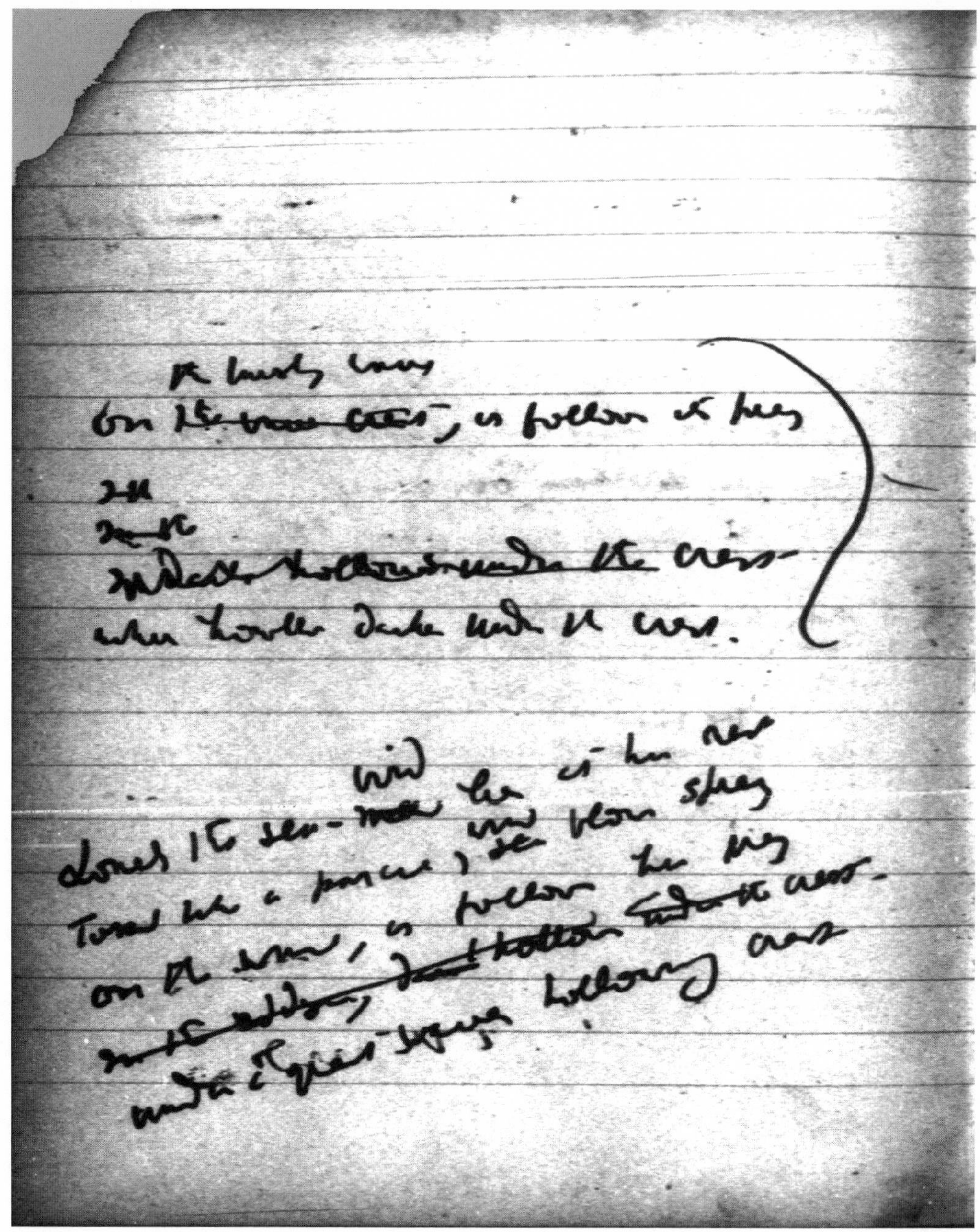

[NLI 30,361, 24^v^]

the cresting wave
On the ~~waves crest~~, it follows its prey
I ll
~~In the~~
~~In dark hollows under the~~ crest
When howlls darken under the crest.

bird
Lonely the sea-~~mew~~ lies at his rest
wind
Tossed like a parcel of ~~sea~~ blown spray
On the wind, it follows his prey
~~In the eddying dark hollows under~~ its crest –
Under the great waves hollowing crest

1–5 Partially inscribed at right with drawn line directing substitution for canceled ll. 3–6 on folio 25^r^.

5 "howlls" for "hollows"? See l. 9.

6–10 Revise ll. 1–5 still further to supersede on 25^r^, ll. 1–6; this sequence of events anticipates the further amendment made in Harvard(C), 12^r^, ll. 9–12.

[NLI 30,361, 25^{r}]

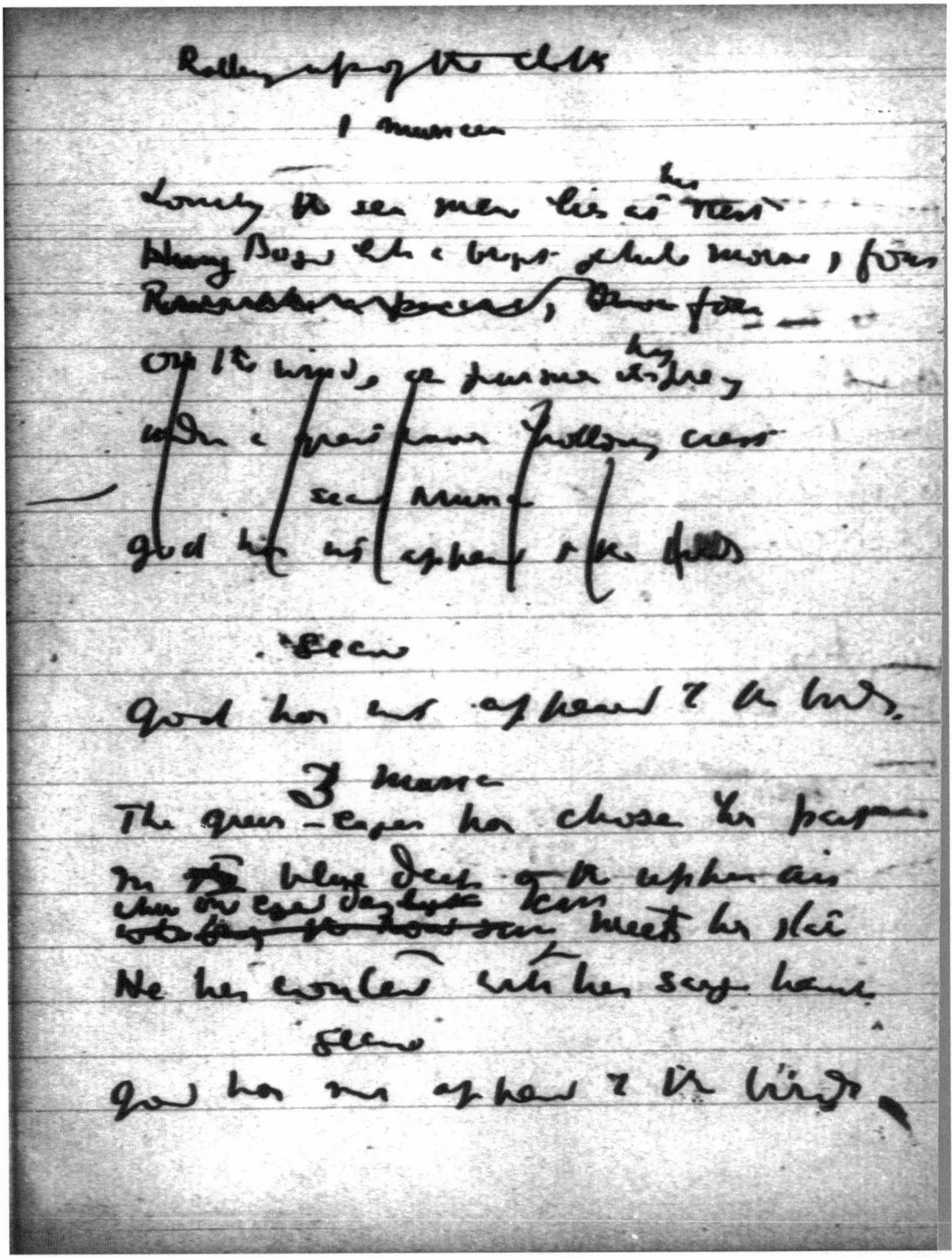

[NLI 30,361, 25[r]]

Rolling up of the cloth

1 Musician

his
Lonely the sea mew lies at nest
~~Hung~~ Boyed like a bright & white morsel of foam
~~Rises like a parcel of driven foam~~
his
On the wind, or pursuing its prey
Under a great waves hollowing crest

Second Musician
God has not appeared to the birds

Second
God has not appeared to the birds.

{3/1} Musician
The geer-eagle has chosen his part
In ~~the~~ blue deep of the upper air
Where one eyed day~~light~~ can
{t/ts}
~~Where only the noon sun~~ ^ mee{t/ts} his stare
He has content with his savage heart

Second
God has not appeared to the birds.

3–6 Incorporate the amendments made on 24[v] as indicated by drawn lines on both pages.

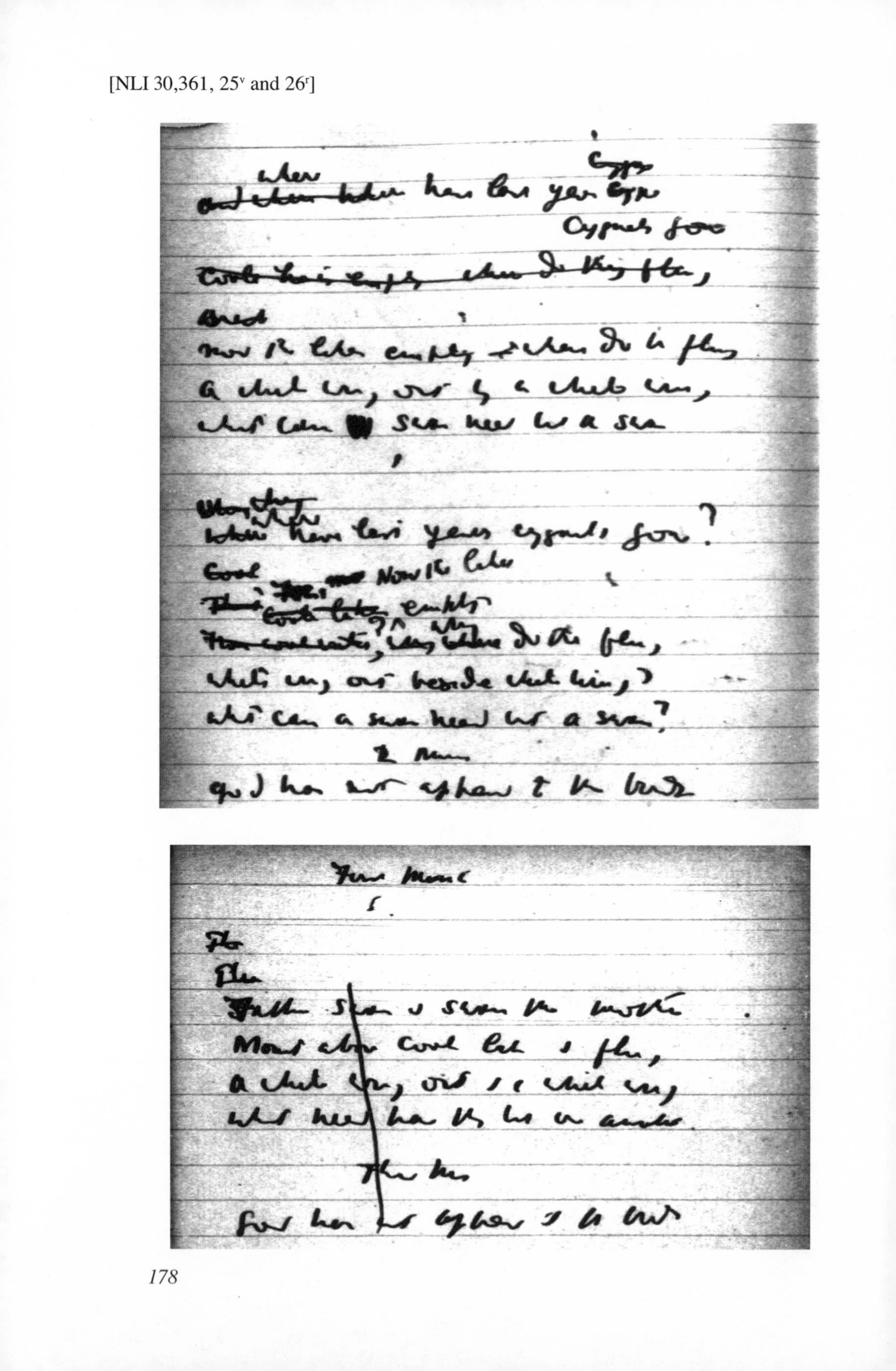

[NLI 30,361, 25^{v} and 26^{r}]

[NLI 30,361, 25v and 26r]

[25v]

where ~~cygn~~
1 ~~And where wher~~ have last years ~~cyn~~
cygnets gone
2 ~~Coole lake is empty where do they fly~~
~~[?]~~
3 Now the lakes empty – where do they fly
4 A white wing out by a white wing
5 what can [~~?a~~] swan need but a swan

1
6 ~~They~~ ~~Why~~
Where
7 ~~Where~~ have last years cygnets gone?
8 ~~Cool~~
9 ~~That~~ ~~For~~ ~~mo~~ Now the lakes
~~Coole lakes~~ ^ empty
{?} Why
10 ~~From cool water~~ {,} ~~Why~~ ~~Where~~ do they fling
11 White wing out beside white wing?
12 What can a swan need but a swan?
{2 1} Music
13 God has not appeared to the birds

[26r]

First Music
1 ~~The~~
2 ~~The~~
3 Father swan & swan the mother
4 Mount above Coole lake & fling
5 A white wing out of a white wing
6 What need have they but one another.

Third Mus
7 God has not appeared to the birds

25v Amends the musicians' dialogue begun on 26r.

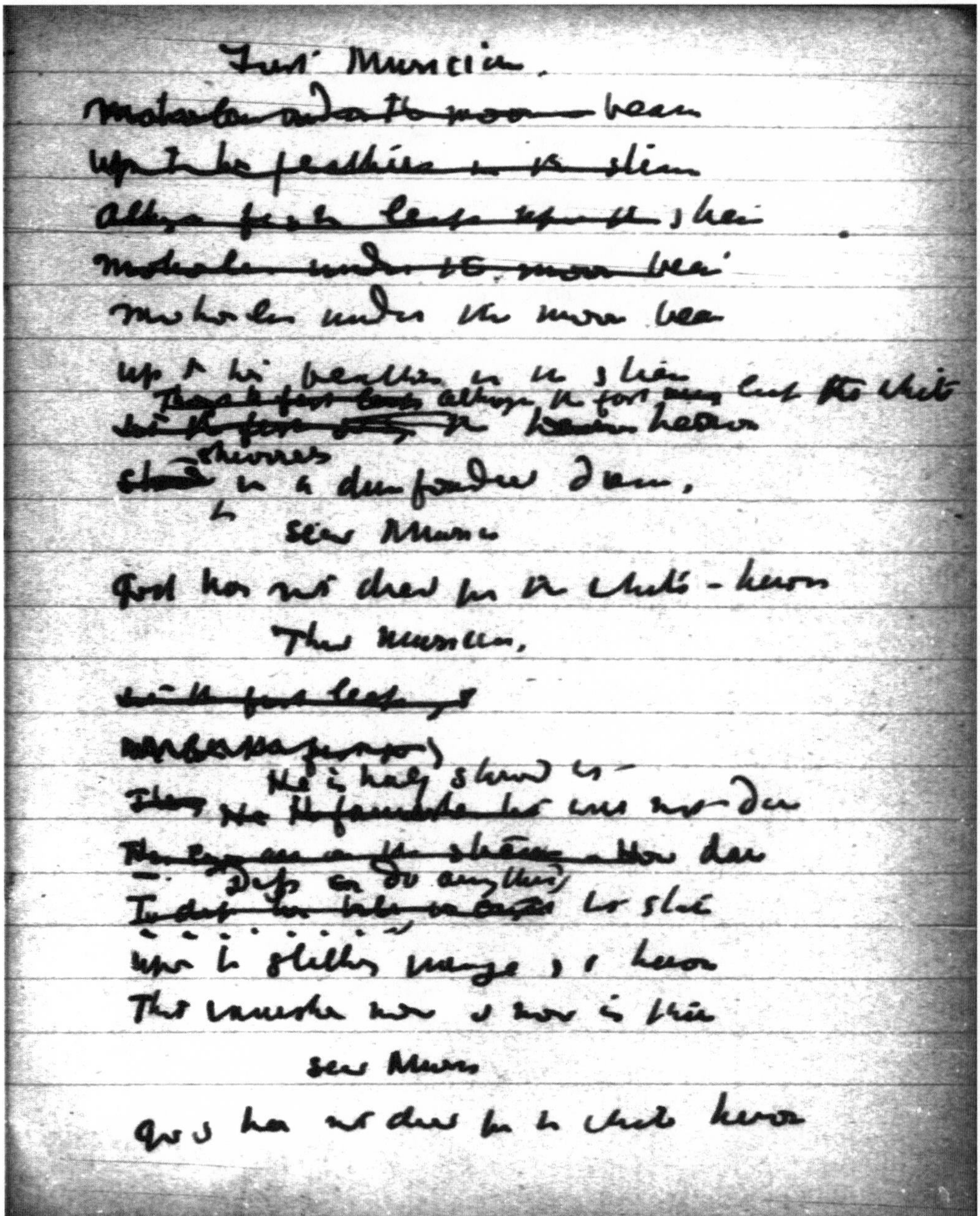

[NLI 30,361, 27^{r} and 28^{r}]

[27^{r}]

[28^{r}]

First Musician.

~~Motionless under the moon~~ beam
~~Up to his feathers in the~~ stream
~~Although fish leap upon the~~ stream
~~Motionless under the moon beam~~
Motionless under the moon beam
Up to his feathers in the stream
~~Though the fish leap~~ Although the fish ~~neep~~ leap the white
~~Let the fish leap~~ the ~~herron~~ hearon
shivers
~~Stands~~ ^ in a dumfounded dream.

Second Musician

God has not died for the white - heron

Third Musician.

~~Let the fish leap, &~~
~~[?He] lets the fish go by~~
He is half starved but
~~They He He famished but~~ will not dare
~~His eyes are on the stream – How~~ dare
Dip or do anything
~~To dip his bill, or ought~~ but stare
Upon the glittering image of a heron
That vanishes now & now is there

Second Music

God has not died for the white heron

Folio 27^{r} is blank but for the two small geometric figures shown above: the left-hand figure is a three-dimensional design for a visor or mask; the right-hand figure is a two-dimensional design for the same. The verso bears the sketch of an open door and dark interior, evidently related to the exit sequence. See the frontispiece to this section.

28^{r}, 15 Marks beneath the canceled phrase "To dip his bill" indicate reinstatement.

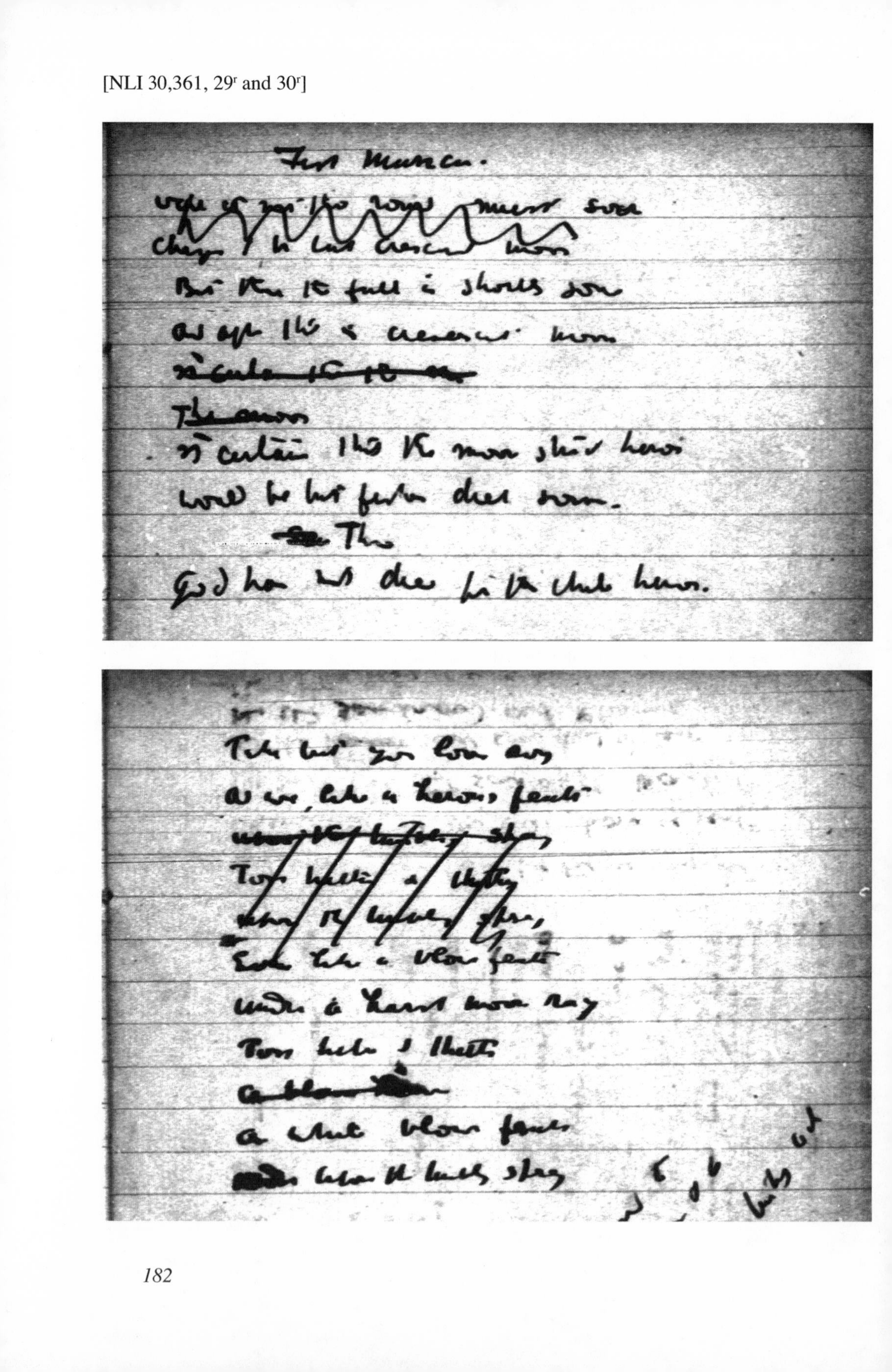

[NLI 30,361, 29^r and 30^r]

[NLI 30,361, 29r and 30r]

[29r]

First Musician.

Were it not that round must soon
Change to the late crescent moon
But that the full is shortly gone
And after that the crescent moon
~~Its certain that the moon~~
~~The moon~~
Its certain that the moon struck heron
Would be but fishes diet soon.

~~Sec~~ Third

God has not died for the white heron.

[30r]

Take but your love away
And we, like a herons feather
~~Upon the tumbling spray~~
Toss hither & thither
upon the tumbling spray
Even like a blown feather
Under a harsh moon ray
Toss hither & thither
~~A blown heron~~
A white blown feather
~~Under~~ Upon the tumbling spray

29v Contains draft materials related to *The Player Queen* and to lines entered at the foot of 29r, likewise with no bearing on *Calvary*.

30r Anticipates the song worked out in Harvard(C), folios 6r–7r. At the foot, written diagonally, are more lines related to *The Player Queen*.

30r, 4 "Toss" for "Tossed"?

30r, 8 "Toss" for "Tossed"?

Folio 30v bears a draft of "Solomon and the Witch," followed on 31v (also sideways) by more of the poem: "As though out of a spider's eye . . . the lamp lack nor wick nor oil." This last relates to *Calvary*, in the second draft, on NLI 30,361, folio 15v, ll. 1–2. Intermittent *Player Queen* materials occur on 31r, thereafter followed by 32r–41r. The notebook concludes with *A People's Theatre* (42r–60r).

II. *Calvary*

Photographs and Transcriptions of the Early Manuscripts (1918–1919)

B. “On the Road to Calvary”—Third Draft and Complete Lyrics, Harvard(C)

1

On the Road to Calvary

Song for the ~~[illegible] & [illegible]~~ unfolding & folding of the cloth.

First musician

Motionless under the moon-beam
Up to his feathers in the stream
Although the fish leap the white heron
~~[illegible]~~ Shivers in a dumb-founded dream

Second musician

God has not died for the white ~~heron~~ herons

Third musician

X ~~He is half starved but cannot dare~~ Although half famished he'll not dare —
Dip or do anything but stare
Upon the glittering image of a heron
That now is lost & now is there.

Second musician

God has not died for the white heron.

First musician

But that the full is shortly gone
and After that is crescent moon
It's certain that the moon-~~[illegible]~~ crazed heron
Would be but fishes' diet soon.

Second musician

God has not died for the white heron.

[Harvard(C), 1^{r}]

1

On the Road to Calvary

Song for the ~~opening & closing~~ & unfolding & folding of
the cloth.

First Musician

Motionless under the moon-beam
Up to his feathers in the stream
Although the fish leap the white heron
Shivers
~~Shivered~~ in a dumb-founded dream

Second Musician

God has not died for the white ~~herron~~ heron

Third Musician

X ~~He is half starved but will not dare~~ *Although half famished*
Dip or do anything but stare *he ll not dare –*
Upon the glittering image of a heron
That vanishes now and now is there

Second Musician

God has not died for the white heron.

First Musician

But that the full is shortly gone
and
^After that is crescent moon
crazed
It s certain that the moon-~~struck~~ heron
Would be but fishers diet soon.

Second Musician

God has not died for the white heron.

---

2 The words "Up to" are elided together?

6 "X" indicates substitution of revision in the right margin (in pencil); both "X" and strikethrough are also in pencil.

[Harvard(C), 1v]

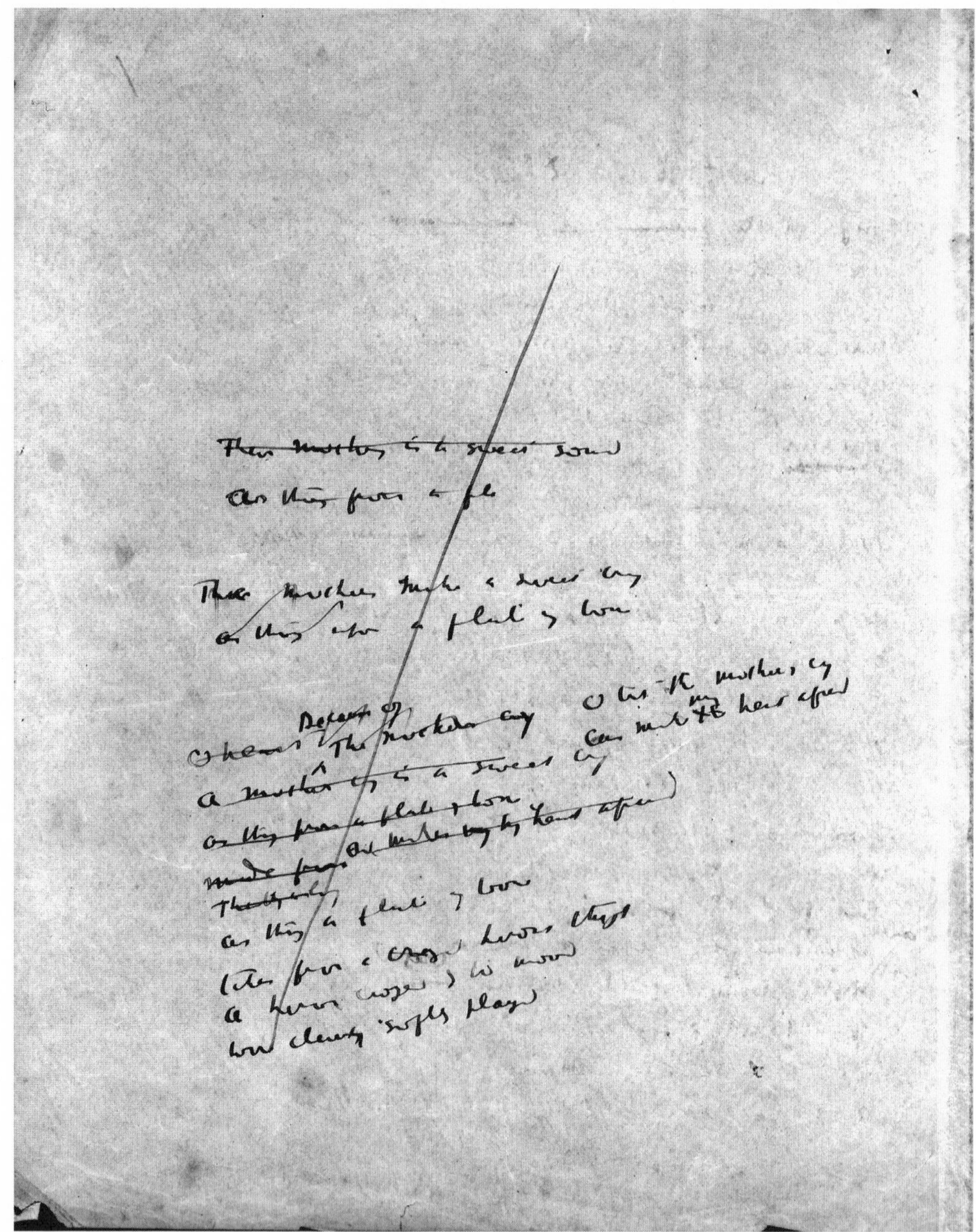

[Harvard(C), 1[v]]

~~Their mockery is a sweet sound~~
~~As though from a flu[te]~~

{e}
Th{eir} mockers make a sweet cry
As though upon a flute of bone

~~Because of~~
O heart ^ ~~The mockers cry~~ O but the mockers cry
my
~~A mocker's cry is a sw~~eet cry Can make ~~the~~ heart afraid
~~As though from a flute of bone~~
~~Made from And makes my my heart afraid~~
~~Though along~~
As though a flute of bone
Taken from a crazed herons thigh
A heron crazed by the moon
Were cleverly softly played

This draft of the lyric sung by the First Musician was canceled once it was incorporated into the fair copy of 2[r]; cf. ll. 5–13 here and ll. 21–26 there.

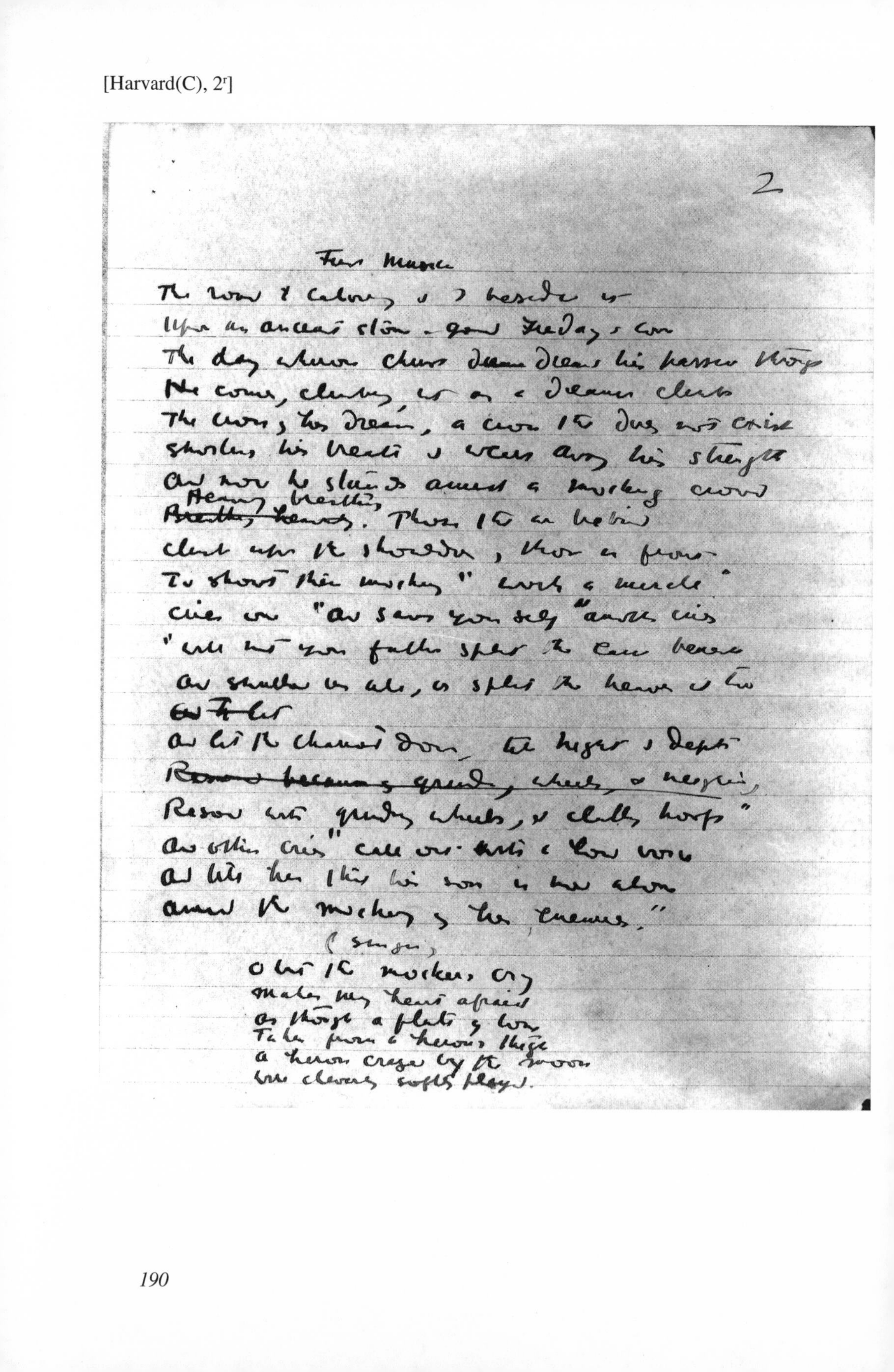

[Harvard(C), 2^{r}]

2

First Musician
The road to Calvary & I beside it
Upon an ancient stone – Good Friday s come
The day whereon Christ ~~dream~~ dreams his passion through
He comes, climbing, not as a dreamer climbs
The cross of his dream, a cross that does not exist
Shortens his breath and wears away his strength
And now he stands amid a mocking crowd
Heavily breathing
~~Breathing heavily.~~ Those that are behind
Climb upon the shoulders of those in front
To shout their mockery "Work a miracle"
Cries one "And save your self" another cries
"Will not your father split the [?earth] beneath
And swallow us all, or split the heavens in two
~~And [?then] let~~
And let the chariot down, till hight & depth
~~Resound because of grinding wheels, & neighing~~
Resound with grinding wheels, & [?clattering] hoofs"
An other cries "Call out with a [?loud] voice
And tell him that his son is now alone
Amid the mockery of his enemies."
(Singing)
O but the mockers cry
Makes my heart afraid
As though a flute of bone
Taken from a herons thigh
A heron crazed by the moon
Were cleverly softly played.

---

18 "loud" or, possibly, "low."
21–26 First composed on 1^{v}.

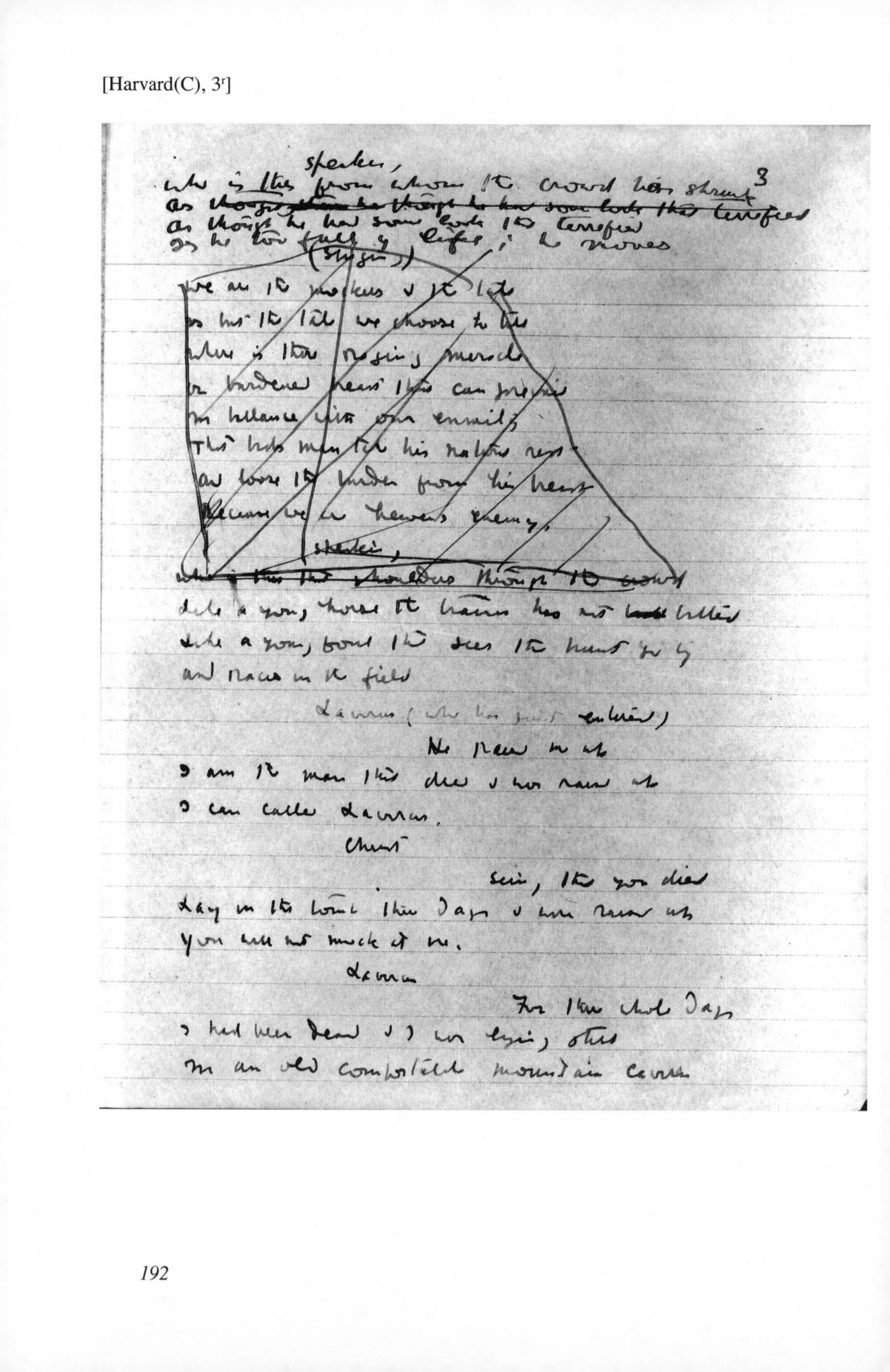

[Harvard(C), 3r]

[Harvard(C), 3r]

3

Speaking
Who is this from whom the crowd has shrunk
~~As though [?then] he though[t] he had some look that terrified~~
As though he had some look that terrified
Is he too full of life; he moves
(Singing)
We are the mockers & the tale
is but the tale we choose to tell
Where is there raging miracle
Or burdened heart that can prevail
In ballance with our enmity
That bids men take his ~~natural~~ rest
And loose the burden from his heart
Because we are heavens enemy.
Speaking
~~Who is this that shoulders through the crowd~~
Like a young horse its trainer has not [?~~bridl~~] bitted
Like a young foul that sees the hunt go by
And races in the field
Lazerus (who has just entered)
He raised me up
I am the man that died & was raised up
I am called Lazarus.
Christ
Seeing that you died
Lay in the tomb three days & were raised up
You will not mock at me.
Lazerus
For three whole days
I had been dead & I was lying still
In an old comfortable mountain cavern

---

14 "bitted" from first thought "bridled"?

4

when you came climbing, there were a great crowd
and dragged me to the light.

Christ.

I called your name
Lazarus come out I said & you came out
Bound up in clothes, your face bound in a cloth

Lazarus

You took my death give me your death instead.

Christ

I gave you life.

Lazarus.

But death is what I ask
alive I never could escape your love
~~[illegible]~~ And when I sickened towards my death I thought
I'll to the desert, & chuckle in a ~~[illegible]~~ corner
mere [illegible] a solitary thing, & I died
And saw no more until I saw you stand
opening the tomb: 'come out ~~[illegible]~~' you called,
~~You came & dragged me out~~ or
It was as though you dragged me out as boys
a rabbit when they have dug its ~~[illegible]~~ hole away
And now [illegible] are the shouting at your heels
You have [illegible] the death I am denied
And this is why I have hurried to this road
and claim the death of you.

[Harvard(C), 4[r]]

4

When you came climbing there with a great crowd
And dragged me to the light.
Christ.
I called your name
Lazarus come out I said & you came out
Bound up in clothes, your face bound in a cloth.
Lazerus
You took my death give me your death instead.
Christ
I gave you life.
Lazerus
But death is what I ask
Alive I never could escape your love
[?~~And~~] And when I sickened towards my death I thought
I'll to the desert, or chuckle in ~~a whole~~ corner
Mere ghost a solitary thing – I died
And saw no more until I saw you stand
In the
Opening of the tomb. 'Come out ~~Come out~~' you called.
^ ~~You came & dragged me out as~~
It was as though you dragged me out as boys
hole
A rabbit when they have dug its ~~whole~~ away
And now with all the shouting at your heels
You travel towards the death I am denied
And that is why I have hurried to this road
And claim the death of you.

---

4 "clothes" for "cloths"?
9 "~~whole~~" for "~~hole~~"? See l. 16, below.

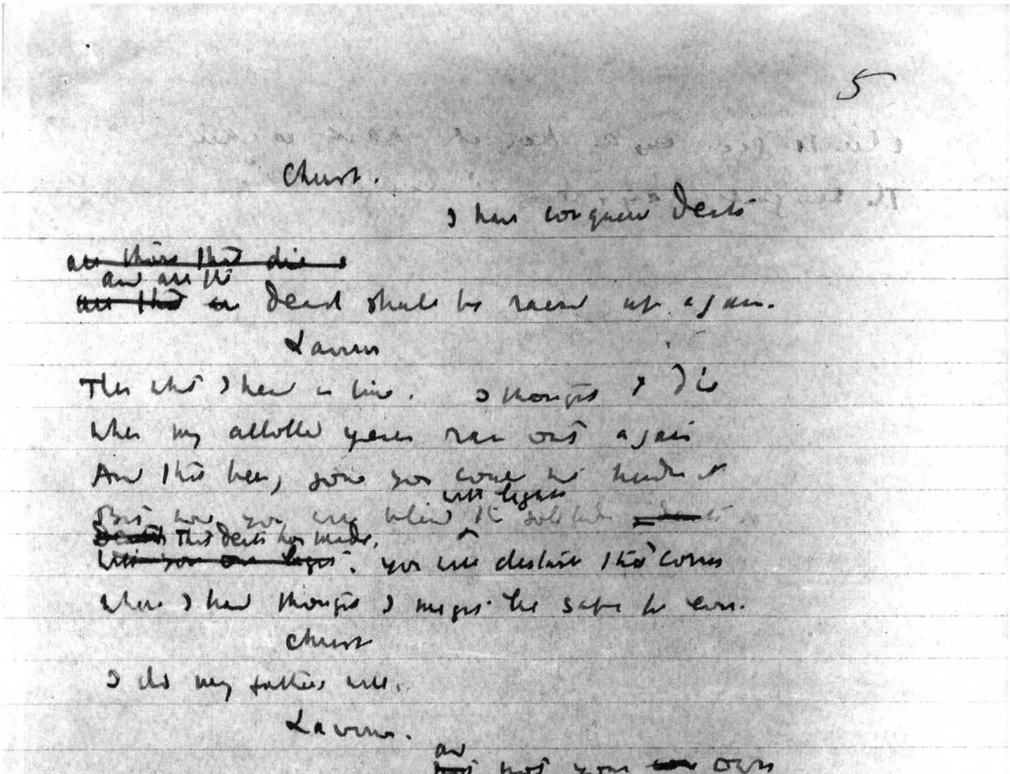

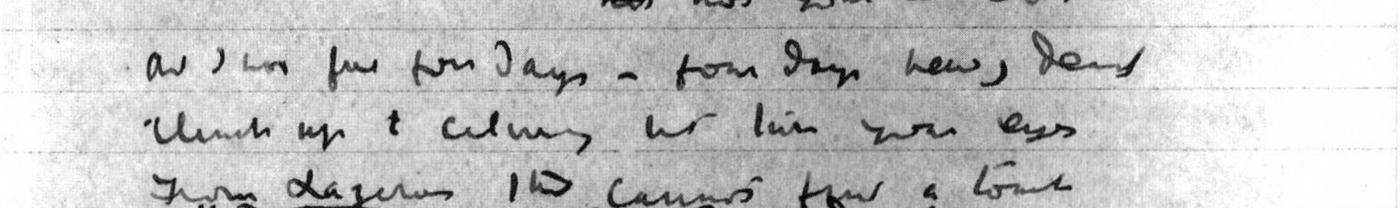

[Harvard(C), 5[r] and 5[v]]

[5[r]]

5

Christ.

I have conquered death
~~All those that die &~~
And all the
~~All that are~~ dead shall be raised up again.

Lazerus
Then what I heard is true. I thought to die
when my allotted years ran out again
And that being gone you could not hinder it
with light
But now you will blind ^ the solitude ~~of death~~
~~Death~~ That Death has made.
~~With your own light~~. You will disturb that corner
~~Where I had thought~~ I might lie safe for ever.

Christ
I did my fathers will.

Lazerus.
And
~~not~~ not your ~~one~~ own
And I was free four days – four days being dead
Climb up to Calvary but turn your eyes
From Lazarus that cannot find a tomb
~~Although he search all heighth, all depth.~~
~~Although he search the world~~ – make way
Make way for Lazerus that has to search
Under the broken mountain side or where
~~The seagull [?] rides,~~ geer eagle rides, or ~~See back~~
~~The jackal howls, or lions eye [?the] skies~~ (See
Where ever the last shadows are – make way

First Musician
The crowd shrinks back ward from the face that seems
Death stricken & death hungry still I know

[5[v]]

Where the geer eagle has its nest is where
The sea gull hangs over the hollow sea.

5[r], 16–17 The note "See back / (See" indicates the interpolation of ll. 1–2 from 5[v], the "back" of this page.

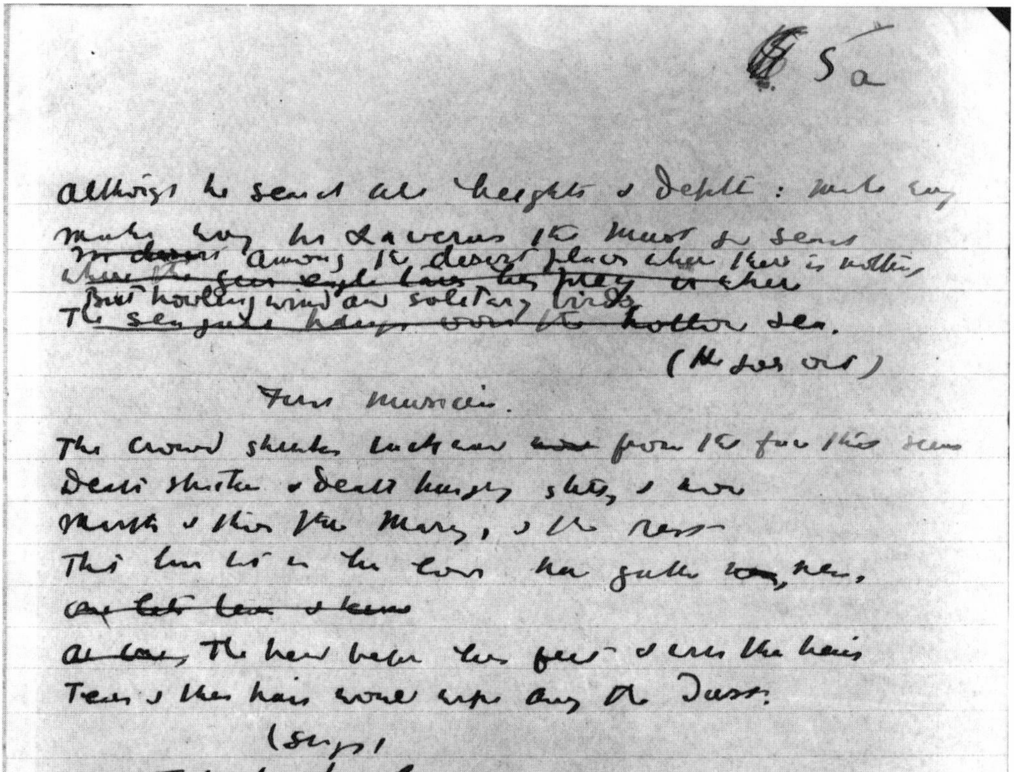

[Harvard(C), 6[r]]

{~~5~~ ~~6~~} 5a

Although he search all heights & depths: make way
Make way for Lazarus that must go search
~~In desert~~ Among the desert places where there is nothing
~~Where the geer eagle tares his prey is where~~
    But howling wind and solitary birds
~~The sea gull hangs over the hollow sea.~~

(He goes out)

First Musician.

The crowd shrinks back ward ~~now~~ from the face that seems
Death stricken & death hungry still, & now
Martha & those three Marys, & the rest
That live but in his love have gathered nea near,
~~One takes leave & kisses~~
~~And one~~, [?Their] head before his feet & with the hair
Tear & their hair would wipe away the dust.

(Sings)

~~Take but his love away~~
Their ~~love were a blown~~ feather
~~Tossed Boyed on the bitter North~~
~~By~~
Take but his love away
Their love becomes a feather
~~or~~
of eagle or ~~of~~ of gull of eagle, swan, or gull,
~~Tossed on the bitter spray~~
Or a drowned heron's feather
~~And Boyed on the bitter spary spray~~
~~And the moon at the full.~~
Tossed hither & thither
Upon the bitter spray
And the moon at the full.

1–4 Spoken by Lazarus.
16, 23 "Boyed" for "Buoyed"?

[Harvard(C), 7r]

6 ~~6~~

1 Martha & those three Marys & the rest
2 That live but in his love nor have a will
3 But when he wills it struggle through the crowd
4 And cry in ~~(he sings)~~ despair half ecstasy.
Sings
5 Take but his love away
6 And we like a heron's feather
7 Under a harsh moon ray
Are tossed
8 ~~Toss~~ ^ hither & thither
even like
9 ^ A white blown feather
10 Upon the
11 Toss hither & thither
12 A white blown feather
13 on tumbling spray.
Christ
At
14 ~~The~~ touching of your lips upon my feet
15 The daylights sweet again – single of heart
how strong the soul of man becomes
16 You know ~~man s soul is an unstable thing~~
When gods love fill it.
17 ~~Lacking gods love~~ – Why have you fled away
18 Why has the street grown empty of a sudden
19 As though all fled from it in terror.
Judas (who has just entered)
I am Judas
20 That sold you for the forty pieces of silver.
Christ
21 You were beside me every day and saw

1–4 Spoken by the First Musician.

[Harvard(C), 8^r]

7

The dead rise up & blind men given their sight
and all that I have said & taught you have known,
yet doubt that I am god.

Judas

I have not doubted

I knew it from the first moment that I saw you
I had no need of miracle to prove it.

Christ.

And yet you have betrayed me. ~~I have believed~~ you

Judas

I have betrayed you

Because you seem all powerful,

Christ.

My father

Even now if I were but to whisper it
would send his horses & his chariots
To set me free.

Judas

And is there not one man

In the wide world you have no power over

Christ

My father put all men into my hands

Judas

That was the very thought that drove me wild
I could not bear to think you had but to whistle
And I must do; but after that I thought

[Harvard(C), 8r]

7

1 The dead raised up & bling men given their sight
2 And all that I have said & taught you have known,
3 Yet doubt that I am God.
Judas
I have not doubted
4 I knew it from the first moment that I saw you
5 I had no need of miracles to prove it.
Christ
you
6 And yet ~~you~~ have betrayed me. ~~I have believe you~~
Judas
I have betrayed you
7 Because you seemed all powerful.
Christ
My father
8 Even now if I were but to whisper it
9 Would send his horses & his chariots
10 To set me free.
Judas
And is there not one man
11 In the wide world you have no power over
Christ
12 My father put all men into my hands.
Judas
13 That was the very thought that drove me wild
14 I could not bear to think you had but to whistle
15 And I must do; but after that I thought

---

1 "bling" for "blind"?

6 The canceled sentence, "I have believe[d in] you," was intended for Judas, hence given to him, immediately below, revised to "I have betrayed you."

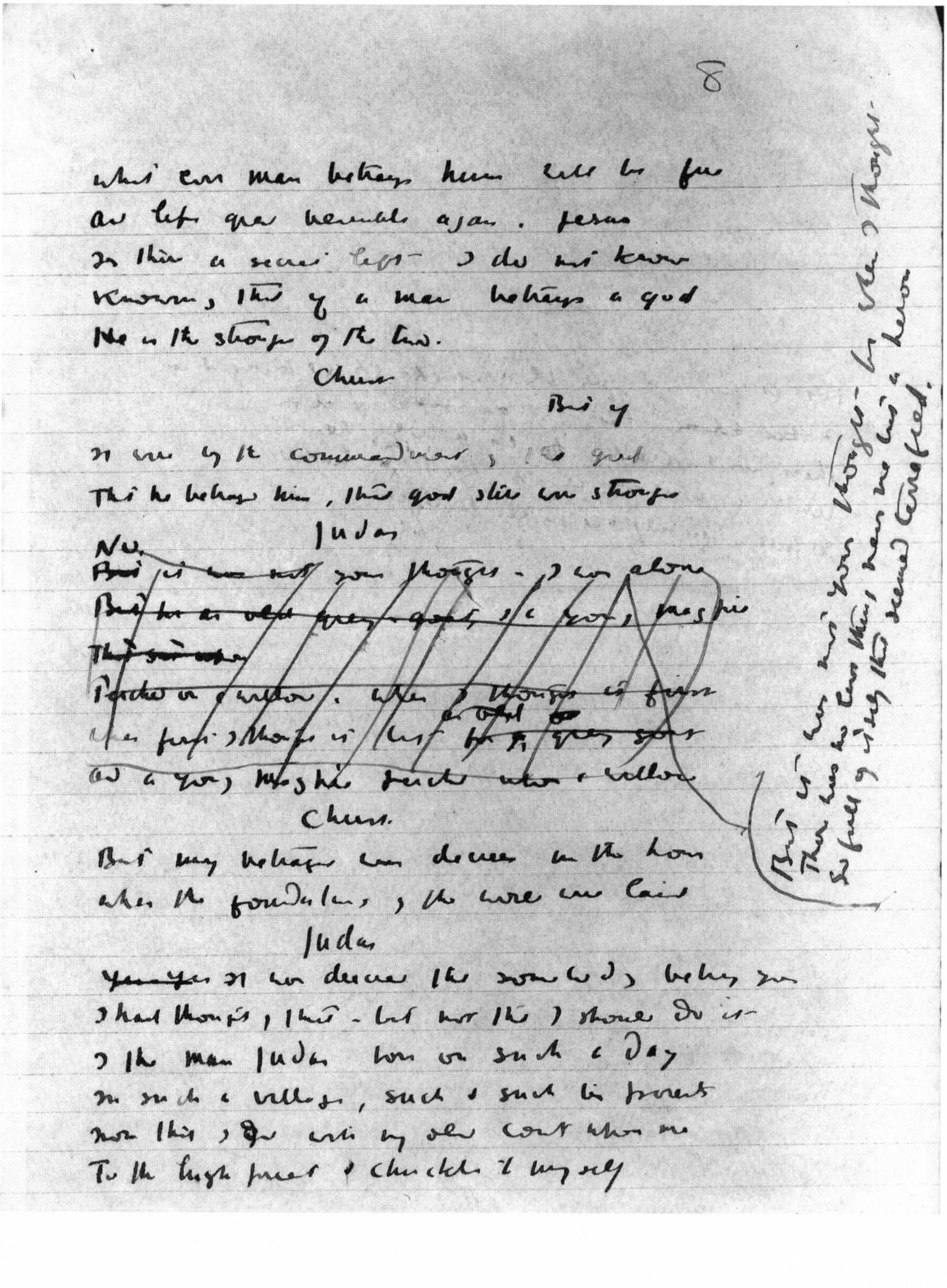

8

what ever man betrays him will be free
and life grow bearable again. Jesus
Is there a secret left I do not know
Knowing, that if a man betrays a god
He is the stronger of the two.

Chorus

But if
It were by the commandment of that god
That he betrays him, that god still were stronger

Judas

No.

Chorus.

But my betrayal was decreed in the hour
when the foundations of the world were laid

Judas

~~Yes yes~~ It was decreed that somebody betray you
I had thought, that – but not that I should do it –
I the man Judas born on such a day
In such a village, such & such his parents
Nor this, I in an old coat about me
To the high priest & chuckled to myself

[Harvard(C), 9[r]]

8

What ever man betrays him will be free
And life grew bearable again. Jesus
Is there a secret left I do not know
Knowing that if a man betrays a god
He is the stronger of the two.

Christ

But if
It were but the commandment of that god
That he betrayed him, that god still was stronger.

Judas

No
~~But~~ it was not your thought – I was alone
~~But for an old grey goat, & a young magpie~~
~~That sat upon~~
~~Perched on a willow when I thought it first~~
~~an old ol~~
When first I thought it but ~~for a grey goat~~
And a young magpie perched ^ upon a willow

But it was not your thought – for when I thought
There was no live thing near me but a heron
So full of itself that seemed terrified.

Christ

But my betrayal was decreed on the hour
When the foundations of the world were laid

Judas

~~Yes. Yes~~ It was decreed that somebody betray you
I had thought of that – but not that I should do it
I the man Judas born on such a day
In such a village, such & such his parents
Nor that I {g / G}o with my old coat upon me
To the high priest & chuckle to myself

13a–c Partially inscribed and inserted, by a leading line, from the right margin into canceled ll. 8–13, as an afterthought first worked out on 9[v].

13c "that [it] seemed"?

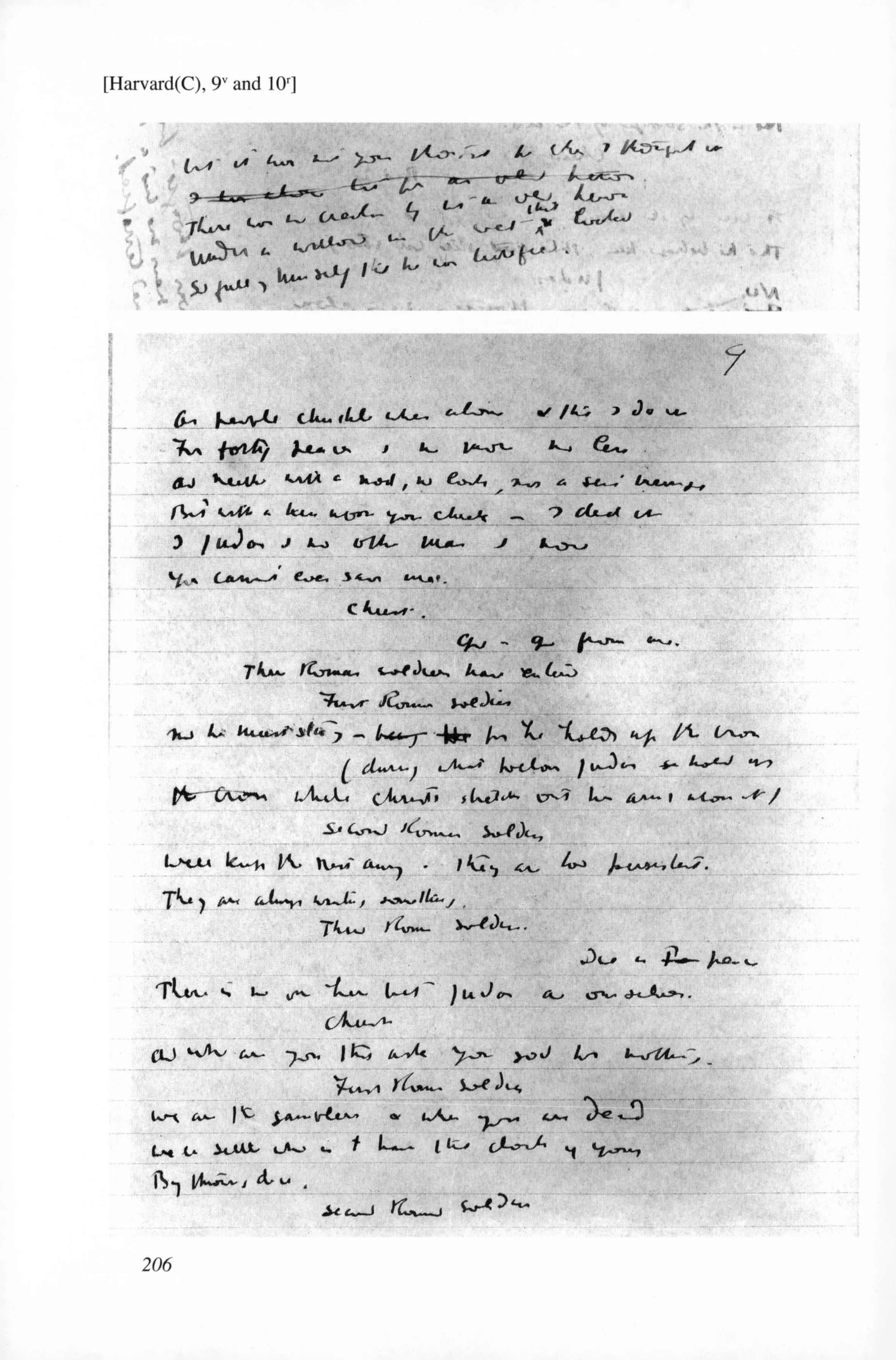

[Harvard(C), 9^{v} and 10^{r}]

[9^{v}]

but it was not your thought for when I thought it
~~I was alone but for an old heron~~
There was no creature by but an old heron
that
Under a willow in the wet ~~&~~ looked
So full of himself that he ^ was terrified

[10^{r}]

9

As people chuckle when alone & that I do it
For forty peaces & no more no less
and neither with a nod, nor look, nor a sent message
But with a kiss upon your cheek – I did it
I Judas & no other man & now
You cannot even save me.
Christ.
Go – go from me.
Three Roman soldiers have entered
First Roman Soldier
Now he must stay – ~~being~~ ~~He~~ for he holds up the cross
(during what follows Judas ~~se~~ holds up
the Cross while Christs stretches out his arms upon it)
Second Roman Soldier
Well keep the rest away. They are too persistent.
They are always wanting something.
Third Roman Soldier
Die in ~~Pe~~ peace
There is no one here but Judas and ourselves.
Christ
And who are you that ask your god for nothing.
First Roman Soldier
We are the gamblers & when you are dead
We ll settle who is to have that cloak of yours
By throwing dice.
Second Roman Soldier

9^{v}, 1–5 Anticipate the nearly fair-hand interpolation on the right margin of 9^{r}.
10^{r}, 1–6 Spoken by Judas.
8 "Well" for "We'll"?

[Harvard(C), 11[r]]

10

They are ivory dice.

Roman
Third ^ Soldier

Some play with wooden dice & some with stone
But ours are ivory. The merchants bring it
after that
In boats along the river & ~~after that afterwards~~
~~& they sleep sound~~
On camels through the desert ~~& all the way I have [?heard] them laugh~~
~~Because they have seen~~
~~They look upon the marvels of the world~~.
^

Roman
First ^ Soldier.

~~one wins~~ the ~~cloa~~
Although but one of us can wil win the cloak
This will not make us quarrel. What does it matter
One day one looses, & the next day wins.

Second Roman Soldier

What ever happens is the best we say
So that it is unexpected.

Third Roman Soldier

Had you sent
a crier through the world you had not found
More peacable companions for a death bed
Than these old gamblers that ask nothing.

First Roman Soldier

They say you are good & that you made the world
But its no matter.

Second Roman Soldier

Come now let us dance.
The dance of the dice throwers for it may be
He cannot live much longer & has not seen it

Second Roman Soldier
I knew a man
18 That delt in ivory & he slept sound
19 Because he had seen the marvels of the world

18–19 The Second Roman Soldier's speech is interpolated from right margin.

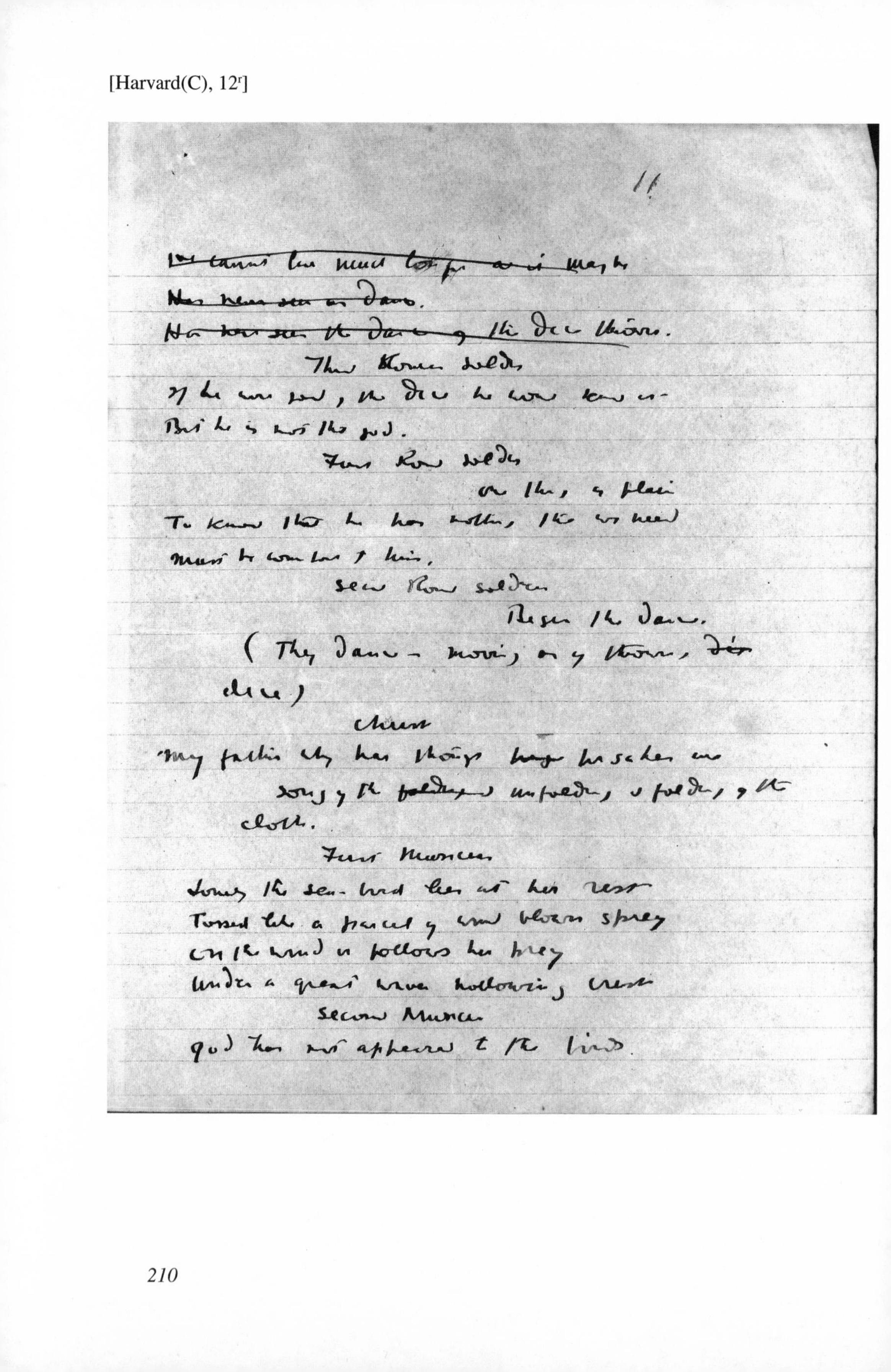

[Harvard(C), 12^{r}]

11

~~He cannot live much longer as it may be~~
~~Has never seen us dance.~~
~~Has never seen the dance of the dice throwers.~~

Third Roman Soldier

If he were god of the dice he would know it –
But he is not that god.

First Roman Soldier

One thing is plain
To know that he has nothing that we need
Must be comfort to him.

Second Roman Soldier

Begin the dance.

(They dance – moving as if throwing ~~dic~~ dice)

Christ

My father why has though ~~forg~~ forsaken me

Song of the ~~folding &~~ unfolding & folding of the cloth.

First Musician

Lonely the sea-bird lies at her rest
Tossed like a parcel of wind blown spray
On the wind it follows her prey
Under a great waves hollowing crest.

Second Musician

God has not appeared to the birds.

---

8 "though" for "thou"?

[Harvard(C), 13^{r}]

12

Third ~~[?]~~ Musician

The ger-eagle has chosen her part
In blue-deep of the upper air
Where one eyed day can meet his stare:
He is content with his savage heart.

Second Musician

God has not appeared to the birds.

First Musician.

Where have last years ~~[?]~~ cygnets gone?
Cool Lake's empty. Why do they fling
White wing out beside white wing
What can a swan need but a swan.

Second Musician

God has not appeared to the birds

[Harvard(C), 13[r]]

12

Third ~~Mer~~ Musician
The geer-eagle has chosen his part
In blue-deep of the upper air
Where one eyed day can meet his stare:
He is content with his savage heart.
Second Musician
God has not appeared to the birds.
First Musician
Where have last year s ~~cyg~~ cygnets gone?
Cool lake's empty. Why do they fling
White wing out beside white wing
What can a swan need but a swan.
Second Musician
God has not appeared to the birds

II. *Calvary*

Transcription of NLI 8776(3) for the Complete Version (1920–1935)

With *apparatus criticus* of variants in NLI 8776(4), BL Add. MS 55879, Texas(E), NLI 30,007, BL Add. MS 55884, BL Add. MS 55891

[NLI 8776(3), 1[r]]

~~ON THE ROAD TO~~ CALVARY.

Song for the folding and the unfolding of the cloth.

1st Musician. ~~“~~**Motionless under the moon-beam**
Up to his feathers in the stream,
Although ~~the~~ fish leap, the white heron,
Shivers in a dumbfounded dream.

2nd Musician **God has not died for the white heron,**
Although famished ~~he will~~ He’ll
3rd Musician. ~~“~~**~~He~~ is half ~~starved but will~~ not dare**
Dip or do anything but stare
Upon the glittering image of a heron,
That vanishes now and now is there.

---

dp PERSONS IN THE PLAY // Three Musicians *(their faces made up to resemble masks)* / Christ *(wearing a mask)* / Lazarus *(wearing a mask)* / Judas *(wearing a mask)* / Three Roman Soldiers *(their faces masked or made up to resemble masks) BL Add. MS 55879, Texas(E), BL Add. MSS 55884 and 55891* PERSONS OF *rev to* PERSONS IN *NLI 30,007*

sd At the beginning of the play the First Musician comes to the front of the bare place, round three sides of which the audience are seated, with a folded cloth hanging from his joined hands. Two other Musicians come, as in the preceding plays, [*rev to* play,] one from either side, and unfold the cloth so that it shuts out the stage, and then fold it again, singing and moving rhythmically. They do the same at the end of the play, which enables the players to leave the stage unseen. *BL Add. MS 55879* preceding plays, one *Texas(E), NLI 30,007, BL Add. MS and 55891*

Song the unfolding . . . cloth.] unfolding . . . cloth *BL Add. MS 55879, Texas(E), BL Add. MSS 55884 and 55891* the unfolding *rev to* unfolding *NLI 30,007*

1 moon-beam] moon-beam, *NLI 8776(4), BL Add. MS 55879, Texas(E), NLI 30,007, BL Add. MSS 55884 and 55891*

2 stream,] stream; *BL Add. MS 55879, Texas(E), NLI 30,007, BL Add. MSS 55884 and 55891*

3 heron,] heron *BL Add. MS 55879, Texas(E), NLI 30,007, BL Add. MSS 55884 and 55891*

5 heron,] heron. *NLI 8776(4)* heron *BL Add. MS 55879, Texas(E), NLI 30,007, BL Add. MSS 55884 and 55891*

6 He’ll] he’ll *NLI 8776(4), BL Add. MS 55879, Texas(E), NLI 30,007, BL Add. MSS 55884 and 55891*

9 that vanishes now and now] that now is lost and now *NLI 8776(4), BL Add. MS 55879, Texas(E), NLI 30,007, BL Add. MSS 55884 and 55891*

Typographical and format differences, as between underscoring and italics, are not reported in the *apparatus criticus*. Neither are the differences in spelling “1st,” “2nd,” and “3rd” (as “First,” “Second,” and “Third”) noted when they occur in the numerous speech headings, which may or may not be followed by a period. The latter is not recorded.

[NLI 8776(3), 1[r] continued]

has
2nd Musician ⁊ ✓**God ~~hath~~ not died for the white heron,**

1st Musician. ⁊ ✓**But that the full is shortly gone**
And after that is crescent moon
Its certain that the moon-crazed heron,
Would be but fishers diet soon.

has
2nd Musician. ⁊ ✓**God ~~hath~~ not died for the white heron,**

(The three musicians are now seated by the drum, flute and zither at the back of stage).

1st Musician. **The road to Calvary and I beside it**
Upon an ancient stone. Good Friday's come.
The day whereon Christ dreams His passion through
He climbs up / **~~he comes climbing~~ but as a dreamer climbs.**
hither / **The cross of His dream, the cross that does not exist,**
Shortens his breath and wears away his strength

---

10 heron,] heron. *NLI 8776(4), BL Add. MS 55879, Texas(E), NLI 30,007, BL Add. MSS 55884 and 55891*

12 moon] moon, *NLI 8776(4), BL Add. MS 55879, Texas(E), NLI 30,007, BL Add. MSS 55884 and 55891*

13 Its] It's *NLI 8776(4)* It's . . . heron *BL Add. MS 55879, Texas(E), NLI 30,007, BL Add. MSS 55884 and 55891*

14 fishers] fishes' *BL Add. MS 55879, Texas(E), NLI 30,007, BL Add. MSS 55884 and 55891*

15 heron,] heron. *NLI 8776(4), BL Add. MS 55879, Texas(E), NLI 30,007, BL Add. MSS 55884 and 55891*

15*sd* stage).] stage.) *NLI 8776(4)* Musicians . . . stage. *BL Add. MS 55879, Texas(E), NLI 30,007, BL Add. MSS 55884 and 55891*

16 Calvary] Calvary, *NLI 8776(4), BL Add. MS 55879, Texas(E), NLI 30,007, BL Add. MSS 55884 and 55891*

17 come.] come, *NLI 8776(4), BL Add. MS 55879, Texas(E), NLI 30,007, BL Add. MSS 55884 and 55891*

18 through] through. *BL Add. MS 55879, Texas(E), NLI 30,007, BL Add. MSS 55884 and 55891*

20 The cross that but exists because He dreams it *BL Add. MS 55879, Texas(E), NLI 30,007, BL Add. MSS 55884 and 55891*

21 strength] strength. *NLI 8776(4)* his . . . his strength.] His . . . His strength. *BL Add. MS 55879, Texas(E), NLI 30,007, BL Add. MSS 55884 and 55891*

[NLI 8776(3), 1[r] continued]

{xxxxxxxx / heavily}

22 **And now he stands amid a mocking crowd,**

23 **Heavily breathing (A player with the mask of**

{xxxxxx / Christ}

Christ and carrying a cross Christ has entered
and now stands leaning upon the cross).

those that are behind

on

24 of the men in front **Climb ~~upon~~ the shoulders ~~of those in front~~**

25 **To shout their mockery. ("work a miracle")**

26 Or **Cries one "and save yourself;" another cries**

27 ~~And~~ open his coach house, **~~Will not your father split the earth beneath~~**

28 And his stable door **~~And smother us all and split the heavens in two~~**

29 ~~call out~~ **~~And let the chariots down till heightened depth~~**

30 ~~And send his chariots~~ **~~Resound with grinding wheels and clattering hoofs~~**

31 ~~till height and depth~~ **Another cries, "Call out with a loud voice**

32 Give up a sign. Call **And tell him that h~~is son is now~~ alone cast away**

33 for the chariots" **Amid the mockery of his enemies"**

"Call on your father now before your bones
bare
Have been plucked ~~clean by~~ the great desert birds"
~~another cries call out with a loud voice~~
~~completes~~

22 he] He *BL Add. MS 55879, Texas(E), NLI 30,007, BL Add. MSS 55884 and 55891*

23 breathing] breathing. *NLI 8776(4), BL Add. MS 55879, Texas(E), NLI 30,007, BL Add. MSS 55884 and 55891*

23*sd* cross).] cross.) *NLI 8776(4)* cross. *BL Add. MS 55879, Texas(E), NLI 30,007, BL Add. MSS 55884 and 55891*

23 those] Those *NLI 8776(4), BL Add. MS 55879, Texas(E), NLI 30,007, BL Add. MSS 55884 and 55891*

25 mockery.] mockery: *NLI 8776(4)* mockery: 'Work a miracle', *BL Add. MS 55879, Texas(E), NLI 30,007, BL Add. MSS 55884 and 55891*

26 "and save yourself;"] and "save yourself"; *NLI 8776(4)* and 'Save *rev to* 'and save *BL Add. MS 55879* [*including marginal query:* Should it be / 'Work a miracle', / Cries one, 'and save yourself';? *answered in another hand:* Yes], *NLI 30,007* 'and save *Texas(E), BL Add. MSS 55884 and 55891*

27–28 *lacking NLI 8776(4), BL Add. MS 55879, Texas(E), NLI 30,007, BL Add. MSS 55884 and 55891*

30 birds"] birds"; *NLI 8776(4)* plucked . . . birds"] picked . . . birds'; *BL Add. MS 55879, Texas(E), NLI 30,007, BL Add. MSS 55884 and 55891*

31 cries, "Call] cries: "call *NLI 8776(4)* cries, 'Call *BL Add. MS 55879, Texas(E), NLI 30,007, BL Add. MSS 55884 and 55891*

33 enemies"] enemies". *NLI 8776(4)* enemies'. *BL Add. MS 55879, Texas(E), NLI 30,007, BL Add. MSS 55884 and 55891*

[NLI 8776(3), 2[r]]

(singing)

34 **“Oh but the mockers cry**
35 **Makes my heart afraid**
36 **As though a flute of bone**
37 **Taken from a heron’s thigh**
38 **A heron crazed by the moon**
39 **Were cleverly, softly played.**

(speaking)
40 **“Who is this from whom the crowd has shrunk**
41 **As though he had some look that terrified**
42 **~~Like a young horse the trainer has not bitted~~**
Maybe he is too full of life.
43 **~~Is he to ful of live~~ {H h}e moves**
44 **Like a young horse the trainer has not bitted**

34*sd* (singing)] (Singing) *NLI 8776(4), BL Add. MS 55879, Texas(E), NLI 30,007, BL Add. MSS 55884 and 55891*

34 “Oh] Oh *NLI 8776(4)* O, but *BL Add. MS 55879, Texas(E)* Oh, but *rev to* O, but *NLI 30,007* O, but *BL Add. MS 55891* O, but *rev to* But *BL Add. MS 55884*

35 afraid] afraid, *NLI 8776(4), BL Add. MS 55879, Texas(E), NLI 30,007, BL Add. MSS 55884 and 55891*

37 thigh] thigh, *NLI 8776(4), BL Add. MS 55879, Texas(E), NLI 30,007, BL Add. MSS 55884 and 55891*

38 moon] moon, *NLI 8776(4), BL Add. MS 55879, Texas(E), NLI 30,007, BL Add. MSS 55884 and 55891*

39*sd* (speaking)] (Speaking) *NLI 8776(4), BL Add. MS 55879, Texas(E), NLI 30,007, BL Add. MSS 55884 and 55891*

40 “Who . . . shrunk] Who . . . shrunk, *NLI 8776(4), BL Add. MS 55879, Texas(E), NLI 30,007, BL Add. MSS 55884 and 55891*

41 terrified] terrified? *NLI 8776(4), BL Add. MS 55879, Texas(E), NLI 30,007, BL Add. MSS 55884 and 55891*

43 life. He] life; he *NLI 8776(4)* He has a deadly face, and yet he moves *BL Add. MS 55879, Texas(E)* deadly] deathly *NLI 30,007, BL Add. MSS 55884 and 55891*

44 bitted] bitted, *NLI 8776(4) lacking BL Add. MS 55879, Texas(E), NLI 30,007, BL Add. MS 55884 and 55891*

The typist evidently lapsed into a different format for speech headings with NLI 8776(3), 2[r]. While maintaining the column set in the same position (perhaps intending to go back to type in character names in a wide left margin), the typist instead identifies the speakers above the speeches (tab centered). The anomaly does not seem to be evidence of different draft states of the play in typescript. However, ribbon and carbon copies are mixed (1[r], 2[r], and 4[r] being ribbon copies), all produced on the same typewriter.

[NLI 8776(3), 2r continued]

Like a young foul that sees the hunt go by
And races in the field.
(A player with the mask of Lazarus has entered)

Lazerus

He raised me up
I am the man that died and was raised up
I am called Lazarus
~~Christ,~~ seeing that you died
Lay in the tomb four days and were raised up
You will not mock at me.

Christ

Laz{a/e}rus

For four whole days
I had been dead and I was lying still
In an old comfortable mountain cavern
When you came climbing there with a great crowd
And dragged me to the light.

Christ

I called your name
Lazerus, Come out I said and you came out
Bound up in cloths, your face bound in a cloth

46*sd* entered)] entered.) *NLI 8776(4)* entered. *BL Add. MS 55879, Texas(E), NLI 30,007, BL Add. MSS 55884 and 55891*

46 Lazerus *rev to* Lazarus. *NLI 8776(4)* Lazarus. *BL Add. MS 55879, Texas(E), NLI 30,007, BL Add. MSS 55884 and 55891*

47 up] up. *BL Add. MS 55879, Texas(E), NLI 30,007, BL Add. MSS 55884 and 55891*

48 Lazarus] Lazerus. *NLI 8776(4)* Lazarus. *BL Add. MS 55879, Texas(E), NLI 30,007, BL Add. MSS 55884 and 55891* Christ. seeing] Christ. Seeing *NLI 8776(4), BL Add. MS 55879, Texas(E), NLI 30,007, BL Add. MSS 55884 and 55891*

49 up] up. *BL Add. MS 55879, Texas(E), NLI 30,007, BL Add. MSS 55884 and 55891*

54 name] name: *BL Add. MS 55879, Texas(E), NLI 30,007, BL Add. MSS 55884 and 55891* name, *rev to* name: *NLI 30,007* [*followed by canceled query mark*]

55 Lazerus, Come out] "Lazerus, Come out" *NLI 8776(4)* 'Lazarus, come out', *BL Add. MS 55879, Texas(E), NLI 30,007, BL Add. MSS 55884 and 55891*

56 cloth] cloth. *NLI 8776(4), BL Add. MS 55879, Texas(E), NLI 30,007, BL Add. MSS 55884 and 55891*

The typist seems to know the correct spelling of Lazarus (in ll. 48, 50, and 46*sd*) though struggling (in l. 55) to remain faithful to the manuscript in spite of it. Yeats's misspellings persist in his corrections until NLI 8776(4), where speech headings are corrected, in pencil and in another hand.

[NLI 8776(3), 2^{r} continued]

Laz{a e}rus

57 |——— **You took my death, give me your death instead**

Christ

58 **I gave you life**

Lazerus

~~**Lazarus said,**~~ **But death is what I ask**

59 **Alive I never could escape your love**

60 **And when I sickened towards my death I thought**

61 **I'll to the desert, or chuckle in a corner**

62 **Mere ghost, a solitary thing. I die**d

63 **And saw no more until I saw you stand**

64 **In the opening of the tomb "come out" You called**

65 ~~**It was as though you dragged me out as boys**~~

66 **A rabbit, when they have dug its hole away**.

You dragged me to the light as boys ~~drgs~~ dra{g gs} out

---

57 instead] instead. *NLI 8776(4), BL Add. MS 55879, Texas(E), NLI 30,007, BL Add. MSS 55884 and 55891*

58 life] life. *NLI 8776(4), BL Add. MS 55879, Texas(E), NLI 30,007, BL Add. MSS 55884 and 55891* Lazerus *rev to* Lazarus. *NLI 8776(4)* Lazarus. *BL Add. MS 55879, Texas(E), NLI 30,007, BL Add. MSS 55884 and 55891* ask] ask. *NLI 8776(4), BL Add. MS 55879, Texas(E), NLI 30,007, BL Add. MSS 55884 and 55891*

59 love] love, *BL Add. MS 55879, Texas(E), NLI 30,007, BL Add. MSS 55884 and 55891*

60 thought *rev to* thought, *BL Add. MS 55879, NLI 30,007* thought, *Texas(E), BL Add. MSS 55884 and 55891*

61 desert,] desert *NLI 8776(4)* I'll . . . corner *rev to* 'I'll . . . corner, *BL Add. MS 55879* 'I'll . . . corner, *Texas(E)* I'll . . . corner *rev to* 'I'll . . . corner *NLI 30,007* 'I'll . . . corner *BL Add. MSS 55884 and 55891*

62 thing. *rev to* thing.' *BL Add. MS 55879, NLI 30,007* thing.' *Texas(E), BL Add. MSS 55884 and 55891*

64 tomb "come out" You called] tomb; "Come out!" You called; *NLI 8776(4)* 'Come out!' you called; *BL Add. MS 55879, Texas(E), NLI 30,007, BL Add. MSS 55884 and 55891*

66 rabbit, . . . away.] rabbit . . . away, *NLI 8776(4)* rabbit . . . away; *BL Add. MS 55879, Texas(E), NLI 30,007, BL Add. MSS 55884 and 55891*

---

58 As elsewhere on 2^{r}, the typist is miscued by a copy text that gives an attribution phrase, as in prose narrative, rather than the customary speech heading.

[NLI 8776(3), 3[r]]

And now with all the shouting at your heels
You travel towards the death I am denied
And that is why I have hurried to this road
└—— And claim~~ed~~ ~~that~~ death of you.
your/

Christ. I have conquered death
And all the dead shall be raised up again.

Lazarus. Then what I heard is true. I thought to die
When my allotted years ran out again
And that being gone you could not hinder it
But now you will blind with light the solitude
That death has made. You will disturb that corner
Where I had thought I might lie safe for ever

Christ. | —— I do My Father's Will

Lazarus. And not your own.
And I was free four days, four days, being dead,
Climb up to Calvary but turn your eyes
From Lazarus that cannot find a tomb,
Although he search all height and depth: make way

---

68 denied] denied. *NLI 8776(4), BL Add. MS 55879, Texas(E), NLI 30,007, BL Add. MSS 55884 and 55891*

69 road; *rev to* road *NLI 30,007*

70 claimed your death of you.] claimed from you your death. *NLI 8776(4)* claimed your death. *BL Add. MS 55879, Texas(E)* and that is why I claim *rev to* And claimed *NLI 30,007* [*with canceled queries:* Long line? / Omit "that is"?] And claimed *BL Add. MSS 55884 and 55891*

70 I . . . death] But I . . . death, *BL Add. MS 55879, Texas(E), BL Add. MSS 55884 and 55891* I . . . death *rev to* But I . . . death, *NLI 30,007*

73 again] again; *NLI 8776(4), BL Add. MS 55879, Texas(E), NLI 30,007, BL Add. MSS 55884 and 55891*

74 that being gone . . . it] that, being gone, . . . it; *NLI 8776(4), BL Add. MS 55879, Texas(E), NLI 30,007, BL Add. MSS 55884 and 55891*

76 made.] made; *NLI 8776(4), BL Add. MS 55879, Texas(E), NLI 30,007, BL Add. MSS 55884 and 55891*

77 ever] ever. *NLI 8776(4), BL Add. MS 55879, Texas(E), NLI 30,007, BL Add. MSS 55884 and 55891*

78 My Father's Will] my Father's will. *NLI 8776(4), BL Add. MS 55879, Texas(E), NLI 30,007, BL Add. MSS 55884 and 55891* own.] own; *NLI 8776(4), BL Add. MS 55879, Texas(E), NLI 30,007, BL Add. MSS 55884 and 55891*

79 days, being dead,] days being dead. *NLI 8776(4), BL Add. MS 55879, Texas(E), NLI 30,007, BL Add. MSS 55884 and 55891*

80 Calvary] Calvary, *BL Add. MS 55879, Texas(E), NLI 30,007, BL Add. MSS 55884 and 55891*

81 Lazarus] Lazerus *NLI 8776(4)* tomb,] tomb *BL Add. MS 55879, Texas(E), NLI 30,007, BL Add. MSS 55884 and 55891*

82 way] way, *NLI 8776(4), BL Add. MS 55879, Texas(E), NLI 30,007, BL Add. MSS 55884 and 55891*

[NLI 8776(3), 3r continued]

83 **Make way for Lazarus that must go search**
84 **Among the desert places where there is nothing**
85 **But howling wind and solitary birds**
(He goes out).

the
86 **1st Musician.** **The crowd shrinks backward from ~~the~~ face that**
and seems
87 **Death stricken, death hungry still, and now**
88 **Martha and those thre Marys and the rest**
round him
89 **That live but in His love hath gathered ~~near~~**
90 **They bend before his feet and with their ~~hair~~**
with
91 **~~Tears~~ and their hair, would wipe away the dust**

tears /

89a He holds his right arm
out & on his arm
89b Their lips are pressed & their
tears fall & now
They
89c ~~He~~ cast them on the ground
before his ~~soiled~~
dirty
~~And blood~~
89d Blood dabled feet & clean
them with their hair

83 Lazarus] Lazerus *NLI 8776(4)*
85 birds] birds. *NLI 8776(4), BL Add. MS 55879, Texas(E), NLI 30,007, BL Add. MSS 55884 and 55891*
85*sd* out).] out) *NLI 8776(4), BL Add. MS 55879, Texas(E), NLI 30,007, BL Add. MSS 55884 and 55891*
87 Death-stricken and death-hungry still; and now *BL Add. MS 55879, Texas(E), BL Add. MSS 55884 and 55891* Death stricken and death hungry still; *rev to* Death-stricken and death-hungry still; *NLI 30,007*
88 Martha and those thre Marys] Martha, and those three Marys, *NLI 8776(4), BL Add. MS 55879, Texas(E), NLI 30,007, BL Add. MSS 55884 and 55891*
89 him] him. *NLI 8776(4)* Him. *BL Add. MS 55879, Texas(E), NLI 30,007, BL Add. MSS 55884 and 55891*
89a out] out, *NLI 8776(4)* His . . . out, . . . His *BL Add. MS 55879, Texas(E), NLI 30,007, BL Add. MSS 55884 and 55891*
89b fall] fall; *NLI 8776(4), BL Add. MS 55879, Texas(E), NLI 30,007, BL Add. MSS 55884 and 55891*
89c his] His *BL Add. MS 55879, Texas(E), NLI 30,007, BL Add. MSS 55884 and 55891*
89d Blood dabled . . . hair] Blood-dabbled . . . hair. *NLI 8776(4), BL Add. MS 55879, Texas(E), NLI 30,007, BL Add. MSS 55884 and 55891*

[NLI 8776(3), 3r continued]

(Sings)

92 **"Take but his love away**
93 **Their love becomes a feather**
94 **Of eagle, swan or gull**
95 **Or a drowned heron's feather**
96 **Tossed hither and thither**
97 **Upon the bitter spray**
98 **And the moon at the full**

~~my feet~~
99 **Christ.** **At touching of your lips upon ~~my feet, heart~~,**
{~~u know how strong the soul~~}
100 **~~Yo {The daylight's sweet again, } of man becomes~~**
101 **~~When God's Love fills it why have you fled away~~**
102 has **Why ~~have~~ the streets grown empty of a sudden** ?
103 **As though all fled from it in terror**?

I felt their hair upon my feet a moment
and then they fled away. Why have they fled?

---

92 "Take] Take *NLI 8776(4)* Take . . . away *rev to* Take . . . away, *BL Add. MS 55879, NLI 30,007* Take . . . away, *Texas(E), BL Add. MSS 55884 and 55891*

94 gull] gull, *NLI 8776(4), BL Add. MS 55879, Texas(E), NLI 30,007, BL Add. MSS 55884 and 55891*

98 full] full. *NLI 8776(4), BL Add. MS 55879, Texas(E), NLI 30,007, BL Add. MSS 55884 and 55891*

99 *lacking NLI 8776(4), BL Add. MS 55879, Texas(E), NLI 30,007, BL Add. MSS 55884 and 55891*

101 and . . . away. Why] And . . . away—why *NLI 8776(4), BL Add. MS 55879, Texas(E), NLI 30,007, BL Add. MSS 55884 and 55891*

102 streets] street *NLI 8776(4), BL Add. MS 55879, Texas(E), NLI 30,007, BL Add. MSS 55884 and 55891*

103 fled from it in] fled in *BL Add. MS 55879, Texas(E), BL Add. MSS 55884 and 55891* fled from it in *rev to* fled in *NLI 30,007* [*including the marginal query, canceled:* long line? / omit "from it"?]

---

99 Almost completely clear of the cancellation scribble of ll. 100–101, this line nevertheless is interpreted as part of the deletion that was only partly balanced by the substitution of two lines inscribed at the foot of the page and arrowed into position as shown. The deletion is confirmed in all succeeding versions of the play.

100 Text within braces indicates overtyping, not authorial revision.

[NLI 8776(3), 4r]

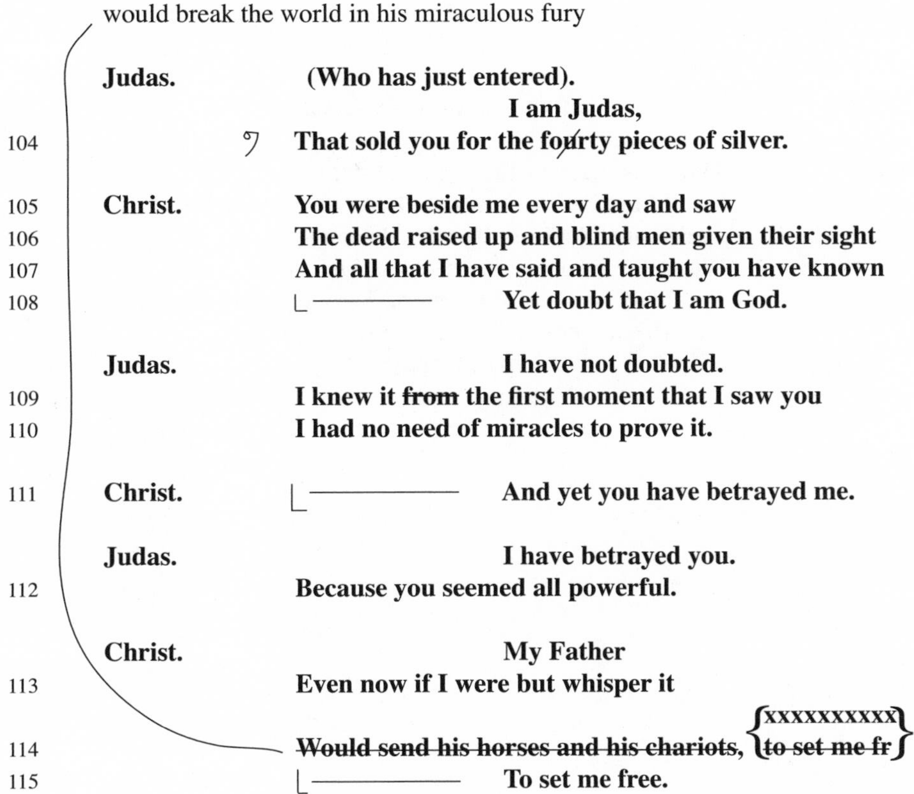

would break the world in his miraculous fury

Judas. **(Who has just entered).**
I am Judas,
104 **That sold you for the fo~~u~~rty pieces of silver.**

105 **Christ.** **You were beside me every day and saw**
106 **The dead raised up and blind men given their sight**
107 **And all that I have said and taught you have known**
108 **Yet doubt that I am God.**

Judas. **I have not doubted.**
109 **I knew it ~~from~~ the first moment that I saw you**
110 **I had no need of miracles to prove it.**

111 **Christ.** **And yet you have betrayed me.**

Judas. **I have betrayed you.**
112 **Because you seemed all powerful.**

Christ. **My Father**
113 **Even now if I were but whisper it**
114 **~~Would send his horses and his chariots,~~** {xxxxxxxxxx / ~~to set me fr~~}
115 **To set me free.**

103*sd* entered).] entered) *NLI 8776(4), NLI 30,007, BL Add. MSS 55884 and 55891*

103 Judas,] Judas *BL Add. MS 55879, Texas(E), NLI 30,007, BL Add. MSS 55884 and 55891*

104 forty] thirty *NLI 8776(4), BL Add. MS 55879, Texas(E), NLI 30,007, BL Add. MSS 55884 and 55891*

105 day] day, *NLI 8776(4), BL Add. MS 55879, Texas(E), NLI 30,007, BL Add. MSS 55884 and 55891*

106 sight] sight, *NLI 8776(4), BL Add. MS 55879, Texas(E), NLI 30,007, BL Add. MSS 55884 and 55891*

107 known] known, *BL Add. MS 55879, Texas(E), NLI 30,007, BL Add. MSS 55884 and 55891*

108 doubted.] doubted; *BL Add. MS 55879, Texas(E), NLI 30,007, BL Add. MSS 55884 and 55891*

109 you] you. *NLI 8776(4)* you; *BL Add. MS 55879, Texas(E), NLI 30,007, BL Add. MSS 55884 and 55891*

111 you.] you *BL Add. MS 55879, Texas(E), NLI 30,007, BL Add. MSS 55884 and 55891*

112 all powerful.] all-powerful. *NLI 8776(4), BL Add. MS 55879, Texas(E), NLI 30,007, BL Add. MSS 55884 and 55891*

113 now if . . . but whisper it] now, if . . . but to whisper it. *NLI 8776(4), BL Add. MS 55879, Texas(E), NLI 30,007, BL Add. MSS 55884 and 55891*

114 would . . . his] Would . . . His *NLI 8776(4), BL Add. MS 55879, Texas(E), NLI 30,007, BL Add. MSS 55884 and 55891*

[NLI 8776(3), 4r continued]

Judas. **And is there not one man**
In the wide world you have no power over.

Christ. **My Father put all men into My Hands.**

Judas. **That was the very thought that drove me wild,**
I could not bear to think that you had but to whistle
And I must do, but after that I thought
‘ **Whatever man betrays him will be free**;’
e/ **And life grøw bearable again. ~~Answer~~** And now
Is there a secret left I do not know
Knowing that if a man betrays a God,

---

116 over.] over? *NLI 8776(4)* world . . . over.] world that is not in your power? *BL Add. MS 55879*, *Texas(E)*, *NLI 30,007*, *BL Add. MSS 55884 and 55891*

117 My Hands.] my hands. *BL Add. MS 55879*, *Texas(E)*, *NLI 30,007*, *BL Add. MSS 55884 and 55891*

118 wild,] wild. *BL Add. MS 55879*, *Texas(E)*, *BL Add. MSS 55884 and 55891* wild, *rev to* wild. *NLI 30,007*

119 think that you] think you *NLI 8776(4)*, *BL Add. MS 55879*, *Texas(E)*, *NLI 30,007*, *BL Add. MSS 55884 and 55891*

120 do,] do; *NLI 8776(4)* do; . . . thought *rev to* do; . . . thought, *NLI 30,007* do; . . . thought, *BL Add. MS 55879*, *Texas(E)*, *BL Add. MSS 55884 and 55891*

121 ‘Whatever . . . free;’] Whatever . . . free; *NLI 8776(4)* Whatever . . . free’ *rev to* ‘Whatever . . . free’; *NLI 30,007* ‘Whatever . . . free;’ *BL Add. MS 55879*, *Texas(E)*, *NLI 30,007*, *BL Add. MSS 55884 and 55891*

122 life] Life *NLI 8776(4)*

123 know] know, *NLI 8776(4)*, *BL Add. MS 55879*, *Texas(E)*, *NLI 30,007*, *BL Add. MSS 55884 and 55891*

124 God,] God *NLI 8776(4)*, *BL Add. MS 55879*, *Texas(E)*, *NLI 30,007*, *BL Add. MSS 55884 and 55891*

---

124 No break between this and the succeeding line.

[NLI 8776(3), 4[r] continued]

He is the stronger of the two.

By ~~It was by~~ ~~But if it were~~ If it were

Christ. **~~But if it were but~~ the commandament of that God** /himself/

him **~~That He betrayed me, that God still was stronger.~~**

That god would still be stronger.

I have thought of that

Judas. **~~But it was not your thought for when I thought.~~**

lc **There was no live thing near me but a heron**

So full of itself that it seemed terrified.

Christ. **But My betrayal was decreed that hour**

When the foundations of the world were laid

Judas. **It was decreed that somebody betray you**

I'd thought of that but not that I should do it.

But when I planned it I was all alone

---

125 two. *rev to* two? *NLI 30,007* two? *BL Add. MS 55879, Texas(E), BL Add. MSS 55884 and 55891*

125/126 If it were / By the commandment of that God himself] But if / 'Twere the commandment of that God Himself *NLI 8776(4)* But if / 'Twere . . . Himself *rev to* But if / 'Twere . . . Himself, *NLI 30,007* But if / 'Twere . . . Himself *BL Add. MS 55879, Texas(E), BL Add. MSS 55884 and 55891*

127 god would still be stronger.] God were still the stronger. *NLI 8776(4), BL Add. MS 55879, Texas(E), BL Add. MSS 55884 and 55891* God were still the stronger. *rev to* . . . stronger? *rev to* . . . stronger. *NLI 30,007*

128 But when I planned it I was all alone] When I planned it *NLI 8776(4), BL Add. MS 55879, Texas(E), NLI 30,007, BL Add. MSS 55884 and 55891*

131 My] my *BL Add. MS 55879, Texas(E), NLI 30,007, BL Add. MSS 55884 and 55891*

132 laid] laid. *NLI 8776(4), BL Add. MS 55879, Texas(E), NLI 30,007, BL Add. MSS 55884 and 55891*

133 you] you – *NLI 8776(4), BL Add. MS 55879, Texas(E), NLI 30,007, BL Add. MSS 55884 and 55891*

134 that but . . . it.] that—but . . . it, *NLI 8776(4), BL Add. MS 55879, Texas(E), NLI 30,007, BL Add. MSS 55884 and 55891*

---

128 The emendment is inscribed at the foot of the page and arrowed into position as indicated.

[NLI 8776(3), 5r]

I the man Judas born on such a day
In such a village, such and such his parents
Nor that I'd go with my old coat upon me
To the high Priest and Chapel to myself,
As people chuckle when alone and that I do it
For fourty pieces and no more, not less
And neither with a nod, a look nor a sent message
But with a kiss upon your cheek I did it.
I Judas and no other man and now
You cannot even save me.

Christ **Go, Go from Me.**
(three Roman soldiers have entered)

---

135 Judas . . . day] Judas, . . . day, *NLI 8776(4), BL Add. MS 55879, Texas(E), NLI 30,007, BL Add. MSS 55884 and 55891*

136 parents] parents; *NLI 8776(4), BL Add. MS 55879, Texas(E), NLI 30,007, BL Add. MSS 55884 and 55891*

138 high Priest and Chapel to myself,] High Priest, and chuckle to myself *NLI 8776(4), BL Add. MS 55879, Texas(E), NLI 30,007, BL Add. MSS 55884 and 55891*

139 alone] alone, *NLI 8776(4)* alone, and that I'd do it *rev to* alone, and do it [*with marginal note, canceled:* Long line? / omit "that I'd"?] *NLI 30,007* alone, and do it *BL Add. MS 55879, Texas(E), BL Add. MSS 55884 and 55891*

140 fourty . . . not less] thirty . . . no less, *NLI 8776(4), BL Add. MS 55879, Texas(E), NLI 30,007, BL Add. MSS 55884 and 55891*

141 nod, a look, nor . . . message, *rev to* nod nor . . . message, [*with marginal note, canceled:* Long line?] *NLI 30,007* nod nor . . . message, *BL Add. MS 55879, Texas(E), BL Add. MSS 55884 and 55891*

142 cheek I did it.] cheek. I did it, *NLI 8776(4), BL Add. MS 55879, Texas(E), NLI 30,007, BL Add. MSS 55884 and 55891*

143 man] man, *NLI 8776(4)* I, Judas, . . . man, *BL Add. MS 55879, Texas(E), NLI 30,007, BL Add. MSS 55884 and 55891*

144 Go, Go from Me.] Begone from me. *NLI 8776(4), BL Add. MS 55879, Texas(E), NLI 30,007, BL Add. MSS 55884 and 55891*

144*sd* (three] (Three *NLI 8776(4)* Three Roman soldiers *rev to* Three Roman Soldiers *BL Add. MS 55879* Three Roman soldiers *circled (with marginal note:* Caps*)* *NLI 30,007* Three Roman Soldiers *Texas(E), BL Add. MSS 55884 and 55891*

---

144 The line (in Judas's speech) should be left justified.

[NLI 8776(3), 5[r] continued]

The has been chosen to

1st Roman soldier **~~No he must stay for he~~ hold~~s~~ up the cross**
(during what follows Judas holds up the cross while Christ stands with his arms stretched out upon it).

2nd Roman soldier **We'll keep the rest away, they are too persistent**
The {yx re}'{xx ll} re always wanting something

3rd Roman Soldier **Die in peace.** └————————
There is no-one here but Judas and ourselves

Christ. **And who are you that ask your God for nothing.**

3rd Roman solider **We are the gamblers, and when you are dead**
We'll settle who is to have that cloak of yours
└———— **By throwing dice.**

2nd Roman Soldier **They are ivory dice.** └————————

---

145 The . . . cross] He . . . cross. *NLI 8776(4), BL Add. MS 55879, Texas(E), NLI 30,007, BL Add. MSS 55884 and 55891*

145*sd* (during . . . it).] (During . . . it.) *NLI 8776(4)* During what follows, . . . His . . . it. *BL Add. MS 55879, Texas(E), NLI 30,007, BL Add. MSS 55884 and 55891*

146 away, . . . persistent] away; . . . persistent; *NLI 8776(4), BL Add. MS 55879, Texas(E), NLI 30,007, BL Add. MSS 55884 and 55891*

147 They're . . . something] They are . . . something. *NLI 8776(4), BL Add. MS 55879, Texas(E), NLI 30,007, BL Add. MSS 55884 and 55891*

148 There is no-one . . . ourselves] There's no one . . . ourselves. *NLI 8776(4), BL Add. MS 55879, Texas(E), NLI 30,007, BL Add. MSS 55884 and 55891*

149 nothing.] nothing? *NLI 8776(4), BL Add. MS 55879, Texas(E), NLI 30,007, BL Add. MSS 55884 and 55891*

152 They are ivory dice.] Our dice were carved *(including marginal note:* Short line?*) BL Add. MS 55879, NLI 30,007* Our dice were carved *Texas(E), BL Add. MSS 55884 and 55891*

---

145 "The" for "He"?

[NLI 8776(3), 5[r] continued]

3rd Roman soldier
~~Some play with wooden dice and some with stone~~
~~But ours are ivory, the merchants bring it~~
~~In boats along the Nile and after that~~
~~On camels through the desert.~~

2nd Roman soldier
I knew a man
That dealt in ivory and he slept sound
Because he had seen the marvels of the world.

1st Roman soldier
Although but one of us can win the cloak
That will not make us quarrel, what does it matter
One day one loses and the next day wins.

2nd Roman soldier
whatever happens is the best we say
⌊———— So that it's unexpected.

---

153 *lacking NLI 8776(4)* Out of an old sheep's thigh at Ephesus. [*continuing from the Second Roman Soldier's speech above*] *BL Add. MS 55879, Texas(E), NLI 30,007, BL Add. MSS 55884 and 55891*

154–158 *lacking NLI 8776(4), BL Add. MS 55879, Texas(E), NLI 30,007, BL Add. MSS 55884 and 55891*

160 matter] matter? *NLI 8776(4)* quarrel; what . . . matter? *BL Add. MS 55879, Texas(E), NLI 30,007, BL Add. MSS 55884 and 55891*

162 whatever] Whatever *NLI 8776(4)* Whatever . . . best we say *rev to* Whatever . . . best, we say, *NLI 30,007* Whatever . . . best, we say, *BL Add. MS 55879, Texas(E), BL Add. MSS 55884 and 55891*

153–158 The radical surgery effected on these lines, which give a reason for the Second Roman Soldier's disclosure that these gamblers use ivory dice and not some other, leaves us a void not filled until "marvels" and mysteries of the ancient world are brilliantly suggested in a one-line substitution made in *Four Plays for Dancers* (1921): [Second Roman Soldier] "Or dice were carved / Out of an old sheep's thigh at Ephesus."

[NLI 8776(3), 6r]

3rd Roman soldier
Had you sent
A crier through the world you had not found
Than three old gamblers that ask nothing at all

1st Roman soldier
They say that you are good and that you made the world,
But its no matter.

2nd Roman soldier
Come now let us dance.
The dance of the dice throwers though it may be
He cannot live much longer and has not seen it.

3rd Roman soldier
If he were God of the dice he'd know itsurely
But he is not that God.

1st Roman soldier
One thing is plain
To know that he has nothing that we need
Must be a comfort to him.

2nd Roman soldier
Begin the dance (they dance round the cross, moving as if throwing dice)

Christ
"My Father why hast Thou forsaken Me".

164a More comfortable companions for a deathbed *NLI 8776(4), BL Add. MS 55879, Texas(E), NLI 30,007* deathbed *rev to* death bed *BL Add. MSS 55884 and 55891*

165 that ask nothing at all] that have asked for nothing. *NLI 8776(4), BL Add. MS 55879, Texas(E), NLI 30,007, BL Add. MSS 55884 and 55891*

166 that you are] you're *BL Add. MS 55879, Texas(E), NLI 30,007, BL Add. MSS 55884 and 55891*

167 its] it's *NLI 8776(4), BL Add. MS 55879, Texas(E), NLI 30,007, BL Add. MSS 55884 and 55891* Come now] Come; now *NLI 8776(4)* Come; now *rev to* Come now; *BL Add. MS 55879, NLI 30,007* Come now; *Texas(E), BL Add. MSS 55884 and 55891*

168 dice throwers though it] dice throwers for it *NLI 8776(4)* dice-throwers, for it *BL Add. MS 55879, Texas(E), NLI 30,007, BL Add. MSS 55884 and 55891*

170 were . . . surely] were but the God of dice he'd know it *NLI 8776(4)* were but the God of dice he'd know it, *BL Add. MS 55879, Texas (E), NLI 30,007, BL Add. MSS 55884 and 55891*

171 plain] plain, *BL Add. MS 55879, Texas(E), NLI 30,007, BL Add. MSS 55884 and 55891*

173 dance] dance. *NLI 8776(4)* Begin . . . dance.] In . . . dance *BL Add. MS 55879, Texas(E), NLI 30,007, BL Add. MSS 55884 and 55891*

173a–c We quarrel for a while, but settle it / By throwing dice, and after that, being friends, / Join hand to hand and wheel about the cross. *BL Add. MS 55879, Texas(E), NLI 30,007, BL Add. MSS 55884 and 55891*

173*sd* (they dance . . . dice)] (They dance . . . dice.) *NLI 8776(4)* They dance. [*lacking* round . . . dice.] *BL Add. MS 55879, Texas(E), NLI 30,007, BL Add. MSS 55884 and 55891*

174 "My Father . . . Me".] My Father, . . . Me. *NLI 8776(4)* My Father, . . . Me. *rev to* My Father, . . . Me? *NLI 30,007* My Father, . . . Me? *BL Add. MS 55879, Texas(E), BL Add. MSS 55884 and 55891*

[NLI 8776(3), 6r continued]

Song of Folding and Unfolding of the Cross.

1st Musician **“Lonely the seabird lies at her rest**
Tossed like a parcel of wind-blown spray,
On the wind or follows her prey
Under a grate wave’s hollowing crest.

2nd Musician **God has not appeared to the birds.**

3rd Musician **The geer-eagle has chosen his part**
In blue deep of the upper air
Where one-eyed day can meet his stare
He is content with his savage heart

2nd Musician **God has not appeared to the birds.**

1st Musician **Where have last year’s sygnits gone**
Cool lakes empty, why do they fling
White wing out this side, white wing
What can a swan need but a swan.

2nd Musician **God has not appeared to the birds.**

174*sd* Song of Folding and Unfolding of the Cross.] (Song of the folding and unfolding of the cloth.) *NLI 8776(4)* Song of the . . . cloth. *rev to* Song for the. . . cloth. [*including marginal note:* as on / pp. 144, 149] *NLI 30,007* Song for the . . . cloth. *BL Add. MS 55879, Texas(E), BL Add. MSS 55884 and 55891*

175 “Lonely . . . seabird] Lonely . . . sea-bird *NLI 8776(4), NLI 30,007, BL Add. MSS 55884 and 55891* rest *rev to* rest, *BL Add. MS 55879, Texas(E)*

176 Tossed like a parcel of wind-blown spray,] Blown like a dawn-blenched parcel of spray, [*rev to* spray] *NLI 8776(4)* Blown . . . spray *BL Add. MS 55879, Texas(E), NLI 30,007, BL Add. MSS 55884 and 55891*

177 On the wind] Upon the wind, *NLI 8776(4), BL Add. MS 55879, Texas(E), NLI 30,007, BL Add. MSS 55884 and 55891*

178 grate] great *NLI 8776(4), BL Add. MS 55879, Texas(E), NLI 30,007, BL Add. MSS 55884 and 55891*

180 geer-eagle *rev to* ger-eagle *BL Add. MS 55891* [*including, in pencil:* elsewhere / ‘ger-eagle’.]

181 In blue *rev to* In the blue *rev to* In blue *BL Add. MS 55879*

182 stare] stare; *NLI 8776(4), BL Add. MS 55879, Texas(E), NLI 30,007, BL Add. MSS 55884 and 55891*

183 heart] heart. *NLI 8776(4), BL Add. MS 55879, Texas(E), NLI 30,007, BL Add. MSS 55884 and 55891*

185 Where . . . sygnits gone] But where . . . cygnets gone? *NLI 8776(4), BL Add. MS 55879, Texas(E), NLI 30,007, BL Add. MSS 55884 and 55891*

186 Cool lakes empty,] The lake is empty; *NLI 8776(4), BL Add. MS 55879, Texas(E), NLI 30,007, BL Add. MSS 55884 and 55891*

187 out this side, white wing] out beside white wing? *NLI 8776(4), BL Add. MS 55879, Texas(E), NLI 30,007, BL Add. MSS 55884 and 55891*

188 swan.] swan? *NLI 8776(4), BL Add. MS 55879, Texas(E), NLI 30,007, BL Add. MSS 55884 and 55891*

189 THE END [*inscribed below the line*] *NLI 30,007, BL Add. MS 55879* [*as printed in Texas(E)*]

Appendixes

Appendix A

Note on *The Dreaming of the Bones* Written for *Four Plays for Dancers* (1921)

Transcription of NLI 8775(5), with List of Variants between NLI 8775(5) and Texas(E)

[NLI 8775(5), 1r]

Pica Caslon Note on the
~~The~~ ^ Dreaming of the Bones 1

I have so written this play that Dervogillas few lines
(if need be) and
can be given ^ to Dermot, ~~so that~~ Dervogillas part
can ~~if need be~~ be taken, ~~if need be~~, by a dancer
who has the training of a dancer alone; nor need ~~that~~
~~dancer~~ that masked dancer be a woman.
The conception of the play is derived from
the world wide belief that the dead dream back for
thoughts & ~~deep~~ deeds of
a certain time, though the more passionate ~~events of~~ ^ life.
The wicked, according to Cornelius Agrippa, dream
to be consumed by flames
~~spi~~ themselves ^ ~~concused by flames~~ & persecuted by
deamons & there is precisely the same thought in a
where
Japanese Noh play, ~~who~~ ^ a spirit advised by a
she has
Buddhist priest, ^ met upon the road, seeks to ~~escape~~
~~in ma~~ to ~~escape~~ escape from the flames, by
ceasing to believe in the dream. The lovers in my
lost
play have ~~found~~ themselves ~~estranged or lost~~
in a different, but still ~~doubtless~~ self created
winding of the ~~labyri~~ ~~lab~~ labyrinth of conscience.
The Judwalis distinguish between the shade,
which dreams back through events in the order of
their intensity
~~the poignancy,~~ becoming happier as the more painful,
and their form more intense, wear themselves away; ~~and~~ and
~~and the soul, though that is not their word,~~
lives
the more spiritual portion of the being, which ~~dreams~~ ^ back
through events in the order of their occurance, ~~as this~~ ~~This~~

12 Cancellation, caret, and correction are in pencil.
24 Cancellation, caret, and correction are in pencil.

[NLI 8775(5), 2r]

~~2~~
2

~~dreaming back is in their eyes~~
through through
not merely ^ their temporal but ^ their intellectual order.
to use their ^ ~~term~~ terms
All solar natures, ~~or as we would say objective natures~~
during life move towards a more ~~& more~~ objective form
towards
of experience ~~& intellect~~, ~~while~~ the lunar ^ [?] a more [?]
subjective. After death a lunar man more solar
~~man, reverses thus moves away from objective experience~~
~~and nearer & nearer to objective subjective experience, which~~
~~in the spiritual world is innocence~~ lunar man, ~~/~~
always
reversing the intellectual order, grows ^ closer ~~& closer~~
to objective experience, which in the spiritual world is wisdom,
to
while a solar man, mounts gradually ^ ~~towards an~~
experience
~~extreme~~ the most extreme subjective ^ possible to him{.,}
{I}
~~and~~ {i}n the spiritual world subjectivity is innocence, and
innocence is
~~which~~ ^ in life an accident of nature ^ now ~~becomes~~
the highest achievment of the intellect. I have already
put the thought in verse.
He grows younger every second
That were all his birth-days reckoned
Much too solemn seemed;
Because of what he had dreamed,
Lpr. Or the ambitions that he served,
Cas Much too solemn & reserved;
Jaunting, journeying
To his own days spring
He unpacks the loaded pern
Of all `twas pain or joy to learn,
Of all that he had made.
The outrageous war shall fade;

9 Closes with a canceled dash.
13 Caret and correction in pencil; also period superimposed on comma and the end of the line.
18–29 Marginal stroke and printer's notation in pencil.

[NLI 8775(5), 3r]

At some winding white thorn root (3
He ll practice on the shepherds flute,
Or on the close-cropped grass
Court his shepherd lass,
Or run where lads reform our day time
Till that is their long shouting play time;
Knowledge he will unwind
Through victories of the mind,
Till clambering at the cradle side,
He dreams himself his mothers pride,
All knowledge lost in trance
Of sweeter ignorance.

The shade is said to fade out at last, but the spiritual
passing
being does not fade, ~~passing~~ on to other states of existence
after it has attained, ~~its~~ a spiritual state, of which the
early
surroundings & aplitudes of ~~eary~~ life are a correspondence
when describing
where ^ we speak of events (as in my poem) ~~to describe~~ ^
its ascent, we but use them as correspondence or symbol.

Robartes writes to John Ahern under the date of May 191{9/7},
a curious letter on this subject. "There is an analogy between instead of
the dreaming back of ^the Body of Passion" (I have used ~~insted of~~ ^
term
this term, the more usual ^ shade) "and ~~its~~ our ordinary dreams
and between the life of Spirit & Celestial body" (I have substituted
though [?useful] term those coherent
the less [?technical] ^ Spiritual being) & ~~the coherent~~ thoughts of
dream-less sleep, which as I know on my personal knowledge,
~~run~~ These dreams are now
~~run concurrent~~ coincide with dreams. ~~which somewhat~~ ^
and now live with an
~~symbolize our~~ their symbols, ~~but some times have an extremely~~ ^ ^
independent life. I have several times been present while
carried
my friend an Arab doctor in Damascus ~~carries~~ ^ on long
conversations with a ~~somnambulist~~ sleeping man. I do not say
hypnotised
a ~~hypnotized~~ ^ man, or even a somnambulist for the sleep
~~seem~~ seemed natural sleep produced by fateigue, though some times

---

16 "aplitudes" for "aptitudes"? Cancellation and correction in pencil, as in l. 14.

[NLI 8775(5), 4[r]]

(4

with a curious suddenness. The sleepers would discuss the most profound truths & yet while doing so make now & again, some movement that suggested dreaming though some dream of [?t] which the part that spoke remained entirely unconscious. On waking he would often describe a long dream,| sometimes a symbolic reflection of the conversation but more often produced by some ~~bodily~~ external stimulus ~~suggestion~~ – a fall in temperature of the room, or some condition of body perhaps. Now & again these dreams would interrupt the conversation as when he dreamed he had feathers in his mouth and began to blow. Seeing therefore that I have observed an almost similar devision during life I find no difficulty in accepting a devision, affirmed by my teachers and supported by so much tradition between two parts of the nature when the body is no longer there to hold them to-gether.

I wrote my play before the Robartes papers came into my hands, and in making the penance of Dermot and Dervogilla last so many centuries I have done something for which I no warrant in those papers but warrant there certainly is in the folk lore of all countries.

At certain moments {T/t}he Spiritual being, or rather that part of it which Robartes calls 'The Spirit', is said to enter into the Shade & during those moments ~~it [?d]~~ can converse with living men, though but within the narrow limits of its dream.

6 The slash marks the beginning of a parenthesis, the conclusion of which is marked by the dash in l. 8.
20 "I no warrant" for "I had no warrant"?

List of Variants between NLI 8775(5) and Texas(E) (by manuscript page and line number)

Page	Line	
1	1	I have so written this play that Dervogilla] Dervorgilla's *Texas(E)*
	2	given if need be . . . Dervogillas] given, if need be, . . . Dervorgilla's *Texas(E)*
	3	can be taken] taken *Texas(E)*
	7	world wide . . . back] world-wide . . . back, *Texas(E)*
	8	though] through *Texas(E)*
	11	deamons & there] demons; and there *Texas(E)*
	12	Noh play, . . . spirit] 'Noh' play, . . . spirit, *Texas(E)*
	14	flames, by] flames by *Texas(E)*
	17	self created] self-created *Texas(E)*
	19	Judawalis . . . shade,] Judawalis . . . Shade *Texas(E)*
	21	painful,] painful *Texas(E)*
	22	and their form more intense . . . away;] and, therefore, more intense . . . away, *Texas(E)*
	24	the more spiritual portion of the being,] the Spiritual Being, *Texas(E)*
	25	occurance,] occurrence, *Texas(E)*
2	2	not merely through their temporal but through their intellectual order.] this living back being an exploration of their moral and intellectual origin. *Texas(E)*
	3	their terms] the Arabian terms, *Texas(E)*
	6	lunar man more solar] *lacking* *Texas(E)*
	12	man,] man *Texas(E)*
	15	innocence . . . nature] innocence, . . . nature, *Texas(E)*
	23	reserved;] reserved. *Texas(E)*
	25	days spring] dayspring, *Texas(E)*
3	1	white thorn] whitethorn *Texas(E)*
	2	He ll practice . . . shepherds] He'll practise . . . shepherd's *Texas(E)*
	5	day time] daytime *Texas(E)*
	6	play time;] playtime; *Texas(E)*
	7	will] shall *Texas(E)*
	9	Till] Till, *Texas(E)*
	10	mothers] mother's *Texas(E)*
	13	shade . . . spiritual] Shade . . . Spiritual *Texas(E)*
	14	being] Being *Texas(E)*
	15	attained,] attained *Texas(E)*
	16	aplitudes . . . correspondence] aptitudes . . . correspondence. *Texas(E)*
	17	where as in my poem we speak of events when describing] When, as in my poem, I speak of events while describing *Texas(E)*
	18	its ascent, we] the ascent of the Spiritual Being, I *Texas(E)*
	19	Robartes writes to John Ahern, . . . 1919,] Michael Robartes writes to Aherne, . . . 1917 *Texas(E)*
	20	subject. "There] subject: 'There *Texas(E)*
	21	Passion"] Passion' *Texas(E)*
	22	term, . . . shade) "and . . . dreams] term . . . Shade), 'and . . . dreams – *Texas(E)*

23 body"] Body taken together' *Texas(E)* substituted] substituted for both terms *Texas(E)*
24 less [? technical] though [? useful] term Spiritual being) &] less technical, though, I fear, vague term Spiritual Being), 'and *Texas(E)*
25 dream-less . . . which] dreamless . . . which, *Texas(E)*
26 are now] are at one time *Texas(E)*
27 and now] and at another *Texas(E)*
29 friend . . . in Damascus] friend, . . . in Bagdad, *Texas(E)*
30 man.] man, and I have myself joined in those conversations *Texas(E)*
31 somnambulist] somnambulist, *Texas(E)*
32 fateigue, though some times] fatigue, though sometimes *Texas(E)*
4 1 sleepers] sleeper *Texas(E)*
2 make] make, *Texas(E)*
3 dreaming though] dreaming, although *Texas(E)*
4 some dream of which the part] the part *Texas(E)*
5 unconscious.] unconscious of the dream. *Texas(E)*
7 conversation] conversation, *Texas(E)*
8 room,] rooms, *Texas(E)*
10 conversation] conversation, *Texas(E)*
11 Seeing] Seeing, *Texas(E)*
12 therefore that I have observed an almost similar division] therefore, that I have observed a separation between two parts of the nature *Texas(E)*
13 life I find no difficulty in accepting a] life, I find no difficulty in believing in a *Texas(E)*
14 devision,] more complete separation, *Texas(E)* teachers] teachers, *Texas(E)*
15 tradition between two parts of the nature] tradition, *Texas(E)*
16 them to-gether.] the two parts put together.' *Texas(E)*
18 hands, and] hands, even before I myself had received much of their thought from a difficult source, and *Texas(E)*
19 Dervogilla] Dervorgilla *Texas(E)*
20 I no . . . in those papers but] I had no . . . in these papers or from that source, but *Texas(E)*
21 folk lore] folklore *Texas(E)*
22 being,] Being, *Texas(E)*
23 Spirit',] Spirit,' *Texas(E)*
24 Shade . . . moments can] Shade, . . . moments it can *Texas(E)*

Appendix B

Note for a Program on a Production of *The Dreaming of the Bones* at the Abbey Theatre

Transcriptions of NLI 30,545 and NLI 30,820

[NLI 30,545]

Note for Abbey Programe (Dreaming of Bones)

I meant
~~When I~~ ~~wrote~~
I ~~wrote have written~~ this & other dance plays
~~with the intent & meant this~~ for performance in private
houses before very small audiences. ~~In especially~~ this
[?~~tells~~] ~~I meant~~ it is essential that there should be no
scenery, no lighting effects; the players ~~should~~
action
describe or suggest^scenery ~~& a~~, light & darkness, by
their movements & their words. To increase the power of
suggestion I have followed ~~th~~ Japanese example
& substituted a dance ~~for the use~~ for the acted climax
~~where ever it seems~~
of more naturalistic drama, & ~~such naturalism,~~ ~~where ever~~ it
And where it
suited to the story, ritual for naturalistic action. ~~The chorus~~
A movement round the stage, to the accompaniment of drum & flute
represents a mountain climbed & a change of scene;
A movement [?~~on~~] from one side of the stage to the other a shorter
climb. There was a time, when I wanted every word sung
~~upon the stage~~ to as audible & intelligible as the spoken dialogue
but now, I let the musician ~~write as the theme~~
do ~~what words & music require~~ write as the theme moves
think half
him, & I ~~look upon~~ my words as a^secret between
myself and the singers. ~~I~~ I do not put the words into the
Programe, ~~because~~ because I do not want my audience to divide
afterwards
their attention between the stage & the programe; they can find them^
possibly ~~in one of~~ in my book "Plays & Controversies".

W.B.Y.

---

16 "to [be] as audible" for sense?
19 "think [of] my words" for sense?

[NLI 30,820]

I wrote this and other dance plays for performance
in private houses before very small audiences.
that
It is essential ^ ~~that~~ there should be no scenery,
no lighting effects; the players suggest
scenery, light and darkness by their movements
and their words. To increase the power of suggestion
I have followed Japanese example and substituted
a dance for the acted climax of more naturalistic
suited
drama, and where it ~~suited~~ the story ritual for
naturalistic ~~acting &~~ action. A movement round the
stage to the accompaniment of drum & flute
represents a mountain climbed, ~~or a change of~~
~~scenery~~ a movement from one side of the stage to the
other a ~~shorter~~ shorter climb. There was a time
when I wanted every word sung to be as audible
& intelligible as the spoken dialogue; but now I
write
let the musician ~~white~~ as the theme moves him;
[?and] I think of my words as a half secret between myself
the print
and ~~the~~ singer. I do not ~~print~~ the words in the
programme because I do ^ not want my audience to
~~its~~ their between
divide ~~their~~ attention ~~between~~ the stage and the programme [~~?~~]:
they can find them afterwards in my book “Plays and Controversies”
W.B.Y

Appendix C

Note on *Calvary* Written for *Four Plays for Dancers* (1921)

Transcriptions of NLI 8776(1) and NLI 8776(2), with List of Variants between NLI 8776(2) and NLI 30,125, NLI 30,789, and Texas(E)

[NLI 8776(1), 1r]

The Road to Calvary
I have written the little songs of the Chorus to please myself
~~cali co~~ confident that singer & composer when the time came
for performance would certainly make it impossible for the
audience to know what the words were. I used to think that singers
should sing a recept for a good desk, or a list of local trains
or something else they wanted to get by heart, but I have changed my
mind & now I prefer ~~that~~ to give here some mystery or secret.
learn
A reader can always ~~turn~~ solve the mystery & ^ the secret by
turning to a note, which need not be as long as those Dante
birds
put to service of the odes in the <u>Convito</u>. I use ~~birds~~ as symbols
of subjective life & ~~I have founded this symbolism in a passage~~
certain
~~among those papers of Michael Robartes over which I have also~~
~~spent several years~~. ~~Probably~~ {M/m}y reason for this & certain other
things ~~will not be clever~~ cannot be explained fully, ~~without~~
~~going into too much detail~~ till I have ~~finished my work as editor~~
~~and published my work as editor. Then~~ published some part
at any rate of those papers of Michael Robartes, over which I have
now spent some years. The following passage in a letter written
by Robartes to Ahearne in the spring of 1917 must suffice. ~~for the~~
~~moment.~~ "At present I rather pride my self on beleiving
all the superstition of the Judwalis, or rather in beleiving that
there is but one amongst them that may not be true, but at
in the early morning
first my west-European mind rebelled. Once ^ when I was living in a
~~tent~~ horsehair tent, among the tents of that tribe, a young Arab
woke me & told me to come with him if I would see a great
wonder. [?He] brought me to level place in the sand just outside
of a certain Arab who had ~~arived~~ arrived the night before & had as
I knew a reputation as a wonder worker, & showed me certain marks
on the sand. I said they were the marks of a jackal but he would not

5 "recept" for "receipt"?

[NLI 8776(1), 2^{r}]

2

have this. He had passed by a little after ~~sun r~~ sunrise & there was not a mark & a few minutes later on his returning the marks were there. No beast could have come & gone unseen. When I asked his explanation he said they were made by the wonder workers “~~daemon” families , or rather~~ “Daimon” or “Angel”. “What” I said “has it a beasts form” “He goes much about the world he has been in Persia, in Afhanistan & as far west as Tripoli~~”~~ He is interested in things, in places, ~~in peoples~~, he likes to be with many people & that is why his daimon has the form of a beast but your daimon if it came would have a birds shape because you are a soletary man”. Later on when I mastered their philosophy I came to learn, when the boy distinguished between the wonder workers & myself he classified ~~us between according to~~ according to their devisions of all mankind into those who are dominated by objects, & those who are dominated by the self, or Zat, or as we would say into objective & subjective natures. Certain birds, especially, as I see things, such lonely birds as the heron, the hawk & eagle, & the swan, are the nature symbols of subjectivity ~~whence I have part of the nature while the beasts, especially those that run in packs, seeing things as we do~~ especially when floating upon the
upon
wind alone, or alighting ~~by~~ some pool or river, while the beasts that run upon the ground especially those that run in packs are the natural symbols of objective men. Objective men though often personally alone, are never alone in their thought, which is always developed in agreement or in conflict with the thought of others, & always seeks the welfare of some cause or institution, while subjective men are ~~soletudes very self~~ the more lonely the more they are true to type seeking always that which is unique or personal. I have used my bird symbolism in these songs, to increase the objective loneliness of Christ, ~~by contrasting it with a loneliness which feels its self as imperfection & a feeling of sorrow, with thing~~ by contrasting it with

[NLI 8776(1), 3[r]]

1 ~~opposite in~~ a loneliness opposite in kind, & that unlike his
2 can whether joyous or sorrowful, be sufficient to itself. ~~They He~~
3 I have surrounded him with the images of those he cannot save,
4 ~~who await none or a different saviour, who have served neither~~
5 ~~God nor ceas Ceasar. The Daimons or Lazerus & Judas~~
~~Lazerus~~
6 ~~Perhaps Zazerus & Judas, are also among those whose~~
7 ~~daimons are birds, though Rom & the Roman soldiers~~
8 ~~are often forms of those for whom he has not died~~
9 ~~or for whom he died in vain~~ not only the birds who
10 have served neither god not Ceasar, & await ~~n~~ for none or a
the
11 different saviour, but Lazerus & Judas &^ Roman soldiers for
12 whom he has died in vain. "Christ" ~~had no~~ writes" Robartes
pitied
13 "~~never pitied intellectual despair but~~ only^ those whose suffering
~~common lot~~ in or in or in sin
14 is ~~from~~ rooted in ~~the general destiny,~~ death, poverty^ sickness ~~sin~~^
15 ~~He takes~~ in some shape of the common lot, & be came especially
16 to the poor, who are most subject to exterior visistude; ~~he was an~~
~~among~~
17 ~~objective, one of those whose nature is symbolized in the Gyraldus' twenty~~
18 ~~eight sybolical human types, by the by those lunar phases in which~~
19 ~~the dark portion of the disk is greater than the light portion~~"^ I
that
20 have therefore represented in Lazerus & Judas types of intellectual despair
that ~~and~~ lay beyond his sympathy
I suggested lay
21 ^while in the Roman soldiers, a form of objectivity that ~~has~~^
22 ~~passed~~ beyond his help. Robartes daid "in one of the conversations
23 recorded by Ahearne "
whom he taught
24 ~~and what is the god, for which^ the saints lacerate their bodies to~~
to starve and to exterminate
25 ~~starved & exterminated themselves, but the spiritual objectivity~~ object of their
26 ~~thought, the Spiritual objective~~" 'I heard much by ~~a certain old Arab~~
27 these songs of joy written by a certain old Arab which owing to the
28 ~~their~~ circumstances of their origin were considered as proof of a
29 peculiar sanctity. He held the faith of Ben Luki but did
30 not live with any of the two or three wandering companies of
31 Judwalis. He was I think the first Judwali I had met

16 "visistude" for "vicissitude."

[NLI 8776(1), 4r]

He lived in the town of [?Hyril] as servant to a rich Arab
merchant. He himself had a rich merchant & had
long
more than one^journey. On his his return from one of these
journeys he had found ~~himself in~~ his house in possession
of an enemy & himself banished by the authorities of the town
on some charge, I think of impiety, & it was then he made his
first song of joy. A few years later his wife & child ~~died~~
~~mur~~ were murdered by robbers in the desert, & after certain
weeks during which it was thought that he must die of
grief his face cleared & his step firm & be made his second
song. He gave away all his goods & became a servant
in Damascus & a year or two later believing that his
death was near [?he] made his third song of joy. He lived
however for several months & when I met him had the
use of all his faculties. I asked him about the three songs
for I knew that even on his death bed, as became the
votary of a small ~~obscure~~ contentious sect he would delight
in ~~expo~~ exposition. “I said, “though I know from the songs
themselves that this was not his thought, but his ~~thought~~ explanation
in his own words “You have rejoiced that the will of god should
be done, even though you & yours ~~mus~~ must suffer” He ~~th~~
answered with some emotion “o no ~~all~~ Ben Luki has taught
us to divide all things into Chance & Choice. ~~O we m~~
can
one ~~must~~ think about the world or about man or any thing
else until all has vanished but these two things. They exist
in god also, for if they did not he would not have freedom
he would be bound ~~h~~ by his own Choice, ~~only a god alone~~
In god alone is each perfect, & without limit or a hindrance.
~~is each infinite is each perfect & without limit.~~ If I
should throw ~~dice~~ from the dice box there would be but six

2 “had [been] a rich merchant” for sense?

[NLI 8776(1), 5r]

possible numbers, six possible sides on each of the dice
have
but when god throws ~~dice~~, he uses dice that ^ all ~~possible nu~~
all possible numbers & sides
~~numbers & sides beyond counting~~. ~~S~~ Some worship ~~hi~~ His
& it is
Choice ^ that is easy, but ^ pleasant to know that he has willed
happens us
for some unknown purpose all that ~~happened happens~~, but I
have spent my life in ~~worshi~~ worshiping, ~~the Chance that~~ is
is
His Chance that ^ equal with his Choice ~~for in~~ & all he
does must be both Chanced & Chosen, though Mankind can but
see it as one or the other, & the moment in which I am
nearest to {H/h}im is that in which I realize its immensity."
~~is that a [?chance]. I cry "blessed be the~~ And because it is very
difficult to do that & because I have put it into a song I
am famous among my people."

[NLI 8776(2), 1[r]]

Pica Cas **Note on ~~the Symbolism of~~ "Calvary".**

I have written the little songs of the Chorus to please
myself, confident that singer and composer when the time came
for performance, would certainly make it impossible for the
{~~xxxxxxxxxxxxxxxxxxxxxx~~}
audience to {understand the words} know what the words were.
a
{~~xxx~~}
I used to think that singers should sing a recipe for {the} good
dish, or a list of local trains, or something else they want to
get by heart, but I have changed my mind and now I prefer to
give him some mystery or secret. A reader can always solve
the mystery and learn the secret by turning to a note, which
need not be as long as those Dante put to several of the odes
in the "Convito". I use~~d~~ birds as symbols of subjective life,
and my reason for this, and for certain other things, cannot be
explained fully till I have published some part at any rate
of those papers of Michael Robartes, over which I have now spent
several years. The following passage in a letter written by
Robartes to Ahearne in the spring of 1917 must suffice. "At
present I rather pride myself in believing all the superstitions
of the Jugwalis, or rather in believing that there is not one
true
amongst them that may not be ~~proved~~, but at first my West Euro-
ed
pean mind rebel~~s~~. Once in the early morning when I was living
among other similar tents
in a horse-hair tent ~~amonst the tents of that tribe~~, a young
Arab woke me and told me to come with him, if I would see a great

6 Comma after "dish" added in black ink.
9 Comma after "which" added in black ink.
11 Comma after "life" added and "d" in "used" stricken, both in black ink.
12 Commas added in black ink.
22 Comma after "him" added in black ink.

[NLI 8776(2), 2[r]]

2

{xx / to}

wonder. He brought me to a level place in the sand, just {xx / to}
outside the tent of a certain Arab, who had arrived the night
before and had, as I knew, a reputation as a wonder-worker, and
showed me certain marks on the sand. I said they were the
When he
marks of a jackal, but he would not have this. ~~He~~ had passed
by a little after sunrise ~~and~~ there was not a mark, and a few
~~his~~
minutes later ~~on / returning~~ the marks were there. No beast
could have come and gone unseen. When I asked his explanation
he said they were made by the wonder-workers "Daimon" or "Angel".
"What" I said, "has it a beast's form?" "He goes much about
he said
the world," "he has been in Persia and in Afghanistan and as far
West as Tripoli. He is interested in things, in places, he
likes to be with many people and that is why his Daimon has the
form of a beast, but your Daimon ~~if it came~~, would have a
bird's shape because you are a solitary man." Later on when
I mastered their philosophy, I came to learn that ~~when~~ the
boy ~~distinguished between the wonder-worker and myself, he~~
had but the wonder worker and myself
classified ~~us~~ according to their division of all mankind into
those who are dominated by objects and those who are dominated
by the self or <u>Zat</u>, or as we would say, into objective and
subjective natures. Certain birds, especially as I see things,
such lonely birds as the heron, ~~the~~ hawk ~~and~~, eagle and ~~the~~ swan,
are
~~or~~ the natural symbols of subjectivity, especially when floating
upon the wind alone or alighting upon some pool or river, while
the beasts that run upon the ground, especially those that run

---

2 Comma after "Arab" added in black ink.
3 Comma after "had" added in black ink.
6 Comma after "mark" added in black ink.
10 Quotation mark added before "He".
11 Quotation marks added, with interpolation, in black ink.
22 Comma added before "eagle" in black ink.
24 Comma after "river" added in black ink.

[NLI 8776(2), 3[r]]

3

in packs are the natural symbols of objective man. Objective
men though often personally alone, are never alone in their
thought which is always developed in agreement or in conflict
with the thought of others and always seeks the welfare of some
cause or institution, while subjective men are the more lonely
the more they are true to type, seeking always that which is
unique or personal. I have used my bird~~s~~-symbolism in these
songs to increase the objective loneliness of Christ, by contrast-
a
ing it with ~~the~~ loneliness opposite in kin~~d and~~d that unlike his
can be, whether joyous or sorrowful, sufficient to itself. I
have surrounded him with the images of those he cannot save/ , ⋏
with
~~N~~ot only ^ the birds, who have served neither God nor Caesar and
with
await for none or for a different saviour, but ^ Lazarus and Judas
and the Roman soldiers for whom he has died in vain. "Christ,"
writes Robartes, "only pitied those whose suffering is rooted in
{xxxx}
death, in poverty, or in {soci} sickness, or in sin, in some shape
of the common lot, and he came especially to the poor who are
most subject to exterior vicissitude~~s~~". I have therefore repre-
sented in Lazarus and Judas, types of that intellectual despair
that lay beyond his sympathy, while in the Roman soldiers, I
suggest a form of objectivity that lay beyond his help. Robartes
{xxxxxx}
said in one of the conversations recorded by {hearn} Ahearne. "I
' "Three Songs of Joy" '
heard much of ~~these songs of joy~~ written by a certain old Arab,
which owing to the circu^mstances of their origin, were considered
{xxxx}
as proofs of great sanctity. He held the faith of {ben} Kusta
ben Luki, but did not live with any of the two or three wandering

---

5 Comma after "institution" added in black ink.
8 Comma after "Christ" added in black ink.
10 Comma after "be" added in black ink.
12 Comma after "birds" added in black ink.
13 Comma after "saviour" added in black ink.
16 Comma after "sickness" added in black ink.
20 Comma after "sympathy" added in black ink.
23 Comma after "Arab" added in black ink.
24 Canceled comma after "origin" may be a stet mark.

[NLI 8776(2), 4r]

4

companies of Judwalis. ~~He was, I think, the first Judwali I had met~~, {H/h}e lived in the town of H   as servant to a rich Arab merchant. He ~~and~~ ^him^self had been a rich merchant and had made more than one long journey. On his return from one of these journeys, he had found his house in posession of an enemy and himself banished by the authorities of the town on some charge I think of impiety, and it was then he made his first song of joy. A few years later, his wife and child were murdered by [?] robbers in the desert and after certain weeks, during which it was thought that he must die of grief, his face cleared and his step grew firm and he made his second song. He gave away all his goods and became a servant {xx/of} in Damascus and a year or two later, believing that his death was near, he made his third song of joy. He lived, however, for several months and when I met him, had the use of all his faculties. I asked him about the "{T/t}hree {S/s}ongs" for I knew that even on his death-bed, as became the votary of a small contentious sect, he would delight in exposition. I said, though I knew from his songs themselves, that this was not his thought, but I wanted his explanation in his own words: "You have rejoiced that the Will of God should be done even though you and yours must {xxxxxx/perish} suffer". He answered with some emotion: "Oh no, Kusta ben Luki has taught us to divide all things into ~~Chants~~ ^Chance^ and Choice; one can think about the world and about men, or anything else until all has vanished but these two things, for they are indeed

9 Comma after "weeks" added in black ink.

17 Comma after "death-bed" added in black ink.

[NLI 8776(2), 5[r]]

5

the first cause of the animate and inanimate world. They exist
in God, **for if they did not [?,] He would not have freedom, He would**
be
can they ~~all~~ united, ~~and~~ yet
be bound by his own Choice. In God alone, indeed, ~~can~~ each be
^{xxxxxx
perfect and without limit or hindrance. If I should {**prove**}
throw from the dice-box, there would be but six possible ~~numbers,~~
~~**six possible**~~ **sides on each of the dice, but when God throws, He**
uses dice that have all numbers and sides. Some worship his
Choice; that is easy to know that he has willed for some unknown
is pleasant
purpose all that happens, ^ **but I have spent my life in worshiping**
Chance
his ~~**Chants that is equal with his Choice for all He does must**~~
~~**be both Chanced and chosen though mankind can but see it as one**~~
~~**or the other and the moment at which I am nearest to Him is that**~~
~~**in which I realise the immensity of His Chance and because it**~~
~~**is very difficult to do that and because I have put it into three**~~
~~**songs, I am famous among my people.**~~ and that moment when
Chance
I understand the immensity of his ~~Coic~~ ~~Choice~~ ^ is the
moment when I am nearest him. Because it is
very difficult & because I have put my understanding
into ~~the Three Songs~~ three songs I am famous
among my people."

2 Comma after "God" added in black ink and, evidently, cancellation of a typed comma after "not."

List of Variants between NLI 8776(2) and Texas(E) (by manuscript page and line number)

Page	Line	
1	1	Chorus] chorus *NLI 30,125*
	2	composer] composer, *NLI 30,125*, *Texas(E)*
	3	performance,] performance *rev to* performance, *NLI 30,125*
	11	"Convito".] Convito. *NLI 30,125*, *Texas(E)*
	17	Ahearne] Aherne *NLI 30,125*, *Texas(E)* "At] 'At, *Texas(E)*
	18	in] on *NLI 30,125*, *Texas(E)*
	19	Jugwalis,] Judwalis, *NLI 30,125*, *Texas(E)*
	21	morning] morning, *NLI 30,125*, *Texas(E)*
	22	him,] him *NLI 30,125*, *Texas(E)*
2	9	wonder-workers] wonder-worker's *NLI 30,125*, *Texas(E)*
		"Daimon" or "Angel".] "Daimon" or "Angel." *rev to* 'Daimon' or 'Angel.' *NLI 30,125* "Daimon" or "Angel." *Texas(E)*
	10	"What" . . . "has . . . form?" "He] "What," . . . "has . . . form?" "He *rev to* 'What,' . . . 'has . . . form?' 'He *NLI 30,125* "What," . . . "has . . . form?" "He *Texas(E)*
	11	world," he said "he] world," he said; "he *rev to* world,' he said; 'he *NLI 30,125* world," he said; "he *Texas(E)*
		Afghanistan] Afghanistan, *NLI 30,125*, *Texas(E)*
	13	people] people, *NLI 30,125*, *Texas(E)*
	15	man."] man.' *NLI 30,125* on] on, *NLI 30,125*, *Texas(E)*
	18	wonder worker] wonder-worker *NLI 30,125*, *Texas(E)*
	20	or] or, *NLI 30,125*, *Texas(E)*
	22	eagle] eagle, *NLI 30,125*, *Texas(E)*
3	1	packs] packs, *NLI 30,125*, *Texas(E)*
	2	men though often personally] men, though often personally *rev to* men, however personally *NLI 30,125*, *Texas(E)*
	3	thought] thought, *NLI 30,125*, *Texas(E)*
	7	personal. I have] personal." ¶ I have *NLI 30,125*, *Texas(E)*
	8	Christ,] Christ *NLI 30,125*, *Texas(E)*
	9	loneliness opposite in kind that] loneliness, opposite in kind, that *NLI 30,125*, *Texas(E)* his] His *NLI 30,125*, *Texas(E)*
	11	him . . . he] Him . . . He *NLI 30,125*, *Texas(E)*
	12	Caesar] Caesar, *NLI 30,125*, *Texas(E)*
	14	he] He *NLI 30,125*, *Texas(E)* "Christ,"] 'Christ,' *Texas(E)*
	15	"only] 'only *Texas(E)*
	17	he] He *Texas(E)*
	18	vicissitude".] vicissitude." *NLI 30,125* vicissitude.' *Texas(E)*
	19	Judas,] Judas *NLI 30,125*, *Texas(E)*
	20	his] His *NLI 30,125*, *Texas(E)* soldiers,] soldiers *NLI 30,125*, *Texas(E)*
	21	his] His *NLI 30,125*, *Texas(E)*
	22	Ahearne. "I] Aherne: "I *NLI 30,125* Aherne: 'I *Texas(E)*
	23	'"Three Songs of Joy"'] *Three Songs of Joy*, *NLI 30,125*
	24	origin,] origin *NLI 30,125*, *Texas(E)*

4 2 H[*blank space*]] H— *rev to* Hâyel *NLI 30,125*, *Texas(E)*

3/4 merchant and had made more than one long journey] merchant, and had been several times to India. *rev to* merchant of Aneyza and had been several times to India. *NLI 30,125*, *Texas(E)*

5 journeys,] journeys *NLI 30,125*, *Texas(E)*

6/7 and himself banished by the authorities of the town on] and was himself driven from . . . on *rev to* and was himself driven from Aneyza by . . . on *(but incorporating revisions, now lost, including* the authorities] the Aneyzan authorities *del) NLI 30,125* was himself driven from Aneyza by the Wahâbies on *Texas(E)*

7 charge] charge, *NLI 30,125*, *Texas(E)*

8 later,] later *NLI 30,125*, *Texas(E)*

9 desert] desert, *NLI 30,125*, *Texas(E)*

12 in Damascus] in Damascus, *rev to* in Hâyel, *NLI 30,125*, *Texas(E)*

15 months] months, *NLI 30,125*, *Texas(E)*

him,] him *NLI 30,125*, *Texas(E)*

16 "Three Songs"] "Three Songs," *rev to* 'Three Songs,' *NLI 30,125* "Three Songs," *Texas(E)*

17 death-bed,] deathbed, *NLI 30,125* , *Texas(E)* small] small, *Texas(E)*

18 said, though] said (though *rev to* said, (though *NLI 30,125* said (though *Texas(E)*

20 words: "You] words): 'You *NLI 30,125* words): "You *Texas(E)*

22 suffer".] suffer." *rev to* suffer.' *NLI 30,125* suffer." *Texas(E)*

"Oh] "Oh, *rev to* 'Oh, *NLI 30,125* "Oh, *Texas(E)*

24 men,] man, *NLI 30,125*, *Texas(E)*

5 2 freedom,] freedom *NLI 30,789*

3 his] His *NLI 30,125*, *Texas(E)*

united, yet] united and *NLI 30,789*

5 dice-box,] dice-box *NLI 30,125*, *Texas(E)*

6 throws,] throws *NLI 30,125*, *Texas(E)*

7 his] His *NLI 30,125*, *Texas(E)*

8 easy] easy; *NLI 30,125*, *Texas(E)*

he] He *NLI 30,789, NLI 30,125*, *Texas(E)*

9 pleasant,] pleasant *rev to* pleasant; *NLI 30,125*, *Texas(E)*

worshiping] worshipping *NLI 30,125*, *Texas(E)*

10 his] His *NLI 30,125*, *Texas(E)*

10–17 Chance and that moment when I understand the immensity of his Chance is the moment when I am nearest him. Because it is] Chance that is equal with his Choice The moment at which I am nearest to Him is that in which I understand the immensity of His Chance. Because it that is *NLI 30,789*

15 and that moment] is the moment *NLI 30,125*

16 his] His *NLI 30,125*, *Texas(E)*

17 him] Him *NLI 30,125*, *Texas(E)*

18 difficult] difficult, *NLI 30,789*

19 songs] songs, *NLI 30,789*

20 people."] people. *NLI 30,789* people.'" *NLI 30,125*, *Texas(E)*

Appendix D

Order of Contents for *Four Plays for Dancers* (1921), NLI 30,079

[NLI 30, 079, 4^{r} and 5^{r}]

[4^{r}]

(1) Preface.
(2) "Dreaming of the Bones"
from "Two Plays for Dancers"
(3) "At the Hawk's Well"
from printed copy enclosed
(4) Calvary
(6) note on first performance of "At the
Hawk's Well"
(7) note on Symbolism of "The Only Jealousy"
(8) note on Symbolism of "Calvary"

[5^{r}]

iv

Print in the following order: –

<u>CONTENTS</u>.

1. Preface.
2. Dreaming of the Bones.

(From "Two Plays for Dancers" which please keep clean.

3 Preface to "At the Hawks Well"

<u>4</u> **~~3~~. At the Hawk's Well. (from printed copy enclosed)**

<u>5</u> <u>~~4~~</u> **~~4~~. The Only Jealousy of Emer. " (from "Two Plays for Dancers")**

<u>6</u> <u>~~5~~</u> **~~5~~. Calvary. (from typed copy enclosed)**

<u>7</u> **~~6~~. Note "On Dreaming of the Bones".**

<u>8</u> **~~7~~. Note on first performance of "The Hawk's Well".**

1^{r}–3^{r} Consist of manuscript notes for *The Only Jealousy of Emer*.

4^{r} Presumably, a number (5) would have consisted of "The Only Jealously of Emer"; this is confirmed in 5^{r}, where the play also follows "At the Hawk's Well."

5^{r} This typed (and amended) contents for *Four Plays for Dancers* is radically different from that used in the book, because *The Dreaming of the Bones* and its notes had yet to be moved. They fell, correspondingly, before the texts and notes of *Calvary*.

[NLI 30,079, 5[r] continued and 6[r]]

[5[r] continued]

9 ~~8~~. **Note on symbolism of "The Only Jealousy of Emer".**

10 **9. Note on symbolism of "Calvary".**

P. S. Mr. Dulac's designs can be placed where convenient. Whichever comes out best had better be frontispiece.

[6[r]]

~~For [?or] from des~~
Four
~~Three~~ designs for masks or costumes
sent
will be ~~done~~ for this book by
Edmond Dulac, & two photographs
of players wearing masks

5[r], P. S. Perhaps the matter of Dulac's designs and the frontispiece to *At the Hawk's Well* had as much to do with Yeats's decision on the final order, which was not entirely chronological, as his wish to pair *The Dreaming of the Bones* and *Calvary*, which treated different aspects of the same themes (temptation and betrayal) and grew from a single conception.

6[r] Further directions related to the postscript on 5[r].

Appendix E

Preface and Contents for *Four Plays for Dancers* (1921)

Transcription of Texas(D), with List of Variants between Texas(D) and Page Proofs of the Coole Edition (NLI 30,007, BL Add. MS 55884, and BL Add. MS 55891)

[Texas(D)]

PREFACE

Two of these plays must be opened by the unfolding and folding of the cloth, a substitute for the rising of the curtain, and all must be closed by it. The others, "The Dreaming of the Bones" and "Calvary," should have the same opening, unless played after plays of the same kind, when it may seem a needless repetition. All must be played to the accompaniment of drum and zither and flute, but on no account must the words be spoken "through music" in the fashionable way; and the players must move a little stiffly and gravely like marionettes and, I think, to the accompaniment of drum taps. I felt, however, during the performance of "The Hawk's Well," the only one played up to this, that there was much to discover. Should I make a serious attempt, which I may not, being rather tired of the theatre, to arrange and supervise performances, the dancing will give me most trouble, for I know but vaguely what I want. I do not want any existing form of stage dancing, but something with a smaller gamut of expression, something more reserved, more self-controlled, as befits performers within arms' reach of their audience.

The designs by Mr. Dulac represent the masks and costumes used in the first performance of "The Hawk's Well." The beautiful mask of Cuchulain may, I think, serve for Dervorgilla, and if I write plays and organize performances on any scale and with any system, I shall hope for a small number of typical masks, each capable of use in several plays. The face of the speaker should be as much a work of art as the lines that he speaks or the costume that he wears, that all may be as artificial as possible. Perhaps in the end one would write plays for certain masks. If some fine sculptor should create for my "Calvary," for instance, the masks of Judas, of Lazarus, and of Christ, would not this suggest other plays now, or many generations from now, and possess one cannot tell what philosophical virility? The mask, apart from its beauty, may suggest new situations at a moment when the old ones seem exhausted; "The Only Jealousy of Emer" was written to find what dramatic effect one could get out of a mask, changed while the player remains upon the stage to suggest a change of personality. At the end of this book there is some music by Mr. Rummell, which my friends tell me is both difficult and beautiful for "The Dreaming of the Bones." It will require, I am told,

[Texas(D)]

either a number of flutes of which the flute-player will pick now one, now another, or an elaborate modern flute which would not look in keeping. I prefer the first suggestion. I notice that Mr. Rummell has written no music for the dance, and I have some vague memory that when we talked it over in Paris he felt that he could not without the dancer's help. There is also music for "The Hawk's Well" by Mr. Dulac, which is itself an exposition of method, for it was written after a number of rehearsals and for instruments that have the most pictorial effect.

"The Dreaming of Bones" and "The Only Jealousy of Emer," bound together as *Two Plays for Dancers*, were printed on my sister's hand-press at Dundrum, County Dublin, and published in a limited edition in the spring of 1919, while "At the Hawk's Well" makes a part of the edition of *The Wild Swans at Coole*, printed at the same press in 1917, though not of the later edition of that book published by Macmillan. "At the Hawk's Well" and "The Only Jealousy of Emer" are the first and last plays of a series of four dealing with Cuchulain's life. The others are my "Green Helmet" and "Baile's Strand." "Calvary" has not hitherto been published.

That I might write "The Dreaming of the Bones" Mr. W. A. Henderson with great kindness wrote out for me all historical illusions to "Dervorgilla"; but neither that nor any of these plays could have existed if Mr. Edmund Dulac had not taught me the value and beauty of the mask and rediscovered how to design and make it.

W. B. YEATS.

July 1920.

[Texas(D)]

CONTENTS

List of Variants between Texas(D) and the Coole Edition (NLI 30,007, BL Add. MS 55884 and BL Add. MS 55891) (by line number)

Line

3/4 "The Dreaming of the Bones"] *The Dreaming of the Bones NLI 30,007, BL Add. MSS 55884 and 55891*

4 "Calvary,"] *Calvary, NLI 30,007, BL Add. MSS 55884 and 55891*

8 "through music"] 'through music' *NLI 30,007, BL Add. MSS 55884 and 55891*

11/12 "The Hawk's Well,"] *The Hawk's Well, NLI 30,007, BL Add. MSS 55884 and 55891*

21 The designs by Mr. Dulac represent] Mr. Edmund Dulac designed *NLI 30,007, BL Add. MSS 55884 and 55891*

22 "The Hawk's Well"] The Hawk's Well *NLI 30,007, BL Add. MSS 55884 and 55891*

24 Dervorgilla *rev to* Dervagilla *(beside canceled reference:* in Vol. II, p. 235*) NLI 30,007* Dervagilla *BL Add. MS 55891* Dervagilla *rev to* Dervorgilla [*with note:* as other Gaelic names, Lady Gregory's spelling, also others] *BL Add. MS 55884*

31 "Calvary,"] *Calvary, NLI 30,007, BL Add. MSS 55884 and 55891*

36/37 "The Only Jealousy of Emer"] *The Only Jealousy of Emer NLI 30,007, BL Add. MSS 55884 and 55891*

41 beautiful] beautiful, *NLI 30,007, BL Add. MSS 55884 and 55891*

44 flute] flute, *NLI 30,007, BL Add. MSS 55884 and 55891*

49 "The Hawk's Well"] *The Hawk's Well NLI 30,007, BL Add. MSS 55884 and 55891*

52 effect.] effect. . . . [*ellipsis added*] *NLI 30,007, BL Add. MSS 55884 and 55891*

Facing the preface, on the blank p. [84] of NLI 30,007, is the following inscription (circled, not in Yeats's hand):

CONTENTS

At the Hawk's Well
The Only Jealousy of Emer
The Dreaming of the Bones
Calvary

put on p. 85

24 A note and cross-reference at the end of Rummell's music, on p. 202 of BL Add. MS 55891, reads as follows:

> Dervorgilla's few lines can be given if / need [X] be, to Dermot, and Dervorgilla's part / taken by a dancer who has the training / of a dancer alone, nor need that dancer, / if masked, be a woman.
>
> [X] cf pp. 85 and 87 where this is corrected by the author / to Dervagilla

As if a rejoinder to this, a slip was attached to the note in BL Add. MS 55884 on "Gaelic names," offering Lady Gregory's precedent as the main authority for reverting the spelling of "Dervagilla" to "Dervorgilla," after it was changed at Yeats's direction in NLI 30,007 and BL Add. MS 55891. The attachment in BL Add. MS 55884 (in the same hand as above): "Dervagilla is impossible!! No / one has ever spelt it like that — / Dervorgilla is universal. // Also Dermot should / really be DIARMUID / though Dermot is just possible. / Lady G. always used / DIARMUID."

40 In NLI 30,007, the word "book" is circled and, in the margin, is inscribed a note to disregard ("Stet."), above the canceled query: "Volume?"

53–60 “The Dreaming . . . Macmillan. *lacking NLI 30,007, BL Add. MSS 55884 and 55891*

60 “At the Hawk’s Well”] *At the Hawk’s Well NLI 30,007, BL Add. MSS 55884 and 55891*

61 “The Only Jealousy of Emer”] *The Only Jealousy of Emer NLI 30,007, BL Add. MSS 55884 and 55891*

62 Cuchulain’s life (see *Plays in Prose and Verse*). *rev to* Cuchulain’s life (see Volume III) *NLI 30,007* Cuchulain’s life (see Volume III). *BL Add. MS 55884 and 55891*

62–64 The others . . . published. *lacking NLI 30,007, BL Add. MS 55884 and 55891*

65 “The Dreaming of the Bones”] The Dreaming of the Bones *NLI 30,007, BL Add. MSS 55884 and 55891*

67 ‘Dervorgilla’; *rev to* ‘Dervagilla’; [*beside canceled query:* Spelling?] *NLI 30,007* ‘Dervagilla’; *BL Add. MS 55891* ‘Dervagilla’; *rev to* ‘Dervorgilla’; *BL Add. MS 55884*

71 W. B. YEATS. *del NLI 30,007* *signature lacking BL Add. MSS 55884 and 55891*

72 1920.] 1920 *NLI 30,007, BL Add. MSS 55884 and 55891*